THE

GLOSSOLALIA PHENOMENON

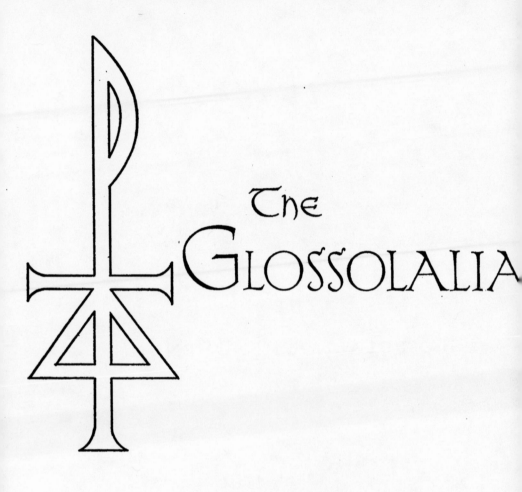

The GLOSSOLALIA

WADE H. HORTON
General Editor

Phenomenon

Contributing Authors

Charles W. Conn

R. Leonard Carroll ● ˙ Vessie D. Hargrave

Ray H. Hughes

James A. Cross ● James L. Slay

Lewis J. Willis

PATHWAY
PRESS

CLEVELAND, TENNESSEE ● PATHWAY PRESS

THE GLOSSOLALIA PHENOMENON

FIRST PRINTING 1966

SECOND PRINTING 1974

THIRD PRINTING 1983

FOURTH PRINTING 1984

FIFTH PRINTING 1986

Library of Congress Catalog Card Number: 66-25794

ISBN: 0-87148-351-3

Printed in the United States of America

This book is affectionately dedicated to

the Pentecostal Pioneers

who suffered both privation and persecution in promulgating a n d preserving the full gospel message, w h i c h includes the Baptism of the Holy Ghost with the evidence of speaking in other tongues as the Spirit gives the utterance.

FOREWORD

Sincere appreciation is hereby expressed in acknowledging the kind assistance given in the preparation of this volume entitled *The Glossolalia Phenomenon*. The writing, reading, correlating, typing, and editing of its pages have been a time consuming and tedious task performed by various persons. The editor's assignment was, however, a pleasant one because of the congenial and understanding attitude of all who participated in preparing it for printing.

Very special thanks go to the writers for graciously consenting to contribute their excellent manuscripts; to the Executive Committee and the Executive Council whose approval and encouragement were strong and undergirding influences; to Charles W. Conn, a valuable editorial assistant, who gave much time and wise counsel; to Lucille Walker for her helpful suggestions and competent assistance in the editing of the manuscripts; to Lewis J. Willis, Duran M. Palmertree, Carmen Holdman and Mary Margaret Holdman, my secretary Margarette Catha, and all others who made worthy contributions; to the publishers who kindly granted permission to quote their works (appropriate footnotes are listed); finally, the greatest and heartiest gratitude is given to God for leading us in beginning this volume and for His leadership in completing it.

The Glossolalia Phenomenon is presented with a prayer that every reader of its pages will experience the joy and satisfaction of speaking in tongues as the Spirit gives utterance, which is speaking "not unto men, but unto God."

WADE H. HORTON

Cleveland, Tennessee
July 1, 1966

CONTENTS

Wade H. Horton

Introduction

For more than half a century the Church of God has been a faithful, though often unheeded, voice with a great experience—the Baptism of the Holy Ghost with the evidence of speaking with other tongues. A tender flock of about one hundred when the outpouring of the Spirit first occurred, the Church of God stands now as a mighty army of approximately a half million members.

This church was born out of and owes her very existence to this marvelous spiritual experience. She has endured the severest persecution and ridicule because of her espousal of this Biblical doctrine and spiritual manifestation and has matured until she can now offer wise counsel and scriptural direction to those who seek understanding and truth. Therefore, it is with deep gratitude to God that we offer this volume, *The Glossolalia Phenomenon.*

It is abundantly evident that there is widespread and sincere interest in the Baptism of the Holy Ghost, with the accompanying manifestation of tongues, in the world today. It is equally evident that there is an urgent need for clarification, so that those interested in the subject may know the viewpoint of a people that have embraced this teaching and experience for many years.

The Glossolalia Phenomenon is therefore presented to meet a desperate need. This need cries aloud for a recognized, authoritative, and thoroughly Pentecostal voice to be heard on

13

glossolalia. The presentation of this study is not only necessary but also extremely urgent because of the variant voices speaking out on this much-discussed and little-understood Biblical subject. Most of them are uncertain and immature voices, and they often do more clouding than clearing the issues on glossolalia. This is regrettable. But, unquestionably, the confusion has augmented the urgency and increased the imperativeness of a sound and seasoned voice to proclaim the position of Pentecostals on this Pentecostal experience.

The writer is strongly convinced and convicted—after much prayer, concern, and consultation with others—that the Church of God should assume this responsibility. And though we do sincerely recognize the right of others to speak out on this important subject, at the same time we respectfully pose the proposition that if any voice has the right to be heard on glossolalia, it should be America's oldest Pentecostal church. And, too, we take this position because the Holy Ghost baptism accompanied by glossolalia is perhaps the one New Testament teaching that distinguishes us more than any other. We are, therefore, most eager for it to be clearly defined and fully understood. Because of its personal experience of glossolalia, its many years spent studying, teaching, and preaching it, and its firsthand observation of the various manifestations of tongues for more than half a century, it seems a reasonable assumption that this church is qualified to speak on the subject. We trust that when the readers will have finished reading this book they will have cause to agree.

Ironically, in recent years the vast majority of Christians, as well as the news media, religious and secular, have principally heard from those who know little about glossolalia theologically and nothing about it experientially; or those who know little about it experientially and almost nothing about it theologically. Those persons have gained much attention either because of opposition to it or because of the supposed uniqueness of receiving the experience in non-Pentecostal churches. This has inadvertently and inappropriately thrust upon them the role of the voice of authority on the subject. This most certainly should not be.

We are neither placing blame for this misdirected attention nor questioning their rights to speak out on glossolalia. It is difficult to understand, however, why it is supposed that these newcomers to Pentecost, who have spent many years either avoiding or opposing the experience, can become such authorities overnight. It seems a little inappropriate for them to almost immediately assume the position of authoritative teachers, pointing out what they claim is an easier, quieter, and more respectable way to receive the Holy Ghost; and at the same time blaming alleged excesses in Pentecost for their past reluctance to accept the Pentecostal message. Would it not be more charitable for them to reexamine the total Pentecostal picture and seek to be taught rather than to teach, at least until they are familiar with spiritual manifestations and have reached a degree of maturity in the Spirit-filled life. These recipients should humbly thank God for the experience and should thank God for the Pentecostals who have long espoused this great truth. The faithfulness of God's promise and the preaching, persuasion, and the permanence of the Pentecostals are the reason they have become partakers of this spiritual blessing. In all probability, if Pentecost in all its ramifications had been accepted in proper Biblical perspective beforehand, many misconceptions and misunderstandings could have been avoided. Most mistakes and immature statements are no doubt made because of a deplorable lack of understanding about the operation of the gifts of the Spirit.

Perhaps we have been at fault for not speaking out louder and clearer and sooner, and for failure to produce a worthy theological treatise on the subject. The failure to write on glossolalia, however, was not primarily because of a lack of interest or a shortage of competent writers, as some claim, but rather because we believed the subject was so clearly taught in the

Holy Scriptures that earnest Christians would have little, if any, difficulty understanding it. And, too, being extremely occupied with the urgency and the passion of preaching the gospel, we just did not see the necessity of producing an extensive documented disquisition on the doctrine of tongues. Perhaps in this we were wrong.

Furthermore we did not, and still do not, place as much importance on glossolalia itself as some do today or as much as others claim we do. We are, however, without question unshakably convinced that glossolalia is a scriptural phenomenon that has its proper place in both private and public worship. We are equally convinced that it is exercised only by consecrated and Spirit-filled Christians, and only then as the Spirit gives the utterance and not at the whim and fancy of human personality.

The uncertain sounds and the many kinds of voices in the world have forced upon us the urgent need and the solemn responsibility of sharing our Pentecostal experience, our historical evaluation, and our theological treatment of the subject even at this late hour in our history. The urgency is now glaringly obvious. The appeal for clarification is unmistakable. The performance of the task is obligatory. To procrastinate longer is inexcusable. It is perhaps more important now than ever before because of a greater diversity of interpretations and because of so many perverted concepts concerning the operation and usage of glossolalia.

It was not nearly so complex in the early days of Pentecost, for there were only two principal voices heard then— the positive voice of Pentecostals and the negative voice of Pentecostal opposers. This has all been changed in recent years. There are additional voices today. These voices, for the most part, are neither altogether for glossolalia nor altogether against it. One is the voice of those who have received the Pentecostal experience outside their denominational structure, but remain in the non-Pentecostal churches where it is neither taught nor accepted. This is the semi-silent voice. It speaks only in off-night prayer meetings and in selected and secluded groups meeting outside the regular announced church services. But in the public worship services this voice blends with the usual ritualistic ecclesiasticisms and is strangely silent. This silence is effected for two reasons: first, because the spiritual climate is not conducive to spiritual manifestations; and second, because of a consciousness that tongues will not be tolerated. How long this can continue, only time will tell.

Another believes in glossolalia, but does not accept it in experience. Though this voice appears to endorse the Pentecostal position, it is only half in and half out at best, and contributes very little, if anything at all, toward clarification of the tongues-speaking phenomenon. And indeed, how can it justifiably try to do so when it has no experiential knowledge of it whatsoever. It speaks from only one side, the outside. And this is the best it can ever do until it comes all the way in.

Another is the voice of one who professes to believe in glossolalia, but casts doubts on some of the accompanying manifestations. Its tongue-in-cheek, half-hearted acquiescence does not strengthen the real Pentecostal position, but rather weakens it. Any positive statement from this source favoring speaking in tongues will be followed by a negative one, either directly or indirectly, disfavoring it.

And still another voice is the one that accepts the mechanical, quiet, sophisticated tongues speaking, but rejects the emotional, unspeakable joy, spiritually intoxicated, rushing-mighty-wind kind of Pentecostal experience. This group wants to be sure that the multitudes are not confounded and amazed at their actions, and most certainly that they are not accused of being drunk as were the first Pentecostal believers. They want to steer their ship clear of the Pentecostal pattern as recorded in Acts 2. This voice says, "I will accept glossolalia, but, please, not as the Pentecostals do."

Finally, another kind of voice, entirely different from all the others, is raised by those who are continually riding on the crest of a miracle. Though this group is very small in number, in all fairness to the whole picture it should be mentioned. These people fully accept the outward manifestations of Pentecost—tongues, interpretations of tongues, miracles, healing—but place emphasis on them all out of proportion to what the Scripture directs. To them it must be either miraculous or mediocre. Nothing short of supernatural outward demonstrations will satisfy them. Their sensibilities are attuned to the sensational, and anything less is shallow, dull, dry, and spiritless. They seem to lay more stress on the physical manifestations than the spiritual experiences. Their actions, attitudes, and declarations seem to propound a superior ministry to their other Pentecostal brethren. This voice speaks long and loud about spiritual liberty, but its concept of this achievement is the come-out-ism, anti-church-government philosophy. Any form of rules, order, or regulations is to them dictatorial and inhibits their initiative, impairs their ingenuity, and interferes with their freedom to operate on what they choose to call a completely spiritual basis. This voice seems reluctant to admit that while the outward gifts and signs have their place in Pentecostal propagation there are other things equally important and some of far greater importance.

We sincerely believe that all this demonstrates the imperativeness of a positive Pentecostal voice, pointing out the proper direction to the reception of the Spirit and the effects of speaking in tongues on the recipient. This we shall prayerfully and conscientiously undertake to do. It is hoped that this exposition written by sane, sound, yet deeply spiritual men will clearly present the Pentecostal picture Biblically, historically, and experientially and will clear up some misconceptions and misunderstandings about the practice of speaking in tongues.

The Glossolalia Phenomenon is a multipurpose book. The purposes are apparent in the light of (1) the confusion surrounding the subject in this day, (2) the evidence of increasing interest being shown in glossolalia, and (3) the need for undistorted scriptural guidance to those who are new in the Pentecostal way. Our earnest desire is to contribute to a better understanding of this apostolic doctrine by establishing a reservoir of sound, scriptural, historical, and empirical information on the subject of speaking in tongues.

One of the main reasons for publishing the book is to assist the earnest inquirer in his search for the truth about the Holy Ghost and speaking in other tongues. Many honest-hearted and spiritually-hungry people are seeking answers, not only to theological questions on glossolalia but also to satisfy a deep yearning in their own hearts. There are perhaps thousands of pastors and parishioners concerned about what the Scriptures teach on glossolalia, and equally concerned because of the vacuum in their own religious experiences. Some have heard of others in similar circumstances coming into the Pentecostal fullness, and they are earnestly seeking for the same spiritual satisfaction. We trust they will find their answer in these pages and that their quest for Pentecostal truth and for spiritual fullness will be fully realized. We are confident too that there are also religious leaders, Christian teachers in colleges, seminaries, and Bible institutes, as well as others from all walks of life who are hungry for a life in the Spirit. It is hoped that this book will be of inestimable value in their search for the deeper life. We pray that it will climax in the Pentecostal experience.

Another purpose is for clarification of our teaching on the Pentecostal doctrine. Since our position has been so grossly misstated and misrepresented by so many, it necessitates a forthright positive expression of our doctrinal declaration. *The Glossolalia Phenomenon* can be used as an informative manual to quote the teaching of the Church of God on glossolalia. Our highest hope is that it will serve the purposes for which it is published. If so, it will be a spiritual gold mine, bringing rewarding dividends to its readers and to the writers of its pages.

The contributing writers of this book were carefully chosen. They were selected because of their personal Pentecostal experience, their acquaintance with the Pentecostal movement, their education and literary qualifications, and their stature and influence both inside and outside of their church. These men are sound in their theology, sober in their thinking, and deeply spiritual in their relationship to their God, their church, and their generation. In short, they were chosen to contribute to this symposium on the charismatic phenomenon because of their competency and conscientiousness in the work of our Lord. They have had this experience of the Baptism of the Holy Ghost with the evidence of speaking with other tongues for an aggregate total of approximately three hundred years. Each has been a Pentecostal preacher for more than twenty-five years. Some of them have preached much longer than this and they are all, without exception, far above the average in pulpit proficiency. Their knowledge of the Pentecostal movement goes back even further than this, for most of them were reared in Pentecostal homes. Some had parents who were Pentecostal preachers before them. That they are qualified from an educational standpoint will be shown in their brief biographies. Their positional and professional stature in their own church and among other Pentecostal and evangelical groups is well known and adds tremendous weight to whatever they write on any subject, and most especially on this one. They all join with me in wishing for this book the success and influence we most assuredly believe it should have. We strongly believe it is a much-needed work and that it will serve well in this day, and perhaps in generations to come. At least it will express the opinion and conviction of America's oldest Pentecostal church.

Glossolalia
and the Scriptures

Charles W. Conn

Charles W. Conn is First Assistant General Overseer of the Church of God and a member of the Executive Committee and of the Executive Council. Before his election to this position he served for ten years as Editor in Chief of Church of God Publications and Editor of the Evangel. *In his broad ministry he has visited sixty-five countries. He has authored eleven books. His first,* Like a Mighty Army, *is a history of the Church of God. Some of the other volumes from his pen are:* Pillars of Pentecost, Where the Saints Have Trod, The Rudder and the Rock, The Bible: Book of Books, Christ and the Gospels, *and* Acts of the Apostles. *He presently serves as Servicemen's Director, and on several important boards and committees. He is currently a member of the National Association of Evangelicals Commission on Theology, and the Pentecostal Fellowship of North America Board of Administration. Because of his outstanding contributions to the outreach of his church, in 1962 Lee College conferred on him the Doctor of Letters degree.*

Charles W. Conn

Glossolalia
and the Scriptures

I. THE PREVALENCE OF TONGUES
IN MODERN TIMES

In recent years there has been a conspicuous increase of glossolalia, the phenomenon of speaking in tongues. Though the phenomenon is not new, its current appearance is so widespread that much attention is given to it. The attention runs from serious study by churches and other interested groups to peripheral notice by the sensation-seeking press.

DEFINITION OF TERMS

The word *glossolalia* is not found in the English translation of the Bible but is based on the Greek word *glossa,* for tongue. The term was used by ancient writers to denote strange or unknown language or speech. The New Testament, written in the Greek, used the expression *glossais lalien* for the tongues spoken in the Spirit by the earliest Christians. Thus, the present practice of speaking in tongues is known as *glossolalia.*

Those who speak with tongues are known as *glossolalists.*

The appearance of glossolalia has been noted in practically every period of Christian history, especially in times of revival and spiritual renewal. Usually these appearances were

23

of sporadic nature and of limited scope. About the turn of this century, however, there was a recurrence of the phenomenon that reached universal proportions. The phenomenon appeared almost simultaneously in many parts of the world. Perhaps the ubiquity of glossolalia was as miraculous as the phenomenon itself. It was as if a new Day of Pentecost had come to the world. The similarity was inescapable. Those who were exercised by the gift of tongues came as a matter of course to be called "Pentecostal" people and their beliefs were called the "Pentecostal" faith. *← not just pentecostals*

The spectacular spread of the modern Pentecostal movement is a marvel of this century—and, for that matter, of Christian history. The rapid growth has understandingly given rise to many legitimate questions. Because of the conspicuous nature of glossolalia, most of the questions concern this manifestation.

THE AUTHORITY OF SCRIPTURE

Before any discussion of glossolalia is entered it should be determined upon what basis or authority that discussion will be conducted. With the Pentecostal believer final authority for all spiritual inquiry rests in the Word of God. The Scriptures are the court of highest and final appeal.

This is well, for Christians should with equal readiness reject whatever lacks scriptural validity and accept those spiritual truths set forth in the Scriptures. We should be willing to measure any belief or any experience by the rule of God's Word. There are extraneous approaches, such as inquiry into the psychological and sociological factors involved, of some value, which may aid in full understanding of the question. These may cast nuances of light and shadow on the subject so as to reveal unsuspected facets and motivations, but they can never fully answer any spiritual question. After these avenues of inquiry are followed to the end, the Pentecostal believer will come still again to the Bible. *← So much freedom need to go back to the word*

why

It is a hallmark of Pentecostal faith that the Bible is the infallible Word of God. Belief in the inerrancy of Scripture may seem naive and unsophisticated in this generation, but this simplicity of faith is the way of life for many today just as it was for the earliest Christians.

In the introduction to his translation of the book of Acts, *The Young Church in Action,* J. B. Phillips had this to say of the apostles and their fellow Christians:

> [The Apostolic Church] surely is the Church as it was meant to be. It is vigorous and flexible, for these are the days before it ever became fat and short of breath through prosperity, or musclebound by overorganization. These men did not make "acts of faith," they believed; they did not "say their prayer," they really prayed. They did not hold conferences on psychosomatic medicine, they simply healed the sick. But if they were uncomplicated and naive by modern standards, we have ruefully to admit that they were open on the God-ward side in a way that is almost unknown today.[1]

The appearance of glossolalia in this day looks directly back to the practices and teachings of the Scriptures. In a time of sophistication and unbelief man hungers for the simplicity of faith and experience revealed in the Bible. He cannot come to divine truth, however, through carnal reasoning. He must turn to the Word of God, for it alone has the answer to man's spiritual needs. ← *scripture alone…*

II. THE PLACE OF TONGUES IN CHRISTIAN EXPERIENCE

We must take care not to attach undue significance to glossolalia. The phenomenon has a valid and proper place in the Christian experience, yet it is not an end in itself and should not be sought for its own sake. Tongues would be

↖ most ppl do this…

---

[1] J. B. Phillips, *The Young Church in Action* (New York: The Macmillan Company, 1955), p. vii.

meaningless in themselves without the deeper Christian life they signify. They would be as meaningless as a herald for a king who does not live or a marker for a place that does not exist.

Tongues are a sign, a witness that accompanies the Holy Spirit when He comes into the human heart. The phenomenon is the initial physical evidence that one has received the Baptism of the Holy Spirit.

is it the initial evidence?

THE HOLY SPIRIT

In Conversion. First, it should be made very clear that the Holy Spirit is active in all aspects of the Christian life. The Spirit, who is the Third Person of the Triune God, participates in the conversion of sinners by bringing conviction of sin: "And when he is come, he will reprove the world of sin, and of righteousness, and of judgment" (John 16:8); and by effecting their union with Christ. From the time of their conversion, the Spirit of Christ dwells in the heart of all Christians: "Now if any man have not the Spirit of Christ, he is none of his. . . . The Spirit itself beareth witness with our spirit, that we are the children of God" (Romans 8:9, 16), for their bodies are the temples of the Holy Ghost (1 Corinthians 6:19). Dwelling in the life of man, the Spirit produces the fruit of love, joy, peace, longsuffering, gentleness, goodness, faith, meekness, and temperance (Galatians 5:22, 23).

fruit in life...

Baptism. There is a further, deepening work of the Spirit, however, that is valid for every regenerated person. It is not the new birth, and it is available only to those who have been born again. This is called the Baptism of the Holy Spirit. It is this baptism that occurred in Acts 2, Acts 8, Acts 10, and Acts 19. It is frequently argued that the experience recorded in these chapters was regeneration or the new birth. Any honest study of the Scriptures will show the error of this position.

WHAT HAPPENED AT PENTECOST?

Regeneration of the Disciples. That which happened on
the Day of Pentecost could not have been the work of regeneration, for the disciples were already converted. The
spiritual integrity of Christ's disciples was attested to in His
directives to them:

"And he called unto him his twelve disciples, and gave them
authority over unclean spirits, to cast them out, and to heal
all manner of disease and all manner of sickness. . . .
These twelve Jesus sent forth, and charged them, saying,
Go not into any way of the Gentiles, and enter not into any
city of the Samaritans: but go rather to the lost sheep of
the house of Israel" (Matthew 10:1, 5, 6 ASV).

"And the seventy returned with joy, saying Lord, even
the demons are subject unto us in thy name. And he said
unto them, I beheld Satan fallen as lightning from heaven.
Behold, I have given you authority to tread upon serpents
and scorpions, and over all the power of the enemy: and
nothing shall in any wise hurt you. Nevertheless in this rejoice not, that the spirits are subject unto you; but rejoice
that your names are written in heaven" (Luke 10:17-20
ASV). *— salvation proclaimed*

Observe that Christ had given His disciples power to do
His works, which could not be done by the unconverted
(Matthew 12:24-27). Unconverted men might attempt to
do the works of Christ (Acts 19:13-16) or even claim to
do them (Matthew 7:22, 23), but such is not possible. What
the disciples did here in measure they would later do abundantly. Note, too, that He sent them to the "lost sheep of the
house of Israel." It is not likely that He would have sent lost
men to lost men—no more than He would have sent blind
men to lead the blind.

Furthermore, Jesus affirmed to the disciples that their
names were written in heaven (verse 20). Revelation 20:15
tells us that those whose names are not written in heaven will

be cast into the lake of fire. The inference is that the disciples were saved from this eternal loss.

Jesus strongly attested the state of grace of the disciples when He spoke to them of the Holy Spirit:

"I will pray the Father, and he shall give you another Comforter, that he may be with you for ever, even the Spirit of truth: whom the world cannot receive; for it beholdeth him not, neither knoweth him: ye know him; <u>for he abideth *with* you, and shall be *in* you</u>" (John 14:16, 17 ASV).[2]

Here the statement is specific that the disciples were (1) separated from the world, (2) that they knew the Spirit already, (3) and that He was already abiding with them. In time to come the Holy Spirit would not only be with them, but He would also be in them. This infilling is the Baptism of the Holy Spirit. It must also be noted that men of the world are not eligible for the Baptism of the Holy Spirit apart from repentance. (Only those who are cleansed from sin can receive this enduement of power.) The indwelling of the Spirit can come only to a <u>regenerated soul</u>.

The Lord, still on the eve of His crucifixion, spoke intimately to His disciples regarding their spiritual relationship to Him:

"Already *ye are clean* because of the word which I have spoken unto you. . . . <u>*I am* the vine, *ye are* the branches:</u> He <u>that abideth in me,</u> and I in him, the same beareth much fruit: for apart from me ye can do nothing. . . . If ye *abide in me,* and my words abide in you, ask whatsoever ye will, and it shall be done unto you" (John 15:3, 5, 7 ASV).[3]

Of equal import is the Lord's prayer for His disciples on His last night with them. This tender, revealing prayer, recorded in John 17, is one of the most sensitive statements we have of the Lord's affection and concern for His own. No one can read this prayer perceptively and sincerely and hold

---

[2] Italics ours.
[3] Italics ours.

any doubts regarding the disciples' regeneration even while Jesus was with them. He committed them to the Father with such affirmations as: "I pray for them: I pray not for the world, but for them which thou has given me; for they are thine. . . . While I was with them in the world, I kept them in thy name: those that thou gavest me I have kept, and none of them is lost, but the son of perdition; that the scripture might be fulfilled. . . . I have given them thy word; and the world hath hated them, because they are not of the world, even as I am not of the world" (John 17:9, 12, 14).

All the foregoing scriptures—each spoken by the Lord Himself — affirm that the disciples were already regenerated men. This work was naturally predicated upon the blood of Jesus, even though He was not yet crucified, which was to be shed for the redemption of man. There is no other power or source for man's salvation (Acts 4:12).

Following His crucifixion and resurrection, yet before the Day of Pentecost, Jesus gave further evidence that the disciples were already saved, this time in the form of a symbol. When He first appeared to them, He "breathed on them, and saith unto them, Receive ye the Holy Ghost" (John 20:22). This act of breathing on the disciples symbolized their spiritual life, as God had first given physical life by breathing into the nostrils of Adam (Genesis 2:7).

Furthermore, immediately before the Ascension, Jesus said to His disciples that ". . . repentance and remission of sins should be preached in his name unto all the nations, beginning from Jerusalem. *Ye are witnesses of these things.*[4] And behold, I send forth the promise of my Father upon you: but tarry ye in the city, until ye be clothed with power from on high" (Luke 24:47-49 ASV). "But ye shall receive power, after that the Holy Ghost is come upon you: and ye shall be witnesses unto me both in Jerusalem, and in all Judaea, and in Samaria, and unto the uttermost part of the earth" (Acts

---

[4] Italics ours.

1:8). This was not a promise of the new birth, of regeneration, of redemption — but of power. The emphasis was not on the Christian life but on Christian service.

Jesus' promise to His disciples was that "ye shall be baptized in the Holy Ghost not many days hence" (Acts 1:5). If they were not already converted, then their conversion would surely have been His great concern during His final hour with them. But in none of His discourses did Jesus indicate any such need. They were already saved. Some men point to Jesus' statement to Peter, "When thou art converted, strengthen thy brethren," as an indication that the apostle was not converted until the Day of Pentecost. Read in context, however, it is seen that the statement anticipated Peter's denial of Christ (Luke 22:31-34). Peter had need of repentance after his cowardly action at the trial of Jesus (Luke 22:54-62).

For about three years, the disciples had partaken of the kingdom; they had listened intently to the saving words of Jesus; they had obeyed Him faithfully; they had lived in communion with the Lord; they had preached the gospel; they had healed the sick and cast out devils. How, in the face of all this, can anyone suggest that they were yet unsaved? They were already saved by His grace. Even so, the Lord told them to remain in Jerusalem until they were endued with power from on high.

The Enduement of Power. The truth becomes very clear. Beyond the regenerative work of the Holy Spirit, there is a further work to be effected in the lives of believers, a baptism in the Holy Spirit.

F. B. Meyer has expressed it in this way:

> . . . As you took forgiveness from the hand of the dying Christ, take your share of the Pentecostal gift from the hand of the Living Christ.
> Don't think that blessed gift is only for elect men and for special work. I want you to understand the fullness of the Spirit is for every believer, to make you the men and women you want to be. The failure of your life that you

complain of is that you are trying to attain the ideal without the power which alone makes the ideal possible.
The blessing of the day of Pentecost is always described as being "filled" with the Holy Spirit. God's will for believers is that they should be filled, women as well as men. As full as the tree is of sap when it rises from the roots and fills the furthermost branches, so we are to be filled with the Spirit until Christian fruitfulness is as natural to us as the flower and fruit to the tree. We may be as full of the Spirit as the tree is of sap, as the body is of life, as the mind is full of thought, as the heart is full of love, as the cold, dull iron is filled with the white flame of the furnace.[5]

The purpose of this baptism is to equip and empower the Christian as a witness for Christ; it is an experience of enlargement and deepening in the spiritual life.

In the book of Acts we find numerous expressions that reveal the nature and power with which the Holy Spirit comes into the hearts of believers:

"ye shall be *baptized with* the Holy Ghost" (1:5)
"ye shall be *baptized with* the Holy Ghost" (11:16)

— — —

"ye shall *receive* the gift of the Holy Ghost" (2:38)
"they might *receive* the Holy Ghost" (8:15)
"they *received* the Holy Ghost" (8:17)
"he may *receive* the Holy Ghost" (8:19)
"which have *received* the Holy Ghost" (10:47)
"Have ye *received* the Holy Ghost?" (19:2)

— — —

"they were all *filled with* the Holy Ghost" (2:4)
"Peter, *filled with* the Holy Ghost" (4:8)
"they were all *filled with* the Holy Ghost" (4:31)
"be *filled with* the Holy Ghost" (9:17)
"Paul, *filled with* the Holy Ghost" (13:9)

---

[5] F. B. Meyer, *Back to Bethel* (Chicago: Moody Press [n.d.]), pp. 94, 95.

"the disciples were *filled with* joy and with the Holy Ghost" (13:52)
"*full of* the Holy Ghost and wisdom" (6:3)
"Stephen, a man *full of* faith and of the Holy Ghost" (6:5)
"*full of* the Holy Ghost" (7:55)
"*full of* the Holy Ghost and of faith" (11:24)

— — —

"the Holy Ghost is *come upon* you" (1:8)
"the Holy Ghost *came on* them" (19:6)

— — —

"the Holy Ghost *fell on* all them which heard the word" (10:44)
"the Holy Ghost *fell on* them" (11:15)

— — —

"the Holy Ghost *was given*" (8:18)
"God *gave them* the like gift" (11:17)

— — —

"on the Gentiles also was *poured out* the gift of the Holy Ghost" (10:45)[6]

These various expressions obviously refer to one and the same impartation of power. Sometimes they are used in close juxtaposition. For instance, in Acts 8:16-18 we have "the Holy Ghost was given," "he was fallen," and "they received the Holy Ghost," all referring to the same outpouring in Samaria. Again, in Acts 10:44-47 we read how "the Holy Ghost fell," "was poured out," and was "received," by the household of Cornelius.

In all these expressions we see the power and dominion with which the Holy Spirit comes to those who will receive Him. He falls on, is poured on, or comes on the believer; the believer is filled with, or baptized with, the Holy Spirit.

---

[6] Italics ours.

This is the believer's immersion in the Spirit, his empowerment for service, his spiritual energizing that enables the
branch to bear the fruit of the Vine (John 15:4, 5). The
Baptism of the Holy Spirit is an enduement of power, a
bestowal of spiritual equipment for the extension of Christ's
ministry.

In his excellent volume *What the Bible Teaches,* R. A.
Torrey says:

> A man may be regenerated by the Holy Spirit and still not
> be baptized with the Holy Spirit. In regeneration there is an
> impartation of life, and the one who receives it is saved;
> in the Baptism with the Holy Spirit there is an impartation
> of power and the one who receives it is fitted for service. . . .
> But not every believer has the Baptism with the Holy
> Spirit, though every believer, as we shall see, may have.
> The Baptism with the Holy Spirit may be received imme-
> diately after the new birth—as e.g., in the household of
> Cornelius. In a normal state of the church every believer
> would have the Baptism with the Holy Spirit. . . .
> In such a normal state of the church the Baptism with
> the Holy Spirit would be received immediately upon re-
> pentance and baptism into the name of Jesus Christ for the
> remission of sins (Acts 2:38). But the doctrine of the
> Baptism with the Holy Spirit has been so allowed to drop
> out of sight, and the church has had so little expectancy
> along this line for its young children, that a large portion
> of the church is in the position of the churches in Samaria
> and Ephesus, where someone has to come and call the at-
> tention of the mass of believers to their privilege in the Risen
> Christ and claim it for them. . . .
> In every passage in the Bible in which the results of the Bap-
> tism with the Holy Spirit are mentioned they are related
> to testimony and service. The Baptism with the Holy Spirit
> has no direct reference to cleansing from sin. It has to do
> with gifts for service rather than with graces of character.
> The steps by which one ordinarily receives the Baptism with
> the Holy Spirit are of such a character, and the Baptism
> with the Holy Spirit makes God so real that this Baptism is
> in most cases accompanied by a great moral uplift, or even
> a radical transformation, but the Baptism with the Holy
> Spirit is not in itself either an eradication of the carnal
> nature or cleansing from an impure heart. It is the imparta-

tion of supernatural power or gifts in service, and sometimes one may have rare gifts by the Spirit's power and few graces.[7]

PREREQUISITES FOR THE INFILLING

Just as there are prerequisites for the forgiveness of sins, so are there for the Baptism with the Holy Spirit. To be saved one must believe on the Lord Jesus (Acts 16:31), repent of sin (Acts 3:19), follow Him in water baptism (Acts 2:38). If the Baptism with the Holy Spirit is subsequent to a clean heart, what, then, are the requirements for this baptism?

First of all, one must be *separated from the world* (Romans 8:1-15; John 14:16, 17). The impartation of the Spirit is not for sinful and unregenerate men. The Holy Spirit cannot fill the heart that is filled with the world. First must come repentance unto salvation and then the infilling of the Holy Spirit (Acts 2:38).

Then there must be a life of *devotion and dedication*, just as we see in the earliest disciples as they tarried in the upper room. These "continued with one accord in prayer and supplication" (Acts 1:14).

The next requirement is an *intense desire* for spiritual fullness. This relates directly to, and stems from, the aforesaid life of devotion. No one can expect to be filled with the Holy Spirit who is indifferent or unconcerned about a deeper dedication to the Christian life. Jesus likened this spiritual desire to physical hunger and thirst (Matthew 5:6; John 7:37-39). This hunger and thirst can become so intense that it allows no distraction. Neither can there be any diminishing of the thirst until the goading pangs of desire be met.

When we are hungry and thirsty for the filling of the Spirit, the next steps come in course. We are to *pray for the*

---

[7] R. A. Torrey, *What the Bible Teaches* (New York: Fleming H. Revell Company, 1933), pp. 271-273.

enduement. Jesus Himself taught this when He said: "If ye then, being evil, know how to give good gifts unto your children: how much more shall your heavenly Father give the Holy Spirit to them that ask him?" (Luke 11:13). On at least three occasions the Holy Spirit came to believers in the wake of earnest prayer—the first disciples (Acts 1:14), Paul (Acts 9:11), and Cornelius (Acts 10:4).

Obedience is necessary for receiving the Holy Spirit. "And we are his witnesses of these things; and so is also the Holy Ghost, whom God hath given to them that obey him" (Acts 5:32). We must obey God in devotion, in conduct, in growth, and in service.

III. THE PROMINENCE OF TONGUES IN SCRIPTURE

In the Scriptures the Baptism with the Holy Ghost was always attended by conspicuous manifestations of the Divine Presence. The common manifestation was speaking with unknown tongues, or languages. This phenomenon was the consistent evidence that the Holy Spirit had come. There were many other evidences that could be observed later, such as a life of spiritual dedication and power, consistent spiritual boldness, an ever increasing effectiveness in His service, and absorption with spiritual things. Whereas these evidences required time, tongues gave immediate witness that the Spirit had come. Speaking in tongues is therefore appropriately called the initial evidence of the Baptism with the Holy Spirit.

Scriptural evidence is not wanting on the subject of tongues. It is, in fact, treated more adequately than any other sign-type phenomenon. Moreover, both the beneficial and adverse aspects are brought into focus in the prophetic, historical, and doctrinal record. This is a fortunate circumstance for anyone seeking understanding and truth.

In reading the New Testament one cannot escape the impression that speaking in tongues was commonplace among the apostolic Christians. It was so much the norm that little moment was made of it. While the recorded incidents of the phenomenon happened with impressive frequence, the matter-of-fact way those incidents are reported is equally impressive. Whether we understand it or not, the fact is clear that the New Testament Christians lived on such an exalted spiritual plane that they accepted the miraculous and the phenomenal as normal aspects of the Christian life.

Only the unbelievers regarded speaking in tongues as abnormal. On the Day of Pentecost they were *amazed*, and *confounded*; they *marvelled* and were *in doubt* (or *perplexed*). But the followers of Christ, the ones exercised by the gift, accepted the incident to be the answer to Christ's promise and the fulfillment of holy prophecy (Acts 2:16).

In Acts 10:45, the disciples were *astonished* when the household of Cornelius spoke with tongues. This was not due to the manifestation of tongues, however, but to the fact that Gentiles had been converted and received the Holy Spirit.

Glossolalia was not confined to one locale, one time, or one people. It was a consistent fact of life among the early Christians. Whether they were Galileans in the holy city of Jerusalem, Samaritans in their own homeland, Romans in the Judean seaport of Caesarea, Jews of the Dispersion in the Asian metropolis of Ephesus, or Grecians in the worldly crossroads of Corinth, the earliest Christians reacted alike as they were wrought upon by the Holy Spirit. However man may rationalize it, that fact stands beyond dispute.

As previously observed, the word *glossolalia* is not found in the English translation of the Scriptures. The term derives from the Greek word for tongue (*glossa*) which is used in various forms to designate the phenomenon of speaking in tongues. There are, in fact, about eight separate expressions in the Authorized Version (the "King James Version") of the Bible. Some of these appellations are as interesting as they are descriptive:

"they shall speak with *new tongues*" (Mark 16:17)
"all . . . began to speak with *other tongues*" (Acts 2:4)
"they heard them speak with *tongues*" (Acts 10:46)
"to another *divers kinds of tongues*" (1 Corinthians 12:10)
"*diversities of tongues*" (1 Corinthians 12:28)
"the *tongues of men* and of *angels*" (1 Corinthians 13:1)
"he that speaketh in an *unknown tongue*" (1 Corinthians 14:2)
"every one of you . . . hath *a tongue*" (1 Corinthians 14:26)[8]

These various expressions presumably refer to one and the same spiritual manifestation, a Spirit-inspired utterance that is not the user's natural language or speech. It is sometimes understood by the hearers but is more often unintelligible unless the Holy Spirit also inspires an interpretation of it. The expression "divers kinds of tongues" refers primarily to different languages. It alludes to another fact that is brought out in the Scriptures—that not all speaking in tongues is the same. In Acts 2:4, for instance, the "other tongues" are languages used in lands other than Palestine. This can be understood in a natural way by anyone who knows the language spoken. On the other hand, the "unknown tongue" of 1 Corinthians 14:2 could not be a language, for it is unintelligible to all hearers unless it is accompanied by a Spirit-inspired interpretation. Known nowadays as ecstatic speech, this is possibly what 1 Corinthians 13:1 calls the "tongues of angels."

There is likewise an apparent distinction between speaking in tongues as *evidence* that the Holy Spirit has come and the manifestation of tongues as a *gift* of the Spirit. The effect may be identical, just as the source is identical, but the one is initial while the other is continual. Because the Holy Spirit gave witness when He came into the human life, all who

---

[8] Italics ours.

received him in Acts spoke with tongues. The same is true today: those who received the Holy Spirit speak with tongues as an initial evidence that He has come. Those who claim to have the Baptism of the Holy Spirit but have never spoken in tongues make a mistaken claim. In 1 Corinthians 12:6-11, where the subject is the gifts of the Spirit, it is implied that the *gift of tongues* is not manifested through all. In verse 30 where the question is asked: "Do all speak with tongues?" it is the gift of tongues that is being considered.

FULFILLMENT OF PROPHECY

The New Testament phenomenon of tongues is the fulfillment of several prophetic promises. Peter explained the events of Pentecost as a fulfillment of prophecy: "But this is that which was spoken by the prophet Joel" (Acts 2:16). It is important that we observe what Joel had actually prophesied: "And it shall come to pass afterward, that I will pour out my spirit upon all flesh; and your sons and your daughters shall prophesy, your old men shall dream dreams, your young men shall see visions: And also upon the servants and upon the handmaids in those days will I pour out my spirit" (Joel 2:28, 29).

The apostle, in quoting Joel, affirmed the outpouring of the Holy Spirit to be positive proof of God's presence among His people, "And ye shall know that I am in the midst of Israel, and that I am the Lord your God, and none else" (Joel 2: 27), and verified the exalted spiritual nature of the Spirit baptism.

Paul, in 1 Corinthians 14:21, also looking back to the Old Testament, related the phenomenon of tongues to the words of Isaiah: "For with stammering lips and another tongue will he speak to this people" (Isaiah 28:11). It should be pointed out that Paul only applied that scripture to the situation in Corinth; he did not actually cite it as a prophecy fulfilled.

Jesus implied and specifically foretold the appearance of

tongues. Of the former we have such statements as: "when the Comforter is come . . . he shall *testify* of me" (John 15:26). "When he, the Spirit of truth, is come . . . he shall not *speak* of himself; but whatsoever he shall hear, that *shall he speak* . . ." (John 16:13).[9]

The words *testify* and *speak* clearly indicate that the Holy Spirit, when He should come to the disciples, would utter praises to Christ. If we had no further record we might miss this suggestion, but when we read what happened on the Day of Pentecost we see the import of Christ's words (Acts 2:4, 11). The Spirit testified or spoke of the wonderful works of God at Pentecost. He did so through the voices of the disciples.

In Mark 16:17, 18, we read a specific prophecy of the glossolalia phenomenon: "And these signs shall follow them that believe; In my name they shall cast out devils; they shall speak with new tongues; They shall take up serpents; and if they drink any deadly thing, it shall not hurt them; they shall lay hands on the sick, and they shall recover."

This is manifestly a prophecy of spiritual power for those who were to continue the work of Jesus. It includes five predictions of physical manifestations of this power. Ample evidence of the fulfillment of three of them is recorded in Acts—casting out of devils, speaking with tongues, and recovery of the sick. It is possible that Acts 28:5 fulfills that which says "they shall take up serpents."

Before proceeding, we must, in honesty, note that some scholars reject the last twelve verses of Mark (16:9-20) as the additions of someone other than Mark because they are not found in the two oldest Marcan manuscripts, Codex Sinaiticus and Codex Vaticanus. All the other ancient manuscripts, on the other hand, do include these verses; and Irenaeus, as early as A.D. 170, ascribed them to Mark. Without entering the textual dispute over the origin of these

---

[9] Italics ours.

verses, let us observe simply that their contents are verified and repeated in other undisputed portions of the Scriptures. Regardless of any possible textual omission or interpolations, the truths of Mark 16:9-20 stand firm.

THE HISTORICAL RECORD

From the prophetic record we turn to the exemplary. The occasion of tongues among the apostles was quite common; there are four rather extensive references to apostolic glossolalia, with other allusions to it. The first three are in a historical context, all in the book of Acts, from which we get clear and inescapable instruction in righteousness (2 Timothy 2:15). The fourth lengthy reference, in 1 Corinthians, is in a didactic context, but laden with historical suggestion. We will first consider the purely historical aspects of these accounts, and later observe their significance for us.

THE DAY OF PENTECOST

The Occasion. The story of the Holy Spirit's coming to the disciples in Acts gives the first account of glossolalia among the apostles. It occurred in this manner:

> Acts 2:1 And when the day of Pentecost was fully come, they were all with one accord in one place.
> 2 And suddenly there came a sound from heaven as of a rushing mighty wind, and it filled all the house where they were sitting.
> 3 And there appeared unto them cloven tongues like as of fire, and it sat upon each of them.
> 4 And they were all filled with the Holy Ghost, and began to speak with other tongues, as the Spirit gave them utterance.

The disciples, about 120 strong, were in Jerusalem between the Lord's ascension and the Day of Pentecost, an interim of about ten days. Their mood was one of great joy (Luke 24:52) as they alternated between the Temple (Luke 24:53) and the upper room (Acts 1:13), probably

where Jesus and the Twelve had shared the last supper (John
20:19). In both places the disciples were in a continual attitude of worship "in prayer and supplication," "praising and
blessing God."

There was an atmosphere of expectancy among the 120
as they waited for the promise of the Holy Spirit. Three
times Jesus had promised that He would send them another
Comforter: twice at the last supper (John 14:16, 26; 16:7),
and once again just before He ascended into heaven (Luke
24:49; Acts 1:8). The disciples fully expected the Spirit to
come, though they could not have known exactly what to expect. The word *suddenly* suggests that the Spirit came with
unexpected power and glory, despite the fact that they were
anticipating the enduement. The extraordinary manner of the
Spirit's coming to them exceeded anything they anticipated.

Although their intense desire prepared them for the Holy
Spirit, it does not imply, as some would have us believe, that
they were victims of autosuggestion. Only a miracle could
cause 120 persons to have a uniform experience and single
reaction to that experience—especially when these persons
were sincere followers of Christ, without guile or hypocrisy.

The Incident. When the Holy Spirit suddenly came upon
the disciples, He was accompanied by three phenomena—the
sound of wind, the appearance of fire, and speaking with
tongues. The sound came from heaven and swept through
the house where the disciples were gathered. The sound
was like a mighty gust, a rush and roar of wind, very strong
and penetrating. There was no actual wind, but only the
sound "as of wind." The appearance of flames of fire filled
the room, then divided and settled upon each of the 120
worshipers. Like the wind, the fire was "like as" of fire. Then
the disciples began to speak in strange languages, as cascades
of praise began to flow from their lips. Thus the hearing, the
sight, and the speech of the disciples were all brought into the
participation of divine worship. The entire personalities of the

worshipers were overwhelmed by the ineffable Spirit of God. They spoke "as the Spirit gave them utterance."

The phenomena of wind and tongues of fire seem to have appeared only in this initial outpouring of the Spirit. They are not mentioned in any of the subsequent accounts of glossolalia, though speaking in tongues did occur again. It is apparent, then, that the wind and fire served an initial purpose only, while tongues was the continuing evidence of the Holy Spirit baptism.

From verse 4 it is clear that *all* were filled with the Holy Ghost and (still *all)* began to speak with tongues. This was the uniform manifestaton of the Spirit's presence. No other sign (Mark 16:17, 18) or gift (1 Corinthians 12:8-10) was in evidence. These came into evidence later, but only tongues gave immediate evidence of the infilling.

The Consequence. Now notice what effect the phenomenon had on the observers and witnesses of the event:

> Acts 2:5 And there were dwelling at Jerusalem Jews, devout men, out of every nation under heaven.
>
> 6 Now when this was noised abroad, the multitude came together, and were confounded, because that every man heard them speak in his own language.
>
> 7 And they were all amazed and marvelled, saying one to another, Behold, are not all these which speak Galilaeans?
>
> 8 And how hear we every man in our own tongue, wherein we were born?
>
> 9 Parthians, and Medes, and Elamites, and the dwellers in Mesopotamia, and in Judaea, and Cappadocia, in Pontus, and Asia.
>
> 10 Phrygia, and Pamphylia, in Egypt, and in the parts of Libya about Cyrene, and strangers of Rome, Jews and proselytes,
>
> 11 Cretes and Arabians, we do hear them speak in our tongues the wonderful works of God.

Because of its importance in Jewish worship, the Feast of Pentecost attracted multitudes of Jews each year. Even then the Jews lived in "every nation under heaven." The presence of this multitude served to the glory of God, for they impressively verified the miracle of tongues. These devout Jews, plus some proselytes (Gentiles who had adopted the Jewish religion) were understandably bewildered when they heard the Galilean followers of Christ speaking in fifteen or more foreign languages.

The fifteen nationalities represented in Jerusalem for the Feast of Pentecost constituted a virtual sweep of the vast Roman Empire. From the Eastern or Babylonian lands of Parthia, Media, Elam or Assyria, and Mesopotamia, the survey scans westward through Syrian and Egyptian lands to the Roman. The major lingual families were represented in the listing—with only a few notable exceptions: Macedonia, Achaia, Cyprus, Cilicia, and others are not mentioned. The Greek language was spoken in most such lands, however, and Greek was one of the common languages (along with Aramaic) spoken in Palestine.

The enumeration of these widely-separated lingual and ethnic families is of great import. It means that a band of provincial Galileans, under the afflatus of the Spirit, spoke in at least fifteen languages they could not have learned and probably had never heard before.

It has been suggested that the glossolalia of the disciples was a mere psychological phenomenon, that these Galileans had heard the listed languages in the marketplaces and on the streets of Jerusalem. These languages were embedded in the subconscious mind and were vented by the impulse of their emotional experience. Such a theory denies the accuracy of the Bible and does injustice to the intellect of the disciples. It reveals the extent to which the unspiritual mind will go in order to discredit the supernatural manifestations of God.

The things spoken by the disciples were not marketplace bargaining or street-scene trivia. They spoke the "wonderful works of God" (v. 11). Their speech consisted of exalted praise, not broken and disconnected catch-phrases. It consisted of syntax and sense, not neurotic jargon.

The reaction of the multitude emphasizes the genuineness of the manifestation. Some felt certain that the ecstatic boldness of the disciples was occasioned by the imbibing of wine (v. 13). Upon Peter's explanation and subsequent sermon, about three thousand persons were converted to Christ.

Here we see an important truth. Tongues drew the multitude's attention and glorified Christ; the phenomenon did not, however, supplant preaching in the winning of the lost. Peter's sermon was necessary for that. The suggestion of some scholars that tongues were given for evangelizing the lost is incorrect. Tongues were given for a sign of the Spirit's indwelling, a sign of the presence of God with man. As we shall see later, however, there would be situations in which glossolalia, combined with interpretation, would serve for edification, exaltation, and comfort (1 Corinthians 14:3).

THE SAMARITAN REVIVAL

The Occasion. In Acts 8 we have the second account of an outpouring of the Holy Spirit. Though glossolalia is not specifically mentioned in this instance, it is so strongly implied that the incident must be taken into consideration.

A period of great persecution against the church in Jerusalem resulted in the Christians' being scattered throughout Judea and Samaria. Except for the apostles, who stayed in Jerusalem, the other disciples departed from the city. Philip, the evangelist (Acts 6:3, 5), went to Samaria and led in a great spiritual awakening. The Bible records it thus:

> Acts 8:5 Then Philip went down to the city of Samaria, and preached Christ unto them.
> 6 And the people with one accord gave heed unto those things which Philip spake, hearing and seeing the miracles which he did.
> 7 For unclean spirits, crying with loud voice, came out of many that were possessed with them: and many taken with palsies, and that were lame, were healed.

8 And there was great joy in that city.

9 But there was a certain man, called Simon, which beforetime in the same city used sorcery, and bewitched the people of Samaria, giving out that himself was some great one:

10 To whom they all gave heed, from the least to the greatest, saying, This man is the great power of God.

11 And to him they had regard, because that of long time he had bewitched them with sorceries.

12 But when they believed Philip preaching the things concerning the kingdom of God, and the name of Jesus Christ, they were baptized, both men and women.

The Incident. Though the Samaritans believed and were baptized, they did not immediately receive the Holy Ghost. The effects of the gospel and the fruit of salvation are evident. Also evident are the effects of the power of the Holy Spirit baptism in the life of Philip: miracles of healing and exorcism were wrought. The whole city was filled with joy. It is striking how the events in Samaria followed the words of Peter on the Day of Pentecost (Acts 2:38):

"Repent, and be baptized every one of you in the name of Jesus Christ for the remission of sins, and ye shall receive the gift of the Holy Ghost."

However, even after the Samaritans had believed unto salvation and were baptized, it remained for them to be filled with the Holy Spirit. That experience also came to them:

Acts 8:14 Now when the apostles which were at Jerusalem heard that Samaria had received the word of God, they sent unto them Peter and John:

15 Who, when were come down, prayed for them, that they might receive the Holy Ghost:

16 (For as yet he was fallen upon none of them: only they were baptized in the name of the Lord Jesus.)

17 Then laid they their hands on them, and they received the Holy Ghost.

The Consequence. While it is not explicitly stated that the Samaritans spoke with tongues when they received the Holy Ghost, any honest reading suggests that possibility. It is strongly implied. Certainly the Spirit was accompanied by observable signs. These signs arrested the attention of Simon the Sorcerer and he sought to buy the power to reproduce them (v. 18). Consistency with the context of this account and with the other outpourings of the Spirit makes it conclusive that these signs included glossolalia.

F. F. Bruce says, "The context leaves us in no doubt that their reception of the Spirit was attended by external manifestations such as had marked His descent on the earliest disciples at Pentecost."[10] A. T. Robertson, commenting on the Greek text, states that the language structure . . . "shows plainly that those who received the gift of the Holy Spirit spoke with tongues."[11] John Trapp, the great Puritan scholar of the seventeenth century, commented that the Holy Spirit fell upon the Samaritans "in those extraordinary gifts of tongues and miracles."[12]

Despite the weight of evidence that the Samaritans spoke with tongues, there are some who insist that if they had done so the fact would be specifically stated. This is not true, for there are two instances in Scripture when the fact of tongues was omitted in one account and graphically related in another. One of these is the case of Paul. In Acts 9:17, 18 we read: "And Ananias went his way, and entered into the house; and putting his hands on him said, Brother Saul, the Lord, even Jesus, that appeared unto thee in the way as thou camest, hath sent me, that thou mightest receive thy sight, and be filled with the Holy Ghost. And immediately there fell from his eyes as it had been scales: and he received sight forthwith, and arose, and was baptized."

Following his conversion on the road to Damascus, Paul

---

[10] F. F. Bruce, *Commentary on the Book of the Acts* (Grand Rapids: Wm. B. Eerdmans Publishing Company, 1954), p. 181.

[11] A. T. Robertson, *Word Pictures in the New Testament* (New York: Harper and Row Company, 1930), III, p. 107.

[12] John Trapp, *Commentary on the New Testament* (Grand Rapids: Zondervan, 1958 reprint of The Richard D. Dickinson edition, London, 1865), p. 438.

received the Holy Spirit when Ananias laid hands on him. Observe here that two things were to happen—Paul was to receive his sight, and he was to be filled with the Holy Ghost. In verse 18, while we read that he indeed received his sight, it is not specified that he was filled with the Holy Spirit. Are we to gather then that he did not receive this impartation? Admittedly, any such suggestion would be ridiculous. We know that he was filled with the Spirit, for Acts 13:9 says "Then Saul, (who also is called Paul,) filled with the Holy Ghost, set his eyes on him."

We follow with the same question regarding glossolalia and arrive at the same answer. We cannot conclude that if Paul had spoken in tongues the Scriptures would have clearly stated it. Though the fact is not recorded in the historic record, it is emphasized in the epistolary literature, where Paul said, "I thank my God, I speak with tongues more than ye all!" (1 Corinthians 14:18).

A similar situation exists in Acts 10, where we have the historic record of how the household of Cornelius received the Baptism of the Holy Spirit, and in Acts 11, where Peter recounted the event to the other apostles. While the manifestation of tongues is pointedly mentioned in the former, it is absent in the latter. We may be sure that Peter mentioned tongues, since we do know that the sign was present (v. 46), for this was the evidence that God had received Gentiles.

What this reveals is that glossolalia was so much a part of the apostolic scene that its presence was assumed in the gospel record. The miracle of tongues was simply an accepted and expected attendant to the Holy Spirit in the lives of the believers.

THE HOUSE OF CORNELIUS

The Occasion. Acts 10 gives a detailed account of how the household of Cornelius received the Baptism of the Holy

Spirit and spoke with tongues. Whereas the Day of Pentecost had concerned only Jews, and even the Samaritans were half Jews, this incident involved an out-and-out Gentile. It is therefore referred to as the "Pentecost of the Gentile world." Cornelius was a Gentile, of great repute among the Jews, a God-fearing man from Italy, a commander in the Roman army. He was a devout, prayerful, charitable man who worshiped the true God of the Jews. He observed the Jewish hours of prayer (Acts 10:3, 30); yet he was not a proselyte, for he did not observe the ceremonial aspects of the Jewish religion (Acts 11:3). Proselytes were circumcised, baptized, and offered Jewish sacrifices. In every way short of circumcision, it may be said, Cornelius satisfied the Jewish requirements. He was what the Jews called a "God-fearer." The impressive list of his religious qualifications marks him as a man of unusual spiritual integrity. If not yet altogether, he was certainly very near to the kingdom.

Notwithstanding the centurian's spiritual excellence, the Jews were so prejudiced against the Gentiles that God had to prepare Peter for his encounter with Cornelius by giving the apostle a miraculous vision (Acts 10:9-16). Consequent to the vision, Peter went to Cornelius in Caesarea, seat of the Roman command in Judea, and preached to him and his household.

> Acts 10:44 While Peter yet spake these words, the Holy Ghost fell on all them which heard the word.
> 45 And they of the circumcision which believed were astonished, as many as came with Peter, because that on the Gentiles also was poured out the gift of the Holy Ghost.
> 46 For they heard them speak with tongues, and magnify God. Then answered Peter,
> 47 Can any man forbid water, that these should not be baptized, which have received the Holy Ghost as well as we?

The Incident and Consequence. While Cornelius and his household listened to Peter's sermon, "the Holy Ghost fell on all them which heard the word" (10:4), "for they [Peter and the Jews] heard them speak with tongues" (10:46). It was the manifestation of tongues that confirmed to the Jews that the Gentiles were converted and had received the Holy Spirit. The Jews acknowledged that they had "received the Holy Ghost *as well as we*" (10:47).[13] Later Peter recounted the incident to the elders in Jerusalem and compared Cornelius' experience with the first manifestation at Pentecost:

"And as I began to speak, the Holy Ghost fell on them, *as on us at the beginning*" (11:15). "God gave them the like gift *as He did unto us,* who believed on the Lord Jesus Christ" (11:17).[14]

The expressions *as well as we, as on us,* and *as He did unto us* draw a pointed parallel between the Jewish experience on Pentecost and the Gentile experience in Caesarea.

It is noteworthy that in this instance the Holy Spirit fell before the act of water baptism. In the other Biblical incidents water baptism came first and then the Baptism with the Holy Spirit. Another similarity is the suddenness with which the Spirit descended. Cornelius and his house seem to have been ready for the outpouring as the original 120 had been.

THE EPHESIAN BAPTISM

The Occasion. In Acts 19:1-7 we have the last mention of glossolalia in the book of Acts. It occurred in the distant Asian city of Ephesus, nearly a quarter of a century after the Day of Pentecost.

> Acts 19:1 And it came to pass, that, while Apollos was at Corinth, Paul having passed through the upper coasts came to Ephesus: and finding certain disciples,
> 2 He said unto them, Have ye received the Holy Ghost since ye believed? And they said unto him, We have not so much as heard whether there be any Holy Ghost.
> 3 And he said unto them, Unto what then were ye baptized? And they said, Unto John's baptism.
> 4 Then said Paul, John verily baptized with the baptism of

---

13 Italics ours.
14 Italics ours.

repentance, saying unto the people, that they should believe on him which should come after him, that is, on Christ Jesus.
5 When they heard this, they were baptized in the name of the Lord Jesus.
6 And when Paul had laid his hands upon them, the Holy Ghost came on them; and they spake with tongues, and prophesied.
7 And all the men were about twelve.

There is a possibility that the twelve men mentioned here had been in some way associated with Apollos. There were at least strong similarities in their experiences; they were all associated with the city of Ephesus, and Apollos' name is mentioned here as a reference point of time.

Apollos, a Jewish Christian from Alexandria, had had incomplete knowledge of the Holy Spirit, though he was a man mighty in the Scriptures and endowed with great abilities (18: 24-28). Apollos had accepted the work of repentance unto salvation—and this he preached with zeal and persuasion—but it remained for Aquila and Priscilla to lead him into the deeper work of the Spirit. They "expounded unto him the way of God more perfectly (18:26)." His understanding had not been inaccurate, only incomplete.

The Incident and Consequence. In Ephesus Paul encountered a group of disciples whose spiritual circumstances were similar to those of Apollos. Whether they were Jews living in Ephesus or converted Gentiles is not known. More likely they were the former. These twelve men had either been baptized in Judea by John the Baptist or by one of his disciples in anticipation of the coming of Christ. This is the obvious meaning of verse 4. There is no doubt that the men were genuine Christians, for Luke called them disciples (19:1), and Paul affirmed that they were believers (19:2). They had not, however, remained in Judea long enough to know of the outpouring of the Holy Spirit on the Day of Pentecost. The statement "We have not so much as heard whether there be any Holy Ghost" does not mean that they had no knowledge of the Person, the dispensation, or the office work of the Holy Spirit. Nor does it mean that they had never experienced His regenerative work. What they had never heard of was the deepening, enriching, infilling of the Spirit available to all believers in Christ. In short, they had never heard of the Baptism in the Holy Spirit.

When Paul baptized the twelve men and laid hands on them, the Holy Spirit came on them, and they spoke with tongues and prophesied (19:6). This recurrence of the glossolalia of Pentecost occurred in the Province of Asia, *under the ministry of one who had not even been present on the Day of Pentecost, to persons who could not have anticipated the experience, for the very reason that they had never heard of it.*

A. J. Gordon, in *The Ministry of the Spirit,* aptly observes:

> This passage seems decisive as showing that one may be a disciple without having entered into possession of the Spirit as God's gift to believers. Some admit this, who yet deny any possible application of the incident to our own times, alleging that it is the miraculous gifts of the Spirit which are here under consideration, since, after recording that when Paul had laid his hands upon them and "the Holy Ghost came upon them," it is added that "they spake with tongues and prophesied." All that need be said upon this point is simply that these Ephesian disciples, by the reception of the Spirit, came into the same condition with the upper-room disciples who received him some twenty years before, and of whom it is written that "they were all filled with the Holy Ghost and began to speak with other tongues as the Spirit gave them utterance." In other words, these Ephesian disciples on receiving the Holy Ghost exhibited the traits of the Spirit common to the other disciples of the apostolic age.[15]

In Ephesus as in Caesarea, there is no indication that the tongues spoken were foreign languages. The disciples' speech was not heard by foreigners, and Paul gave no indication of

---

[15] A. J. Gordon, *The Ministry of the Spirit* (Philadelphia: The Judson Press, 1950), pp. 71, 72.

understanding what was said. These men also prophesied, however, and that would have been understood. As we shall see, prophecy is ecstatic speech in the understood language of any group.

It is interesting to note that in Ephesus the disciples were baptized in water before they received the Holy Spirit. So it was also in Samaria, as well as with the earliest disciples at Pentecost. The household of Cornelius received the Holy Spirit, however, and then were baptized. It is not likely that Peter would have been willing to baptize Cornelius before the speaking in tongues gave evidence that God accepted Gentiles (Acts 10:46-48).

In both Samaria and Ephesus the disciples received the Holy Spirit when Peter and John, in the former instance, and Paul, in the latter, laid hands on them. It is in no way implied that the apostles imparted the Spirit to the people, or that they had power to do so in themselves. The laying on of hands is significant as a token of confirmation, of encouragement or blessing, but not as a means of dispensing any grace. No hands were laid on the disciples at Pentecost; they were filled with the Holy Spirit as they worshiped. Nor were hands laid on Cornelius and his family; the Holy Spirit fell on them as they listened to Peter preach. The Holy Spirit comes as a response to personal faith. For some that point of effective faith is reached through the stimulus of prayer. For others it is reached through the hearing of the Word, and still others through the touch of anointed hands.

Regardless of the setting or the antecedent, the consistent effects of the Spirit's coming were manifestations of spiritual power. And glossolalia was the most conspicuous and arresting of these.

IV. THE PROBLEM OF TONGUES IN THE CORINTHIAN CHURCH

Having looked at the several occurances of glossolalia in the book of Acts we now turn to a treatment of didactic nature. Occasioned by certain abuses of the gift in Corinth, 1 Corinthians 12-14 is the only extensive discussion of glossolalia in the Scriptures. Frankly corrective in purpose, the perceptive analysis treats with candor both the benefits and problems of the gift of tongues.

The church in Corinth was by no means ideal; it was in many regards a "problem church." That is not surprising when you consider the populace from which it was hewn.

Corinth was situated at one of the major crossroads of the ancient world. The situation of the city at the narrow Isthmus of Corinth exposed the people to heavy sea traffic, east and west, and a stream of land traffic north and south. The influences of many lands and cultures molded a community of polyglot, carnal men and women. Paul indicated the nature of the Corinthian people when he wrote: "Know ye not that the unrighteous shall not inherit the kingdom of God? Be not deceived: neither fornicators, nor idolaters, nor adulterers, nor effeminate, nor abusers of themselves with mankind, Nor thieves, nor covetous, nor drunkards, nor revilers, nor extortioners, shall inherit the kingdom of God. And such were some of you: but ye are washed, but ye are sanctified, but ye are justified in the name of the Lord Jesus, and by the Spirit of our God" (1 Corinthians 6:9-11).

As David Smith observed, however, "With all their faults the Corinthians were not lacking in distinguished and precious endowments. They were an intellectual community, delighting in eloquence and wisdom, 'speech' and 'knowledge.' "[16]

As Paul preached the gospel to them, many of these earthen vessels were cleansed and filled with the Holy Spirit (1 Corinthians 6:19). Notwithstanding the grace and power given to them, the people were imperfect in knowledge and understanding (1 Corinthians 14:20). It was in an effort to correct

---

[16] David Smith, *The Life and Letters of St. Paul* (New York: Harper and Row Company, [n.d.]), p. 243.

these misunderstandings and guide them toward spiritual maturity that Paul wrote the letter we know as 1 Corinthians. The apostle wrote from Ephesus, where news of the Corinthian problems had reached him. Evidently, numerous questions were forwarded to him by the confused congregation.

The pressure of the Corinthian confusion elicited from Paul some of Scripture's most eloquent doctrinal statements. One Pentecostal writer has observed that

> There are those who would point out to us that the Apostle Paul was not establishing doctrine in 1 Cor. 12-14. He was rather correcting the confusion of a "Corinthian" church. "The carnality of the Corinthians" is always emphasized by those who would discount the value of the charismatic gifts. It should be pointed out, however, that these same critics have overlooked the fact that the greatest doctrines of the Bible find their theological background in this same book. Christian unity, the cross, and spiritual verities are found in the first three chapters. The seventh chapter teaches the sacredness of marriage. Chapter eleven is read on almost every communion Sunday. "The greatest thing in the world" is found in chapter 13 according to Henry Drummond. The greatest chapter in the Bible on the resurrection is the fifteenth chapter of 1 Corinthians. The emphasis given to spiritual gifts in chapters 12, 13, and 14 is certainly for the purpose of "doctrine, for reproof, for correction, and for instruction in righteousness."[17]

GIFTS OF THE SPIRIT

A prominent feature of 1 Corinthians is the attention given to the subject of spiritual gifts, or the charismatic nature of the Holy Spirit. It is clear that one of the problems in the church was incomplete knowledge concerning the gifts; therefore, Paul introduced the subject by saying: "Now concerning spiritual gifts, brethren, I would not have you ignorant" (1 Corinthians 12:1).

1 Corinthians 12:4 Now there are diversities of gifts, but the same Spirit.

---

[17] Frank W. Smith, "What Value Tongues?" *Message . . . of the Open Bible,* XLV (June, 1963), p. 4.

> 5 And there are differences of administrations, but the same Lord.
> 6 And there are diversities of operations, but it is the same God which worketh all in all.
> 7 But the manifestation of the Spirit is given to every man to profit withal.
> 8 For to one is given by the Spirit the word of wisdom; to another the word of knowledge by the same Spirit;
> 9 To another faith by the same Spirit; to another the gifts of healing by the same Spirit;
> 10 To another working of miracles; to another prophecy; to another discerning of spirits; to another divers kinds of tongues; to another the interpretation of tongues:
> 11 But all these worketh that one and the selfsame Spirit, dividing to every man severally as he will.

The gifts of the Spirit are supernatural operations in the lives of those thus endowed. They are not permanently vested in individuals so that a person can exercise them at will; they are spiritual powers manifested through individuals as he wills (12:11).

It must also be emphasized that the gifts are *of the Spirit.* No natural abilities or human approximations are to be reregarded as spiritual gifts. The gifts are supernatural in manifestation and effect. They operate through human channels but are never human in origin. It is true that at times a gift is manifested through an individual whose natural disposition fits him for it; for instance, a person who is naturally discerning may be exercised·by the discerning of spirits or a person naturally wise, with the word of wisdom. The exceptions to this, however, are too numerous to make it even close to a rule. When the gift of tongues is manifested, it is rarely through a linguist. When the gifts of healing are manifested, it is rarely through a physician.

The point is that, while human abilities and powers are admirable, they are not to be equated with or substituted for the dispensation of spiritual gifts.

An apparent fault among the Corinthians was their preference for the spectacular gifts over those of less conspicuous character. Paul enumerated nine gifts, all of which are important to the Christian witness and necessary for the branches to do the work of the vine. Whether great or small, the nine are alike sacred. None should be disparaged or neglected and none should be accorded disproportionate prominence. Paul admonished the Corinthians to "covet earnestly the best gifts" (12:31) without specifying which are the best. All are valid for the Christian community and should be desired by every Christian believer (12:31; 14:1).

For the purpose of analysis and retention it should be observed that there are three categories of gifts—(1) those that reveal the mind of God to man, (2) those of spiritual power and performance, (3) those manifested through the spoken voice as the Spirit inspires the individual. There are three gifts in each category as follows:

Gifts of revelation—the word of wisdom, the word of knowledge, and the discerning of spirits;

Gifts of operation—faith, the gifts of healing, and the working of miracles;

Gifts of inspiration—prophecy, divers kinds of tongues, and the interpretation of tongues.

At this point let us note briefly the function of these charismatic manifestations. Although our primary study at this time is the gift of tongues, we will do well to observe it in relationship to the other eight.

The Word of Wisdom. This gift illustrates the importance of wisdom in all the functions of life. Proverbs 4:7 says: "Wisdom is the principal thing; therefore get wisdom: and with all thy getting get understanding." The wisdom here is neither a native faculty nor a permanent impartation; it is a word of wisdom manifested in a time of need.

The Word of Knowledge is similarly a Spirit-borne manifestation in a time of urgency. Neither is it a permanent impartation, as though God gives a package of ready-made knowledge for the believer to glory in or to use at his own discretion. The term "word of" implies the nature of both gifts; they are manifestations of the Spirit that come as a stroke of insight and understanding when urgency demands them. The word of knowledge is a revelation of facts or situations, and the word of wisdom is a revelation of solutions or insights. They were no doubt clearly in mind when Christ said: "But beware of men: for they will deliver you up to the councils, and they will scourge you in their synagogues; And ye shall be brought before governors and kings for my sake, for a testimony against them and the Gentiles. But when they deliver you up, take no thought how or what ye shall speak: for it shall be given you in that same hour what ye shall speak. For it is not ye that speak, but the Spirit of your Father which speaketh in you" (Matthew 10:17-20). Read also Luke 12:11, 12 and Luke 21:12-15.

Faith. Faith is the only Christian grace mentioned both as a fruit of the Spirit (Galatians 5:22) and as a gift of the Spirit. The obvious reason is that there are various forms and expressions of faith in the spiritual life. We must, first of all, have that faith by which the just shall live (Hebrews 10:38) and without which it is impossible to please God (Hebrews 11:6). That is living faith, the fruit of the Spirit.

We may then have the gift of faith, a faith that manifests God's power in special ways. It is an intercessory faith by which healings are effected (James 5:14) and miracles are performed (1 Corinthians 13:2, Matthew 17:20; 21:21). Both A. T. Robertson[18] and Conybeare and Howson[19] speak of this as "wonder-working faith."

Gifts of Healing. This is mentioned in the plural for the

18 A. T. Robertson, *op. cit.,* IV, p. 169.
19 W. J. Conybeare and J. H. Howson, *The Life and Epistles of St. Paul* (Grand Rapids: Wm. B. Eerdmans Publishing Company, 1957), p. 405.

very reason that sicknesses and diseases are so numerous and varied. As it was in apostolic days, the gifts of healing constitute one of the most conspicuous of all the gifts. The very omnipresence of disease brings it into sharp focus at all times, and the suffering of mankind makes it one of the most beneficial and desired of all the gifts.

Once again it must be pointed out that this is an impartation of the Spirit's power. Healings cannot always be wrought at the will of those exercised by the gift. The will of God and the faith of the sick person play a great part (John 5:19, 20; Acts 14:8-10).

The Working of Miracles. Some illness is caused by organic malfunction and some by demon possession. Whereas mere sickness can be cured by the gift of healing, the exorcism of a demon requires the working of a miracle (Acts 16:16-18). Divine healing works in harmony with natural processes, but a miracle requires a change or even a reversal of the wonted laws of nature. It is a deviation from normal physical processes that could happen only through supernatural intervention. In Ephesus God wrought special miracles through Paul (Acts 19:11). In Acts 13:8-11 the apostle effected a miracle that was a healing in reverse, when Elymas the Sorcerer was struck with blindness.

Prophecy. Contrary to common opinion, prophecy is not just foretelling the future; it is also forth-telling, or speaking forth God's message under the control and guidance of the Holy Spirit. Neither is it ordinary pulpit preaching, which is the product of human study and insight touched by the anointing Spirit of God. There is a difference between the most anointed preaching and the manifestation of prophecy.

Howard P. Courtney in a study of *The Vocal Gifts of the Spirit* observes: "The Holy Spirit, through the gift of prophecy, uses the voices of yielded believers to speak to His people. The gift of prophecy never goes beyond the Word . . . Prophecy may be defined as speaking one's own language in the power of the Spirit, or as divine ability to forth tell. It is speaking for God; being a mouthpiece for God; being God's spokesman. It is a flowing forth, a springing forth, a heavenly overflow in intelligent, God-inspiring utterance."[20]

Prophecy is an ecstatic utterance in the speaker's own language. It is as electric and dynamic as speaking in tongues, except that it is understood by those who hear, and it achieves in one operation that which is achieved by the combination of tongues and interpretation. Because of this similarity tongues and prophecy are frequently mentioned together (Acts 19: 6; 1 Corinthians 14:4, 5, 6, 22, 23, 24).

Prophecy may be only a short message or it may be of extended sermon length. Whether brief or at length, however, it is spoken as the Spirit gives utterance.

Discerning of Spirits. As has been mentioned, some sickness is caused by demon possession and other is organic disorder. The gift of discerning of spirits enables one to recognize the difference and thus know whether a healing or a miracle of deliverance is required.

By the discerning of spirits the believer is also able to recognize true spiritual utterance and false or spurious imitations. So Peter saw through Ananias (Acts 5:3) and Simon the Sorcerer (Acts 8:20-23), and so Paul discerned the spirit that tormented the girl of Philippi (Acts 16:16-18).

It is manifest that this is one of the most beneficial of the gifts, and one that is sorely needed in these times.

Tongues. The expression "divers kinds of tongues" in addition to referring to different languages, indicates the ecstatic praise to God that edifies the speaker (1 Corinthians 14:2, 4) and the utterance that is interpreted for the church's edification (1 Corinthians 14:5). It also has in view the use of a specific human language, which, though unkown to the speaker, can be understood by those who know the language (Acts 2:4-8).

---

[20] Howard P. Courtney, *The Vocal Gifts of the Spirit* (Los Angeles: B. N. Robertson Company, 1956), p. 38.

J. H. King, one of the early leaders of the Pentecostal revival observed in his classic study *From Passover to Pentecost:*

> The sign is an evidence of the incoming of the Spirit to dwell within us. The gift is that which the Spirit Himself bestows. The sign was universal; the gift was given individually. The sign was the Spirit speaking in praise to God the Father, and God the Son. The gift was used in addressing men for their edification. The sign was ecstatic speech, the person being lifted out of himself with great joy. While speaking, the gift was exercised soberly; the person having complete control of himself while speaking. The gift must always be interpreted; the sign was not accompanied with interpretation. When the Spirit bestowed the Gift of Tongues, He also bestowed a corresponding Gift of Interpretation. The one was essential to the other. In that form of speaking as associated with the outpouring of the Spirit, no corresponding interpretation was given; therefore we conclude that it was quite different from the Gift of Tongues, which always has its corresponding Gift of Interpretation.[21]

Interpretation of Tongues. For the church to receive full benefit from an occurrence of glossolalia, it is necessary that the tongue be understood. Unless persons are present who have intellectual understanding of the language employed, the only other means of understanding is through interpretation. When a person gives the interpretation of a tongue, he speaks in ecstacy as he, like the glossolalist, is moved upon by the Spirit. There is no mental process by which the interpreter translates the unknown to the known and then reveals this to the church. Interpretation is supernatural in impulse and operation; the interpreter is as wondrously wrought upon by the Spirit as the one who speaks in tongues.

It should also be observed here that the exercise is an *interpretation* rather than a verbal *translation* or *transliteration* of what is spoken in tongues. For this reason the interpretation may vary in length from the message in tongues and may

---

[21] J. H. King, *From Passover to Pentecost* (Franklin Springs, Georgia: Publishing House of The Pentecostal Holiness Church, 1955), pp. 184, 185.

contain modes of expression peculiar to the interpreter or to the people. In this operation the Spirit interprets to the church the message, the meaning, the import of what has been spoken in tongues.

In addition to these spiritual gifts, which are in reality empowering graces for Christian service, there are other ministrations of the Spirit which are not involved in this present study. These are the ministry gifts mentioned by Paul in 1 Corinthians 12:28, Romans 12:6-8, Ephesians 4:11-13.

THE SUPREMACY OF LOVE

As observed earlier, the Corinthian church had scrambled its spiritual values by an inaccurate evaluation of the gifts. Some of the people apparently felt that the exercise of certain spectacular gifts gave proof of spiritual excellence or even supremacy. This erroneous concept was divisive and led to the neglect of basic Christian love. Love, not spiritual gifts, was the proof of spiritual integrity (John 13:35, 1 John 2:5; 3:14; 4:7-13, 20). So Paul proceeded from his discussion of the gifts to a discussion of love: "Covet earnestly the best gifts: and yet shew I unto you a more excellent way" (1 Corinthians 12:31).

Love is that more excellent way. The apostle did not advocate love in place of the gifts, but love and the gifts working together. He constantly reminded the Corinthians that they were to exercise the gifts (1 Corinthians 12:31; 14:1, 5, 12, 39) with love. Boldly Paul stressed that without love even the gifts would be meaningless:

"If I speak with the tongues of men and of angels, but have not love, I am become sounding brass, or a clanging cymbal. And if I have the gift of prophecy, and know all mysteries and all knowledge; and if I have all faith, so as to remove mountains, but have not love, I am nothing" (1 Corinthians 13:1, 2 ASV).

Paul, while endeavoring to correct an error, no more discounted the validity and value of these gifts than he discredited charity and martyrdom when he continued: "And if I bestow all my goods to feed the poor, and if I give my body to be burned, but have not love, it profiteth me nothing" (1 Corinthians 13:3 ASV). He was graphically, impressively showing the supremacy of love over all other Christian graces and gifts. The gifts are to be exercised in addition to love, not in lieu of it. Follow after love *and* desire spiritual gifts (1 Corinthians 14:1), for love is eternal and the gifts are not:

> 1 Corinthians 13:8 Love never faileth: but whether there be prophecies, they shall be done away; whether there be tongues, they shall cease; whether there be knowledge, it shall be done away. 9 For we know in part, and we prophesy in part; 10 But when that which is perfect is come, that which is in part shall be done away. (ASV)

These verses are often misunderstood to mean that the gifts of the Spirit were temporary and ceased with the apostolic age. Such is not the case. The view here is manifestly of eternity, when the earthly life and its necessities are ended (13:10, 12). The gifts are for the work of the kingdom in this life, until the eternal kingdom shall be established and Christ enthroned. There will be no need then of knowledge when knowledge is full and complete. We will no longer need a *manifestation* of prophecy, or knowledge, or tongues when we have the perfection or fullness of their benefits? The perfect will then have come.

It is different with love. This is eternal. Heaven is made of love so there can be no end to it. The gifts are manifestations of God's power, given so that we can continue the ministry of Christ on earth (John 14:12; 15:1-8). Love is the very essence of God (1 John 4:7, 8). Because He lives, there is love; wherever His Spirit is, in heaven or on earth, there is love. It never ends.

REGULATION OF TONGUES

With the admonition to "Follow after love: yet desire earnestly spiritual gifts" (ASV), Paul went on to a long, careful discussion of the gift of tongues (1 Corinthians 14). The Corinthian errors necessitated the apostolic regulation of the gift. It should be stressed here that Paul neither prohibited nor discouraged the exercise of the gift. Nor did he attempt to disparage or devalue it. He merely endeavored to show the Corinthians its proper function in the church. We err, therefore, when we try to read into Paul's words any intent to dismiss or discard the gift.

The Corinthians also had erroneous attitudes regarding the sacraments, especially the Lord's Supper, and Paul devoted much attention to those irregularities (1 Corinthians 10-11). His intent was to correct the errors, not to abolish or discourage the Lord's Supper. So it was with the glossolalic manifestation. Let us look at his words:

> 1 Corinthians 14:1 Follow after love; yet desire earnestly spiritual gifts, but rather that ye may prophesy. 2 For he that speaketh in a tongue speaketh not unto men, but unto God; for no man understandeth; but in the spirit he speaketh mysteries. 3 But he that prophesieth speaketh unto men edification, and exhortation, and consolation. 4 He that speaketh in a tongue edifieth himself; but he that prophesieth edifieth the church. 5 Now I would have you all speak with tongues, but rather ye should prophesy. (ASV)

Unless tongues are interpreted for the edification of the church, prophecy is to be preferred, which is very similar in function to tongues. It is, however, in an intelligible language and is directed to the hearers. Tongues are ordinarily for praise and worship directed to the Lord.

We must conclude that the almost invariable function of uninterpreted tongues is praise and adoration. Men pray in tongues (14:14), sing in tongues (14:15), give thanksgiving and blessing in tongues (14:16). Obviously all of these are basically personal in nature and primarily edify the individual rather than the congregation.

Prophecy, on the other hand, is for edification, exhortation, and comfort (14:3); and by prophecy men learn and are comforted (14:19, 31). Tongues with interpretation can achieve the results of prophecy; therefore the glossolalist should pray that he may interpret (14:12, 13). Notwithstanding the several advantages of prophecy over uninterpreted tongues, the latter also has its specific purpose: tongues edify the believer and are a sign to unbelievers (14:22).

Although tongues are a sign to the unbeliever (14:22), if the manifestation continues without interpretation for a prolonged period, the effect will be reversed and the observer will conclude that the glossolalists are mad (14:23). Paul clearly detailed the order that should be followed so the benefits of glossolalia will not be lost (14:23-33). When the gift of tongues is manifested in a service there should be an interpretation. If it becomes apparent that there is no interpretation, the glossolalist should not continue until the worship of others is hindered (14:28). Instead, he should speak quietly to himself and to God (14:28).

In his establishing of order, Paul took care not to impair that which is good and beneficial (14:39). Perhaps most telling was his reminder to the Corinthians that he was the most frequent glossolalist of them all: "I thank God, I speak with tongues more than you all" (11 Corinthians 14:18 ASV).

This was no weak and pallid admission to a dubious or shameful practice; it was a hearty and willing affirmation to a manifestation of great worth. The apostle was aggrieved that the misdirected zeal of a few had abused something of power and value to the church. Paul was concerned lest the abuse of tongues bring disrepute to a worthy spiritual gift and hinder its freedom of operation in the church.

SUMMATION

Our brief study of glossolalia in the Scriptures gives abundant proof that speaking in tongues is a Biblical fact, that it originated with God, and that it was not only present at the birth of the Church, but that it also continued in widespread operation in the growing Church. As with any Christian truth, abuses arose which had to be corrected. Correction of the abuses, however, in no way discounted the experience, but on the contrary served to establish its extensity and historicity.

Glossolalia is undiminished in its value to the Church today. It brings edification to the speaker at all times and to the congregation whenever it is interpreted. It is still a sign of the Spirit's presence in the Church as He declares to our generation the wonderful works of God.

Glossolalia: Apostles to The Reformation

R. Leonard Carroll

R. Leonard Carroll is Third Assistant General Overseer of the Church of God and a member of the Executive Committee and of the Executive Council. He served as President of Lee College for five years, was listed in Who's Who in American Education and in Who's Who in Tennessee, and was elected to membership in Phi Delta Kappa, a national honorary fraternity for educators. He received his Bachelor of Arts degree from Furman University, his Master of Science degree and Doctor of Education degree from the University of Tennessee. He has served on the Home for Children Board and is currently serving as Chairman of the General Board of Education. He has traveled and preached in twenty-eight foreign countries. Among the numerous booklets which he has written are: The Holy Trinity, That I May Know Him, *and* Keeping the Foundation. *He is presently writing a book on* Stewardship.

R. Leonard Carroll

Glossolalia: Apostles to The Reformation

When subjected to criticism, any report of historical data is apt to undergo a great variety of judgments. Some people honestly praise the trustworthiness of an authority whom others decry as utterly unreliable. It is acknowledged that in a sphere where the feelings of mankind are so deeply involved, where opposing emotions and tendencies are concerned—as in the domain of religion—that diversity of opinion will be glaringly evident.

The character of the long dispute about the recurrence and authenticity of the glossolalia phenomenon has been colored by those who have entered the discussion with their minds already made up, and with their feelings deeply stirred. Even scholars render diverse judgments according to their idiosyncrasies and frequently come to opposite conclusions on the same evidence. Being cognizant of this very fact, a forthright attempt has been made to maintain a just sense of direction and to exercise great care in the presentation of the subject so as not to go beyond documented evidence.

If personal predilections and prejudices are valued more

69

than proper research, it will be difficult to predetermine
who will praise and who will condemn this study. The same
evidence which convinces one may fail to convince another.
The individual, therefore, must estimate the value of the
presentation according to his own insights and understand-
ings. The effectiveness of the material, then, will vary according to the total makeup of the individual and to his
willingness to understand and accept the findings of this study.
(It is believed, nevertheless, that the discovery of evidence
can refine the judgments and reshape the opinions of those who
desire to know and to live by the truth.)

During the past decade, tongues speaking has gained un-
precedented recognition and enlarging acceptance in the religious world. It is significant that large numbers of earnest
Christians who hold church membership outside the ranks of
Pentecostal groups have discovered a new dimension of joy
and expression through the operation of the glossolalia phenomenon. The recent widespread outburst of tongues speaking among long established non-Pentecostal denominations has,
however, stimulated an urge to determine the origin, continuation, value, purpose, and reality of the experience. Because the speaking with tongues has been often viewed with
suspicion and branded as heresy, the operation of glossolalia
in some religious circles has been subtly avoided, suppressed,
or totally ignored. As a result, few attempts have been made
toward developing objective studies which focus directly upon the glossolalia phenomenon. It is evident that the revival of
tongues speaking has accentuated the need for supporting
testimony from historical data which may help to clarify the
subject.

(The Holy Scriptures are clear and unmistakable with reference to glossolalia.) Confusion and dissension have, nevertheless, arisen over whether or not the glossolalia phenomenon
ceased with the apostles. The historical record, therefore, is
a vehicle of great significance provided there is an honest

endeavor to ascertain the scope of tongues speaking among the children of God since the Day of Pentecost. If the glossolalia phenomenon terminated with the birth of the Christian church, such evidence should be beyond reasonable dispute. On the other hand, if the Word of God and the records of history reveal the continuing and purposeful operation of tongues speaking through the ages, the matter of glossolalia should be carefully considered and respectfully received. It would be a grave mistake to discredit documented evidence and to nonchalantly dismiss tongues speaking as a vague, emotional, and irrational experience.

The Holy Bible is believed to be the very truth. It is further maintained that the records of sacred and secular history complement the Biblical record. As such, formal records become a definitive factor of paramount importance with regard to the actual occurrence of tongues speaking throughout the development of the Christian church. The specific purpose of this chapter is to trace the operation of tongues speaking from the days immediately following the ministry of the apostles through the experiences and writings of the Church Fathers into the Reformation. A secondary objective of this study is to analyze and appraise historical data in an attempt to point up meaningful implications for the church and believers today.

Basic Convictions

Foundational concepts determine the direction and the intelligent development of any inquiry. It is to be noted, however, that true research forgoes prejudicial bias, tradition, or private interpretation. Sober conclusions are relative to the deliberate consideration of facts. In order to enhance the possibility of a meaningful and factual presentation of research, a framework of basic truths undergirds this study.

First, the Holy Bible is accepted as the inspired, everlasting, and infallible Word of God. The Sacred Record, there-

For all
, Scared in case
disappointed

fore, is the <u>final authority</u> on the subject of glossolalia. This conviction is an objective truth which transcends all subjective interpretations. It is extremely significant therefore to determine whether or not tongues speaking occupies a place in the New Testament and, if so, of what prominence and consequence.

Second, the records of religious and secular history disclose objective truth and facts generally accepted as authoritative. History has a way of preserving and reflecting happenings very nearly as they occurred. If succeeding generations can openly accept the authenticity of previous reports of events in one area of experience, could not the same records be trusted when dealing with other matters? The critical scrutiny of the ages has dignified the works of the Church Fathers with meritorious status. Although much of this literature is seldom read, it nevertheless reveals that these men were capable writers who possessed unquestionable intellectual acumen. Thus, the experiences and writings of the Church Fathers and other historical literature are accepted as reliable sources of authoritative data. Since their writings have been commonly accepted, would it be reasonable to discount their trustworthiness when they discuss glossolalia?

Third, the glossolalia phenomenon has continued within the framework of the Body of Christ since the inception of the Church. That the Holy Ghost baptism, with the accompanying speaking in tongues, operated within the church of the apostles is beyond dispute. Can it be assumed that tongues speaking was simply to give the Early Church a triumphant entree into a hostile world? If the church needed such a unique and heavenly manifestation to begin an effective ministry, would it not be reasonable to reckon how desperately the church needed such a phenomenon in order to maintain a meaningful and continuing service to Christ within the confines of an increasingly sinful and contrary world? (The plan of God for the Spirit-filled life has been portrayed through the fact that the glossolalia phenomenon has survived determined opposition, peril, privation, suppression, and ridicule. The very *continuance* of tongues through the annals of the ages reflects divine association and approval!)

AN OVERVIEW OF HISTORY

Does sacred history really make sense? If accepted without private interpretation, the significance of historical data, including that segment which relates to the permanency of the promises of God (1 Corinthians 14; Acts 2:17, 18, 39), is self-evident. Special abilities or adept intellectual penetration are not necessary to properly evaluate the historical record. It is to be clearly understood, however, that objective analysis is distinct from merely responding to propaganda as so often the case has been. A superficial point of view may be intriguing but it is an unrealistic approach to truth. To discover truth has always been one of the main desires of sincere Christians. When there is this desire to arrive at the truth, there will be no hesitancy in accepting what proper research may disclose. That goes right to the heart of the mystifying quandries which have been allowed to develop around spiritual tongues speaking. This study urges the use of intelligence and the deliberate focusing upon facts.

It is absolutely necessary to recognize the evidence of God in history if the record is to have value; otherwise the history of man may appear to be an endless devouring cycle. This study projects the idea that the historical record is a matrix out of which emerges undeniable evidences of the truth of the Word of God. It is admitted, however, that the spiritual benefits derived from history are relative to the degree that the records may be correlated with the Word of God.

Truth is never discovered, however, simply by relying on popular consensus *per se!* Our task is to find, accept, and follow truth, and to translate it into everyday living. Though many may have denied the miracle of utterance, it does not follow that everyone must deny; though many have been frustrated by prejudice and bias, this is no indication that all must be ensnared; though a highly vocal segment of professed Christianity may have refused to "walk in the light," this need not prevent other believers—once freed—from receiving the inheritance of the saints!

A REWARDING ADVENTURE

To trace the recurrence of tongues speaking through the centuries is a most enlightening experience. An elementary observation, however, reveals that it is a mistaken assertion that the manifestation of glossolalia completely disappeared shortly after the Day of Pentecost. The facts of church history, on the other hand, reveal that this concept, for the most part has been based upon a deliberate and structured effort to circumvent tongues speaking, or the concept was erected upon stark ignorance. But it is profitable to review the annals of man for historical evidences which relate to the miracle of tongues speaking. It is clearly evident that many times since Pentecost the glossolalia phenomenon has broken out of its institutional container—the church—and has reworked the religious landscape.

It might be well to state here that the scope of this survey is limited to authenticated instances of tongues speaking rather than to compiling a voluminous report. The central aim of this study, then, is to present reliable witnesses to the manifestation of the miracle of utterance during respective periods of time following the first-century church until the Reformation. *The Interpreter's Dictionary of the Bible* states: "through the centuries glossolalia has frequently reappeared among Christian groups."[1] G. B. Cutten, author of *Speaking With Tongues* writes: "Many isolated examples of speaking

—tongues··
reliable
witnesses
that it has
not died
out

---

[1] *The Interpreter's Dictionary of the Bible* (New York: Abingdon Press, 1962), IV, p. 672.

with tongues might be given, extending down through the ages . . . In most cases the appearance of speaking with tongues has been connected with revival experiences. . . ."[2] *The Encyclopaedia Britannica* asserts that miraculous utterances recur in Christian revivals in every age.[3] Lefferts A. Loetscher is clear and emphatic in his statement: "The phenomenon of 'speaking with tongues as the Spirit gives utterance' (Acts 2:1-13) has appeared in all ages of the Church."[4]

A news reporter, McCandlish Phillips wrote concerning the modern charismatic revival, "Praying in tongues has recurred at intervals throughout the Christian era, although it did not affect large masses until early in this century."[5] Is not this candid evidence that when a person is not colored by prejudice, bias, tradition, or petty interpretation that he has little difficulty in seeing the perseverance of the miracle of utterance?

Burton Scott Easton states,

> If the modern history of estatic utterances has any bearing on the Apostolic age, the speaking in foreign languages could not have been limited only to Pentecost. . . . Tongues are a Divine gift, the exercise is not to be forbidden ([1 Corinthians] 14:39) . . . Indeed, to those who treat them simply with scorn they become a "sign" that hardening is taking place (14:21-23). . . . A purely intellectual and ethical religion is rather a dreary thing. A man who has never allowed his religious emotions to carry him away may be in a high state of grace—but he has missed something, and something of very great value.[6]

JUST WHAT WAS HAPPENING?

Dr. Philip Schaff, universally acknowledged historian, has

---

[2] G. B. Cutten, *Speaking With Tongues* (New Haven: Yale University Press, 1927), p. 113.

[3] "Tongues, Gift of" *Encyclopaedia Britannica*, 1958, XXII, p. 283.

[4] Lefferts A. Loetscher (ed.), *Twentieth Century Encyclopedia of Religious Knowledge* (Grand Rapids: Baker Book House, 1955), II, p. 1118.

[5] McCandlish Phillips, "And There Appeared to Them Tongues of Fire," *The Saturday Evening Post* (May 16, 1964), p. 32.

[6] Burton Scott Easton, "Tongues, Gift of," *International Standard Bible Encyclopaedia*, James Orr, gen. ed. (Grand Rapids: Wm. B. Eerdmns Publishing Company, 1943), V, p. 2997.

won the acclaim of all discerning scholars. It is evident that he also had the unique ability to recognize the vital trend of the times and to judge the inconsequential in its proper perspective. In his *History of the Apostolic Church,* he wrote

> The speaking with tongues, however, was not confined to the Day of Pentecost. . . . This gift perpetuated itself. We find traces of it still in the second and third centuries.[7]

In *Harper's Bible Dictionary,* Madeleine S. and J. Lane Miller state very pointedly:

> That this phenomenon is by no means restricted to early Christianity is universally recognized. It was common in the Christian movement as late as Tertullian and Irenaeus. By the time of Chrysostom it had apparently died out; at least the good bishop found difficulty in understanding what it really was. This, however, was but temporary. In later years it appeared again, and has been the seemingly inevitable consequence of all extended seasons of "revivals."[8]

John E. Steinmueller and Kathryn Sullivan make the following statement in the *Catholic Biblical Encyclopedia:*

> In regard to the perpetuation of these charisms, it may be said that, although they were manifested more frequently in the infant Church and the first few centuries, they have never been completely lacking in the Church.[9]
> . . . glossolalia was a true charism of the Holy Spirit.[10]

F. L. Cross, in *The Oxford Dictionary of the Christian Church,* says, "Similar phenomena are constantly met with in religious revivals."[11]

These references strike a death blow to the protracted assertion that tongues speaking had been filed away after the birth of the New Testament church. We are reminded that

---

[7] Philip Schaff, *History of the Apostolic Church,* Book I, Section 55, cited by Elmer C. Miller, *Pentecost Examined* (Springfield, Missouri: Gospel Publishing House, 1936, p. 18.

[8] Madeleine S. Miller and J. Lane Miller, *Harper's Bible Dictionary* (New York: Harper & Brothers, 1952), p. 768.

[9] John E. Steinmueller and Kathryn Sullivan, *Catholic Biblical Encyclopedia* (New York: Joseph F. Wagner, 1956), p. 101.

[10] *Ibid.,* p. 258.

[11] F. L. Cross, "Glossolalia," *The Oxford Dictionary of the Christian Church* (London: Oxford University Press, 1958), p. 564.

if these gifted writers can be trusted in one area of reporting, it follows that they can also be trusted when they discussed tongues speaking.

If tongues speaking had not ceased to occur, what forces
contributed to much of the silence on the subject? Evidence
comes to us from Eusebius of Caesarea, the "father of church
history," who lived from about A.D. 260 to 340. The *Church
History* of Eusebius presents a low estimation of a certain
sect of tongues speakers.[12] This segment of historical data
discloses far more, however, than the disrepute of a few
disorderly people. It is highly significant that the record also
reveals startling trends in religious interpretation and emphasis at this particular period of time. It is evident and
noteworthy, however, that the sarcasm and ridicule focus
directly upon the very *fact* that the glossolalia phenomenon
was actually in operation.

Mr. Arthur Cushman McGiffert,[13] in the notes which
accompany the text, presented supplementary information
which opens enlarging avenues of concern. Prophecy was refuted *not because of its substance* but because of the *form* of
its presentation. It was agreed that the prophecies contained
much that was true, but a reserved segment of the church
proper found the jubilant tongues speaking distasteful. The
form and method of delivery disturbed the mute formalism
that was rapidly infiltrating the church. It was now evident
that the vibrant apostolic church was being affected by a
subtle influence. Of no little significance is the fact that the
rich enthusiasm and vocal testimony which marked the Early
Church had almost disappeared by the middle of the second
century. Yet, in the midst of an atmosphere that was not
conducive to spiritual phenomena, tongues speaking continued!

---

[12] Eusebius, "Montanism" *Nicene and Post-Nicene Fathers,* Second Series
(Grand Rapids: Wm. B. Eerdmans Publishing Co., 1952), Vol. I, Book V,
Chapter XVI, p. 231.
[13] *Ibid.*

The Didache, a brief manual of instruction entitled *Teaching of the Twelve Apostles* (or Didache), and *The Shepherd of Hermas*, an apocalyptic work by Hermas, a Roman Christian, are early second century writings which indicate that the prophets spoke in a similar kind of vocal ecstasy that characterized Paul's time. There were still prophets, according to Justin and Clement of Alexandria,[14] who were not *generally* moved upon by the same miracle of utterance that marked their predecessors. Is not this an admission that tongues speaking was in operation even though it was forced to resist an entrenched system of formalism? The miracle of utterance may have become decidedly the exception, but when has it been required that any spiritual gift justify its significance or validity by the degree to which it is accepted? It is clearly evident that this Early Church Age had so completely departed from accepted practices of the church of the apostles that the old method of tongues speaking appeared to be a decided innovation. Prophecy, in itself, was nothing strange to them; but, due to the fact that the miracle of utterance had been so suppressed, its operation was not recognized as a revival of the New Testament form. The manner in which the spiritual tongues were delivered was revolting to the congealed form of worship; therefore, the bishops and other leaders of the church viewed the occurrence with suspicion.

The situation was further aggravated by the fact that the prophetic utterances of the tongues speakers claimed that the anointing of the Holy Ghost superseded the power of the constituted church authorities. Contrary to the operational pattern which had already been established in the church, these prophets insisted that the body of Christians must be guided by revelations from the Spirit rather than by legalistic impressions. The leaders of the church took the matter in hand and straightway condemned tongues speaking as out of order and pronounced its prophecy a fraud.

---

[14] *Ibid.*

Let us face a simple inquiry. Should the reaction have been so stringent that *all* prophecy and miracles of utterance should fall into discredit? Was it not clearly evident that when the enemies of Holy Ghost manifestations could not veil the truth of the Holy Scriptures, the next approach would be to create a breach between the will of God for the ministrations of the Holy Ghost within His church and the management of the Lord's estate? Since the original fall of man, Satan's chief aim has been to destroy the plan of God, to incapacitate God's children, and thereby retard the accomplishment of the kingdom of God in the earth!

The temperament of the age was reflected in fragments from an anonymous writer which were preserved by Eusebius.[15] The writer tacitly admits in one paragraph (v; Ch. 16) exactly what he had already denied in another: In one instance he charged that the lack of martyrs among the tongues-speaking group proved that they were heretics. In a following reference he admits the existence of such martyrs but vigorously maintains that this certainty did not in any way argue for their orthodoxy. The inconsistency was glaringly apparent and pointed up the caustic opposition to the operation of the glossolalia phenomenon. It is plain that the bitter catholic hostility took precedence over regard for the truth. Too often there has been a designed and persistent effort to paint the miracle of utterance as black as possible. Is it not entirely feasible that this religious reactionary resistance perpetuated itself from one generation of church leaders to succeeding ones?

Irenaeus, Bishop of Lyons, was a student of Polycarp and lived about A.D. 115 or 125 to 202. This association takes on added significance when it is realized that Polycarp had direct contact with Saint John. That Irenaeus was familiar with tongues speaking was obvious and his source of information dependable. The Bishop was not making an idle and ambiguous reference when he discussed the miracle of ut-

---

[15] *Ibid.*, pp. 231-233.

terance. Neither was he attempting to conjure up a vague, mystical, indefinite experience with which he had no Biblical connection. This is clearly seen in his writings from *Against Heresies*

> For [God] promised, that in the last times He would pour Him [the Spirit] upon [His] servants and handmaids, that they might prophesy. . . . This Spirit . . . also, as Luke says, descended at the day of Pentecost upon the disciples after the Lord's ascension . . . from whence also, with one accord in all languages, they uttered praise to God.[16]

Not only did this esteemed churchman have the ability to make a systematic exposition of the church's beliefs, but he also possessed a rare ability to relate the past to his own day. As an impartial reporter of contemporary events, Irenaeus gave an explicit testimony in his *Against Heresies* to the recurrence of the miracle of glossolalia.

> In like manner we do hear [or have heard] many brethren in the Church, who possess prophetic gifts, and who through the Spirit speak all kinds of languages, and bring to light for the general benefit the hidden things of men, and declare the mysteries of God, whom also the apostle terms "spiritual," they being spiritual because they partake of the Spirit.[17]

A careful reading of the reference extracts the thorn of critics and should silence them forever. There was no speculation in the report. The tongues speaking was actually heard. Brethren spoke all kinds of languages through the anointing of the Holy Ghost. This is a complete refutation of the common charge that the gifts of the Spirit are based upon some dreamy inoperative sentiment. "Many brethren" denotes that the miracle of tongues was not relegated to a *few outcasts*. They were warmly listed as "brethren," not brawlers. The occasion centered within the confines of the living church. Perhaps it was alarming to some people that the

---

16 Irenaeus, "Against Heresies." *The Ante-Nicene Fathers,* American Series (Grand Rapids: Wm. B. Eerdmans Publishing Co., 1956), Vol. I, Book III, Chapter XVII, p. 444.
17 *Ibid.,* Book V. Chapter VI, p. 531.

operation of the glossolalia phenomenon was not an isolated occurrence. The stage for tongues speaking was the church, not a dark alley. The miracle of utterance was not an aimless occurrence; it was to declare the mysteries of God and to reveal hidden things of men for the *general benefit* of all concerned. In the final analysis, the hallmark of the tongues speakers was that they were spiritual people.

> For this reason does the apostle declare, "We speak wisdom among them that are perfect" (1 Corinthians 2:6), terming those persons "perfect" who have received the Spirit of God, and who through the Spirit of God do speak in all languages, as he used Himself also to speak.[18]

Tertullian, a North African (150-220 or 240), is referred to by some historians as the father of Latin theology and church language. Some scholars esteem him as one of the greatest men of Christian antiquity. He received a liberal Graeco-Roman education and distinguished himself as a lawyer of rare genius who possessed keen discernment. He was a man of strong convictions and never hesitated to express them without fear or favor.[19]

In referring to the certainty of spiritual gifts, Tertullian said,

> . . . the apostle most assuredly foretold that there were to be "spiritual gifts" in the church. Now, can you refuse to believe this, even if indubitable evidence on every point is forthcoming for your conviction?[20]

This is a powerful appeal of a brilliant lawyer for a fair appraisal of the evidence on every point. Can we honestly refuse to believe that spiritual gifts, which include tongues speaking, are an integral part of church life? The gifts of the Spirit were not veiled entities to Tertullian. His works do not suggest in the slightest degree that any of Paul's list of gifts had

---

18 *Ibid.*
19 Philip Schaff, *History of the Christian Church* (Grand Rapids: Wm. B. Eerdmans Publishing Co., 1952), II, pp. 818-827.
20 Tertullian, "A Treatise on the Soul," *The Ante-Nicene Fathers*, American Edition, *op. cit.*, Vol. III, Chapter IX, p. 188.

been lost; neither do they forecast that their operation would cease. On the contrary, his convictions were positive and his thrust deliberate. In *Tertullian Against Marcion,* Tertullian asks Marcion to

> . . . exhibit . . . such as have not spoken by human sense, but with the Spirit of God, such as have both predicted things to come, and have made manifest the secrets of the heart . . . produce a psalm, a vision, a prayer—only let it be by the Spirit, in an ecstasy, that is, in a rapture, whenever an interpretation of tongues has occurred.

Then Tertullian declares:

> Now all these signs (of spiritual gifts) are forthcoming from my side without any difficulty; and they agree, too, with the rules, and the dispensations, and the instructions of the Creator; therefore without doubt the Christ, and the Spirit, and the Apostle, belong severally to my God. Here, then is my frank avowal for any one who cares to require it.[21]

This statement made by Tertullian is a classic example of the fact that the glossolalia phenomenon did not cease with the apostles. That the miracle of utterance was in operation in his day cannot be refuted. In essence, the Dean of Western Christianity was graphically defending the fact of tongues speaking against contemporary heretical views. His insight into the Holy Scriptures, his sincerity, and his personal integrity are clearly evident when he said, all these signs . . . agree with the rules, the dispensations, and the instructions of God.[22]

At this juncture it may be illuminating to pose a few simple questions. Do the rules, verities, and instructions of God change? Can the rules be adjusted for the sake of comfort or convenience? Can the instructions of God be tailored to fit the whims of any given age? Can a just God favor one group above another with the *benefits* of the Holy Ghost?

---

[21] Tertullian, "Tertullian Against Marcion," *The Ante-Nicene Fathers,* American Edition, *op. cit.,* Vol. III, Book V, Chapter VIII, p. 447.

[22] *Ibid.*

Contrary to the allusion of some sages that tongues speaking was the result of a frenzied emotional reaction, Tertullian avowed that the glossolalia phenomenon belonged to God! The passage indicates that tongues speaking was a normal part of the Christian experience and that if spiritual growth was allowed to proceed unhampered, the gifts would be freely forthcoming.

Pachomius, an Egyptian archimandrite, "was reported to have spoken the language of angels."[23] According to Dr. Philip Schaff, "tradition ascribes to him all sorts of miracles, even the gift of tongues."[24] Dr. Alban Butler in his *Lives of the Saints* related that this devoted monk "after seasons of prayer, under the power of the Spirit, was able to speak languages which he had never learned."[25] These references are unquestionable, conclusive. Tongues speaking had not been filed away.

Origen, a Christian philosopher, gave evidence that he knew about tongues speaking when he defended the Christian prophets of his day who were being attacked by Celsus. Celsus had ridiculed: "To these promises are added strange, fanatical, and quite unintelligible words, of which no rational person can find the meaning."[26]

Even though this brilliant philosopher did not make a strong defense for the miracle of utterance, he did disclose the fact that the phenomenon was still occurring.

Augustine's writings reflect more than an historical acquaintance with tongues speaking. In *Homilies on the First Epistle of John,* he appeared anxious "to make up the church's mind and get the matter out of the way."[27]

---

[23] Alban Butler, *The Lives of the Saints* (Baltimore: Murphy & Co., 1889), II, p. 218.

[24] Schaff, *op. cit.,* III, p. 197.

[25] Butler, *op. cit.,* Vol. II, p. 218.

[26] Origen, "Origen Against Celsus," *The Ante-Nicene Fathers* (New York: Charles Scribner's Sons, quoting Celsus, 1907), Vol. IV, Book VII, Chapter IX, p. 614.

[27] From *Tongues Speaking,* by Morton T. Kelsey. Copyright © 1964 by Morton T. Kelsey. Reprinted by permission of Doubleday & Company, Inc., p. 40.

In the earliest times, "the Holy Ghost fell upon them that believed: and they spake with tongues," which they had not learned, "as the Spirit gave them utterance." These were signs adapted to the time. For there behooved to be that betokening of the Holy Spirit in all tongues, to shew that the Gospel of God was to run through all tongues over the whole earth. That thing was done for a betokening and it passed away.[28]

The tone and direction of Augustine's presentation was *aimed* at disquieting what appeared to him to be a contemporary problem of the church which merited grave concern. Had there not been a point of reference there would have been no need for his pointed discussion. There would have been futility of purpose in his structured effort to convince the people that tongues speaking had passed away *if* they had actually ceased. A wise man never spends his time and energy at the tombs of the dead with a treatise which anxiously attempts to prove that the tombs are the residence of the dead *unless* there has been evidence of a resurrection!

A basic conviction of this study has been duly established. Tongues speaking occurred during the first century. Tongues speaking occurred during the second century. Tongues speaking occurred during the third century. Tongues speaking occurred during the fourth century. The facts from history have brought to naught the false assertion that the miracle of utterance ceased with the apostolic church.

Gregory Nazianzen,[29] an eloquent Cappadocian theologian and a teacher of the fourth century, recognized that the glossolalia phenomenon was the miraculous working of the Holy Ghost. In his discussion of tongues speaking in *On Pentecost* he relates,

They spoke with strange tongues, and not those of their native land; and the wonder was great, a language spoken by

---

[28] Augustine, "Homilies on the First Epistle of John," *The Nicene and Post-Nicene Fathers*, First Series (Grand Rapids: Wm. B. Eerdmans Publishing Co., 1956), Vol. VII, pp. 497, 498.
[29] Schaff, *op. cit.*, III, pp. 908-921.

those who had not learnt it. And the sign is to them that believe not, and not to them that believe, that it may be an accusation to the unbelievers, as it is written, With other tongues and other lips will I speak unto this people, and not even so will they listen to Me saith the Lord. But they heard . . . the Spirit wrought a miracle in the matter of the tongues.

But as the old Confusion of tongues was laudable, when men who were of one language in wickedness and impiety, even as some now venture to be, were building the Tower; for by the confusion of their language the unity of their intention was broken up, and their undertaking destroyed; so much more worthy of praise is the present miraculous one. For being poured out from One Spirit upon many men it brings them again into harmony. And there is a diversity of Gifts, which stands in need of yet another Gift to discern which is best, where all are praiseworthy.[30]

In the fourth century, Gregory Nazianzen verified the operation of many *praiseworthy gifts* which prompted concern and contemplation as to which gift was best. His discussion exhibits clarity as to the origin of glossolalia. "The Spirit wrought a miracle"[31] refutes the idea that tongues speaking is psychogenic. He also focuses attention upon the fact that the miracle of utterance had meaning and purpose—"a sign to them that believe not."[32] His report further discloses that there were *many* recipients of the gift of tongues who received desirable benefits from the miracle.

Basil the Great[33] was a distinguished church teacher of the fourth century from the Asiatic province of Cappadocia. In classical culture he holds a conspicuous place as a pulpit orator, theologian, shepherd of souls, and church ruler. The book of Basil the Great, *On the Spirit,* consigns the gifts of the Spirit, inclusive of diversities of tongues, to the arranging of the church. The church was the designated container of the gifts that are of the Holy Ghost. It is interesting to note that

---

[30] Gregory Nazianzen, "On Pentecost," *The Nicene and Post-Nicene Fathers,* Second Series, *op. cit.,* VII, pp. 384, 385.
[31] *Ibid.*
[32] *Ibid.*
[33] Schaff, *op. cit.,* III, pp. 893-903.

Basil without hesitation affirmed that the Spirit is the keystone in ordering, directing, and arranging the church.

> And is it not plain and incontestable that the ordering of the Church is effected through the Spirit? For He gave, it is said, "in the church, first Apostles, secondarily prophets," thirdly teachers, after that miracles, then gifts of healing, helps, governments, diversities of tongues," for this order is ordained in accordance with the division of the gifts that are of the Spirit.[34]

Basil's burden for the care of souls is sharply reflected in his words,

> It follows that the Spirit is verily the place of the saints and the saint is the proper place for the Spirit, offering himself as he does for the indwelling of God, and called God's Temple. So Paul speaks in Christ, saying "In the sight of God we speak in Christ," and Christ in Paul, as he himself says, "Since ye seek a proof of Christ speaking in me." So also in the Spirit he speaketh mysteries, and again the Spirit speaks in him . . . then, the Spirit is said to be in them "in divers portions and in divers manners," . . . For the grace flowing from Him when He dwells in those that are worthy, and carries out His own operations, is well described as existing in those that are able to receive Him.[35]

The ability to receive the ministrations of the Holy Spirit is relative to worthiness and the intent of the individual to carry out His operations.

Hilary of Poitiers, of the fourth century, "was a man of thorough biblical knowledge, theological depth and acuteness, and earnest, efficient piety. . . . an independent thinker and investigator. . . . He had an effective hand in the development of the dogma of the consubstantiality of the Son with the Father, and the dogma of the person of Christ."[36] His strong and earnest presentation of the powers and functions of the Holy Ghost are depicted in his writings *On the Trinity*:

---

[34] Basil, "The Book of Saint Basil on the Spirit," *The Nicene and Post-Nicene Fathers*, Second Series, *op. cit.*, VIII, p. 25.

[35] *Ibid.*, p. 39.

[36] Schaff, *op. cit.*, III, p. 960.

The next step naturally is to listen to the Apostle's account of the powers and functions of this Gift. . . . *Now to one is given through the Spirit the word of wisdom, to another the word of knowledge according to the same Spirit, to another faith in the same Spirit, to another gifts of healing in the One Spirit, to another workings of miracles, to another prophecy, to another discerning of spirits, to another kinds of tongues, to another interpretation of tongues.* . . . Here we have a statement of the purpose and results of the Gift; and I cannot conceive what doubt can remain . . .[37]

Hilary's words ring with a tonal quality of certainty. Tongues speaking, as well as the other gifts, has design and purpose. According to his explanation these precious treasures are functional.

The urgency of his appeal is disclosed when he exhorts the people of his own day and of succeeding generations,

Let us therefore make use of this great benefit, and seek for personal experience of this most needful Gift.[38]

Hilary was admonishing contemporary believers to take advantage of a spiritual benefit. It is not difficult to observe that tongues speaking, among other things, was felt to be a most needed and useful gift. Merely drifting along in an indifferent and vague state of heart was not enough. His advice was that believers should seek for a warm and invigorating personal experience.

In referring to Acts 1:4-8 and 1 Corinthians 12, Hilary reflects the tenor of his spiritual emphasis. He not only indicates that tongues speaking was in vogue, but he goes a step further: The speaking in tongues was a sign of the Holy Ghost.

We may be sure that here [1 Corinthians 12] we have a reference to the Father's same promise. Hence it is by these miraculous workings that the manifestation of the Spirit

[37] Hilary of Poitiers, "On the Trinity," *The Nicene and Post-Nicene Fathers,* Second Series, *op. cit.,* Vol. IX, Book II, p. 61.
[38] *Ibid.*

> takes place. For the gift of the Spirit is manifest . . . by kinds of tongues, that the speaking in tongues may be bestowed as a sign of the gift of the Holy Spirit . . . Thus in all these things distributed to each one to profit withal there is the manifestation of the Spirit being apparent through these marvelous advantages bestowed upon each. Now the blessed Apostle Paul in revealing the secret of these heavenly mysteries, most difficult to human comprehension, has preserved a clear enunciation and a carefully worded caution in order to show that these diverse gifts are given through the Spirit and in the Spirit.[39]

Attention is called to the fact that tongues speaking is a portion of the heritage of God's children. The spiritual manifestation of the miracle of utterance carries marvelous advantages with it. This gift is not carnal; neither is it a work of the flesh. Tongues speaking is given through the Holy Ghost and in the Holy Ghost.

Hilary further clarifies his position: Tongues speaking is clearly one of the Church's agents of ministry and work. God has ordained glossolalia:

> For God hath set some in the Church, first apostles, in whom is the word of wisdom; secondly prophets, in whom is the gift of knowledge; thirdly teachers, in whom is the doctrine of faith; next mighty works, among which are the healing of diseases, the power to help, governments by the prophets, and gifts of either speaking or interpreting divers kinds of tongues. Clearly these are the Church's agents of ministry and work of whom the body of Christ consists; and God has ordained them.[40]

Ambrose,[41] (340-397) son of the governor of Gaul, was educated for high civil offices; and, after distinguishing himself as a rhetorician, was elected imperial president of Upper Italy. He became one of ancient Christendom's greatest bishops who was full of dignity, energy, administrative wisdom, and the unction of the Holy Ghost. His exegesis Of the

---

[39] Ibid., Vol. IX, Book VIII, p. 146.
[40] Ibid., p. 147.
[41] Schaff, op. cit., III, pp. 961-967.

Holy Spirit plainly substantiates that tongues speaking was a continuing phenomenon received by the believer according to his capacity as he desired or deserved it.

> Lastly, it is the same God Who worketh all in all, that you may know that there is no diversity of operation between God the Father and the Holy Spirit; since those things which the Spirit works, God the Father also works, "Who worketh all in all." For while God the Father worketh all in all, yet "to one is given through the Spirit the word of wisdom; to another the word of knowledge, according to the same Spirit; to another faith, in the same Spirit; to another the gift of healings, in the one Spirit; to another the workings of miracles; to another prophecy; to another discerning of spirits; to another divers kinds of tongues; to another the interpretation of sayings; but all these worketh one and the same Spirit, dividing to each one as He will."
>
> There is then no doubt but that those things which the Father worketh, the Spirit worketh also. Nor does He work in accordance with a command, as he who hears in bodily fashion, but voluntarily, as being free in His own will, not the servant of the power of another. For He does not obey as being bidden, but as the giver He is the controller of His own gifts.
>
> . . . .
>
> See, God set apostles, and set prophets and teachers, gave the gift of healing . . . gave divers kinds of tongues. . . . each, according to his capacity, receives that which he either desires or deserves. . . . You see, the Father and Christ also set teachers in the Churches; and as the Father gives the gift of healings, so, too, does the Son give; as the Father gives the gift of tongues, so, too, has the Son also granted it.
>
> In like manner we have heard also above concerning the Holy Spirit, that He too grants the same kinds of graces. For it is said: "To one is given through the Spirit the gift of healings, to another divers kinds of tongues, to another prophecy." So, then, the Spirit gives the same gifts as the Father, and the Son also gives them.[42]

Ambrose's exegesis focuses upon other areas which are

---

[42] Ambrose, "Of the Holy Spirit," *The Nicene and Post-Nicene Fathers*, Second Series, *op. cit.*, Vol. X, Book II, Chapter XII, pp. 132-134.

worthy of consideration. The Triune God, of His own will, is the giver and controller of the glossolalia phenomenon. Tongues speaking, therefore, operates not at the command of man but in accordance with the power of God who controls and directs the miracle.

Leo,[48] who bears the title of "the Great" in the history of the Latin hierarchy, indicates in a sermon that the gift of glossolalia still continued as common property in the mouth of the Church.

> For as the Apostles' story testifies: "while the days of Pentecost were fulfilled and all the disciples were together in the same place, there occurred suddenly from heaven a sound as of a violent wind coming, and filled the whole house where they were sitting. And there appeared to them divided tongues as of fire, and it sat upon each of them. And they were all filled with the Holy Spirit, and began to speak with other tongues, as the Holy Spirit gave them utterance." Oh! how swift are the words of wisdom, and where God is the Master, how quickly is what is taught, learnt. No interpretation is required for understanding, no practice for using, no time for studying, but the Spirit of Truth blowing where He wills, the languages peculiar to each nation became common property in the mouth of the Church. And therefore from that day the trumpet of the Gospel—preaching has sounded loud: from that day the showers of gracious gifts, the rivers of blessings, have watered every desert and all the dry land, since to renew the face of the earth the Spirit of God "moved over the waters," and to drive away the old darkness flashes of new light shone forth, when by the blaze of those busy tongues was kindled the Lord's bright Word and fervent eloquence, in which to arouse the understanding, and to consume sin there lay both a capacity of enlightment and a power of burning. . . .
>
> . . . .
>
> By these and other numberless proofs, dearly beloved, with which the authority of the Divine utterances is ablaze, let us with one mind be incited to pay reverence . . . Let the minds of the faithful rejoice, that throughout the world One God, Father, Son, and Holy Ghost, is praised by the confession of all tongues, and that that sign of His presence,

---

[48] Schaff, *op. cit.*, III, pp. 314-323.

which appeared in the likeness of fire, is still perpetuated in His work and gift.[44]

Ronald A. Knox, a Roman Catholic prelate, admits in his exhaustive study of enthusiasm, that the fact of tongues speaking could not be denied. In the same frame of reference, he also confesses that glossolalia was a symptom of divine inspiration.

> I do not mean to deny the existence of glossolaly all through the period under dispute. . . . What does not appear is that it was ever claimed, at least on a large scale, as a symptom of divine inspiration, until the end of the seventeenth century.[45]

The *Encyclopaedia Britannica* states that the miracle of utterance recurred "among the mendicant friars of the 13th century."[46]

In his comprehensive work on *The History of the Christian Church*, Dr. Philip Schaff refers to Vincent Ferrer, who died in 1419, as a devoted missionary and one of the greatest Spanish preachers.[47] According to Dr. Schaff, "his name is also associated with the gift of tongues."[48] Ferrer preached through Spain, Northern Italy, and France; and thousands, especially Jews and Mohammedans, yielded to his persuasions. Dr. Schaff further explained that although the great missionary Ferrer was

> able to speak only Spanish, his sermons, though they were not interpreted, are reported to have been understood in France and Italy. The gift of tongues was ascribed to him by his contemporaries as well as the gift of miracles.[49]

The Reverend Alban Butler, in his voluminous works on the *Lives of the Saints*, discloses some very interesting in-

---

[44] Leo the Great, "Sermons of Leo the Great," *The Nicene and Post-Nicene Fathers*, Second Series, *op. cit.*, Vol. XII, Sermon LXXV, pp. 190, 191.

[45] Ronald A. Knox, *Enthusiasm: A Chapter in the History of Religion* (New York: Oxford University Press, 1950), p. 551.

[46] "Tongues, Gift of," *Encyclopaedia Britannica*, *op. cit.*, p. 283.

[47] Schaff, *op. cit.*, VI, pp. 229-231.

[48] *Ibid.*, p. 229.

[49] *Ibid.*, p. 230.

formation. He recorded a publication made by Boniface IX in 1391 which said, "to speak the language of angels, was the happy privilege of Saint Bridget."[50] Saint Bridget was a daughter of Birger, a prince of Sweden.

In his discussion of the life of Saint Lewis Bertrand who was born at Valencia, Spain, in 1526, he records,

> The gifts of tongues, of prophecy, and of miracles, were favors conferred by heaven on this new apostle, as the authentic history of his life . . . assures us.[51]

In compiling materials relative to the life of Saint Camillus De Lellis, who was born in 1550 in Naples, Butler relates,

> God testified his approbation of the saint's zeal by the spirit of prophecy and the gift of miracles, on several occasions, and by many heavenly communications.[52]

The summation of the life of Saint Francis Xavier, apostle to the Indies, discloses an interesting and suggestive reference:

> At Amanguchi, God restored to St. Francis the gift of tongues; for he preached often to the Chinese merchants, who traded there, in their mother-tongues, which he had never learned.[53]

During the Reformation, the weary centuries rebelled against the religious regimentation and rediscovered a neglected dimension of spiritual living. Burton Scott Easton caught the spirit of the times when he quotes a reference from *Philo, Quis rerum. divine.*, li-lii, 249-266,

> The best [ecstasy] of all is a Divinely infused rapture and "mania," to which the race of the prophets is subject. . . . The wise man is a sounding instrument of God's voice, being struck and played upon invisibly by Him. . . . As long as our mind still shines [is active]. . . . we are not possessed [by God]. . . . but . . . when the Divine

---

[50] Butler, *op. cit.*, IV, p. 67.
[51] *Ibid.*, p. 73.
[52] *Ibid.*, III, p. 74.
[53] *Ibid.*, IV, p. 444.

light shines, the human light sets. . . . The prophet. . . . is passive, and another [God] makes use of his vocal organs.[54]

Whether honored or opposed, none can deny Martin Luther's preeminent place in the history of the church. This man of vivid, compelling faith and heroic courage is spoken of in Souer's first writings on the history of the Christian church: "Dr. Martin Luther was a prophet, evangelist, speaker in tongues and interpreter, in one person, endowed with all the gifts of the Holy Spirit."[55]

VERIFICATION OF THE GLOSSOLALIA PHENOMENON

The operation of the glossolalia phenomenon has been a neglected area in Christian dogma. Even though the church has possessed, in common, the content of the Holy Scriptures, very little effort has been focused upon a critical analysis of the miracle of utterance. Neither has research been aimed at correlating the evidence of spiritual tongues speaking throughout history with the Holy Bible; therefore, l i t t l e consideration has been given to the attempt to determine whether or not historical facts are related to the Scriptural phenomenon of tongues speaking.

This study verifies the fact of tongues speaking through recorded history. It discloses the evidence that glossolalia was recognized by those who laid the foundations of the church and that the miracle of utterance has continued among Spirit-filled people down through the ages. A current viewpoint that tongues speaking is merely an outgrowth of an undisciplined psychological and physiological reaction is totally discredited.

Speaking in tongues is the initial evidence of the Baptism in the Holy Ghost and, in its true form, has never been con-

---

[54] Easton, *op. cit.*, p. 2996.
[55] Souer's *History of the Christian Church*, Vol. III, p. 406, cited by Elmer Miller, *Pentecost Examined, op. cit.*, p. 19.

trolled by human manipulations. When viewed in the light of documented data, this research disquiets the assertion that tongues speaking terminated with the apostles. In the final analysis, the findings of research make clear the fact that the glossolalia phenomenon has been an integral part of church life and a contributing factor to spiritual culture. The operation of the miracle of utterance is emphasized in the fact that the phenomenon continued when resisted and when it was ignored. It has survived the caustic holocaust of being assigned to works of the flesh or to psychic powers.

History confirms the fact that there can be no substitute for a creative spiritual experience in the Holy Ghost. Through the centuries tongues speaking has been a hallmark of Spirit-filled Christians.

It is clearly evident that the glossolalia phenomenon has had a distinctive capacity for spiritual survival and reappearance. Tongues speaking has revealed some aspects of Christianity's inner struggle to be more than an extension of some social or secular movement. Of all the tragedies of Church history, none is sadder than the failure to explore the deeper realities of God. If modern Christians are to bear a dynamic witness in our confused generation, those who are called by His name must declare that the acceptance of New Testament promises is a decisive proof of spiritual growth and maturity. The Holy Ghost baptism with accompanying tongues speaking is the heritage of every believer and represents the fellowship that is the gift of God!

Glossolalia: Reformation to the Twentieth Century

Vessie D. Hargrave

Vessie D. Hargrave is General Director of Church of God World Missions and a member of the Executive Committee and of the Executive Council. He was Supervisor of the Church of God in Europe before his election to his present position. He served as state youth director, missionary, Superintendent of the Church of God in Latin America for nineteen years, and has traveled in ninety-two countries. He was instrumental in beginning several Bible schools in the Latin American territory. He has served as editor of Spanish church magazines and Sunday school literature, and has authored the following books in English: Undaunted by Obstacles, Moved by the Spirit, *and several books of sermons. He is a graduate of Lee College and holds the Bachelor of Arts and Master of Science degrees from Trinity University where he majored in Spanish and sociology. He is one of the best informed men in his church on missions.*

Vessie D. Hargrave

Glossolalia: Reformation to the Twentieth Century

Most theologians acknowledge the phenomenon of glossolalia at Jerusalem, Ephesus, and Corinth, even though they
may not agree upon the mode of exercise. The Early Church ⚓
practiced "speaking in tongues" as is evident by the Scriptures
and the writings of the Church Fathers. Even the heathen
philosopher and controversalist against Christianity, Celsus
(A.D. 177), scornfully describes the procedures at Christian
meetings "where prophecy often passed into tongues as the
speaker worked himself up."[1] Origen quotes Celsus to the
effect that, "both in and outside the sanctuaries people ex-
hibited ecstatic phenomena and uttered unknown, unintelligible speech."[2]

This study proposes to call to the reader's attention the occurrences of tongues speaking and the writings of eminent
scholars on the subject of glossolalia since the Reformation.
Tongues speaking as the initial, but certainly not the exclusive,

---

[1] W. K. Lowther Clarke, *Concise Bible Commentary* (New York: The Macmillan Company, 1953), p. 847, citing Celsus.
[2] *Schaff-Herzog* *Encyclopedia of Religious Knowledge* (Grand Rapids:
Baker Book House, 1953), XI, 38, citing Origen, *Contra Celsum* VII., ix.

evidence of the indwelling of the Holy Spirit in the believer is commonly agreed upon by many writers; and, further, the "gift of tongues," as described in 1 Corinthians, chapters 12, 13 and 14, is recognized as being in operation today by an ever enlarging segment of Christianity. Illustrious men have spoken out clearly and unequivocally since the Reformation relative to these important Biblical projections. These scholars have spoken from varied professions and confessions in each of the centuries embraced in this study.

The writers introduced in this century-by-century survey may not all agree on every phase of glossolalia with the traditional Pentecostal position; nevertheless, their works in each age denote serious thinking and make applicable and acceptable contributions to a more thorough understanding of the spiritual manifestation of "tongues speaking." Furthermore, the influence of some of their theological works laid the groundwork for the twentieth-century "latter rain."

I. THE SIXTEENTH CENTURY

The sixteenth century introduced many revolutionary changes in the social, political, and religious life of Europe. In the latter, the pronounced voice of Martin Luther (1483-1546), the indomitable reformer, resounded not only in his beloved fatherland, but the echoes reverberate until this day in many lands.

According to Souer's writings on the Christian church, "Dr. Martin Luther was a . . . speaker in tongues and interpreter . . . endowed with all the gifts of the Holy Spirit."[3]

When Luther was asked about the phenomenon that occurred on the Day of Pentecost, he replied, " 'They could speak diverse languages . . . This was one of the greatest miracles that ever happened, that poor fishermen should re-

---

[3] Carl Brumback, "What Meaneth This?" (Springfield, Mo.: Gospel Publishing House, 1947), p. 92, citing Souer's History of the Christian Church, III, p. 406.

ceive such splendid gifts. It is just as if I were to awaken a stone and make it talk in all manner of languages.' "[4]

John Calvin (1509-1564), the Swiss exiled French reformer, recognized in glossolalia the God-instituted way of reaching the world of a "diversity of tongues:"

> The diversity of tongues did hinder the gospel from being spread abroad any farther; so that, if the preachers of the gospel had spoken one language only, all men would have thought that Christ had been shut up in the small corner of Jewry. . . . the disciples spake indeed with strange tongues; otherwise the miracle had not been wrought in them, but in the hearers.[5]

In discussing the scripture "in the spirit he speaketh mysteries" (1 Corinthians 14:2), Calvin declares with Chrysostom that man in this state does speak "by a spiritual gift." However, Calvin interprets *the mysteries* as being "dark sayings, that are obscure and involved;" but Chrysostom understands this to be "special revelations from God." Calvin admits:

> . . . he [Paul] does not give such a preference to prophecy, as not to leave some place for foreign tongues. . . . God has conferred nothing upon His Church in vain . . . although the Corinthians, by a misdirected eagerness for show, had rendered that gift partly useless.[6]

As Calvin continues, there is no fight with him. He frankly admits that it is *the Spirit that does the speaking.* He says, "The meaning is now obvious. 'If, therefore, I frame prayers in a language that is not understood by me, and the *spirit* supplies me with words, the *spirit* indeed itself, which regulates my tongue, will in that case *pray.* . . .' "[7]

---

[4] W. Robertson Nicoll, *et al.* (eds.), *The Expositor's Dictionary of Texts* (New York: George H. Doran Company, 1910), II, 377, quoting E. Kroker, *Luther's Tischreden* (1903), p. 325, who quotes Luther.

[5] John Calvin, *Calvin's Commentaries: Commentary Upon the Acts of the Apostles,* Vol. I (Grand Rapids: Wm. B. Eerdmans Publishing Company, 1949), pp. 75, 77.

[6] *Ibid.,* Corinthians, Vol. I, pp. 436, 437.

[7] *Ibid.,* p. 446.

Calvin, in referring to tongues, says about the theologians who disdained the practice:

> . . . at present great theologians . . . declaim against them [use of tongues] with furious zeal. As it is certain that the Holy Spirit has here honoured the use of tongues with never-dying praise, we may very readily gather, what is the kind of spirit that actuates these reformers, who level as many reproaches as they can against the pursuit of them. . . . Paul, nevertheless, commends the use of tongues. So far is he from wishing them abolished or thrown away.[8]

The church of the reformation period was in the throes of a great struggle to survive, and there is little evidence of revival and spiritual manifestation during that time. This is understandable in the light of strong, and at times violent, ecclesiastical opposition to any form of freedom in religious expression. Christian leaders and patriots were few, but they were strong and outspoken. They spoke decidedly upon several important doctrines, some of which influence the church until this day. It is worthy of notice that theologians like Calvin would project for his day and ours, "Paul commends the use of tongues," and further indicates that Paul did *not* want tongues "abolished or thrown away." The church of our day should be thankful that the church of the reformation period, though small and struggling to exist, did make its mark on the pages of religious history and contributed to the end-time revival.

II. THE SEVENTEENTH CENTURY

Calvin became the leader of French Protestantism, and Geneva in Switzerland became the training center from which hundreds of ministers returned to France. This was a period of intensified efforts for the extermination of heresy. The Waldenses were ordered exterminated in 1545. Twenty villages were destroyed; thousands were massacred. Many Calvinists were executed during this time. Evangelists traveled dis-

---

[8] *Ibid.*, p. 437.

guised, holding secret meetings and distributing literature. The inquisitorial tribunal, "the burning chamber," was established. The French Protestants, the Huguenots (1525-1700), possibly suffered more than any group during the long period of persecution following the advent of the Reformation in Europe.

In June, 1551, the Edict of Chateaubriand gave more power to ecclesiastical judges. The inquisition was reinstituted. The burning of heretics (the Huguenots) continued for over one hundred years. The Edict of Nantes (May 2, 1598) was to provide, if not equality, at least token religious freedom for the Huguenots. The provisions of this governmental document were flagrantly violated many times during the reigns of both Louis XIII and Louis XIV. It was during the rule of Louis XIV, at the close of the seventeenth century, that stringent restrictions were imposed upon the Huguenots.

Many of these people were cruelly tortured and executed; others died in prison or of extreme hardship. In spite of this, thousands of Frenchmen professed conversion. Some, disregarding laws prohibiting emmigration, found homes in Holland, England, Ireland, Germany, Switzerland, and America. Those remaining in France, although severely persecuted, took all risks and met secretly for worship. The greatest numbers found asylum in the mountains of the Cevennes. "The spiritual gifts of the Apostolic Church reappeared—miracles of healing, prophecy, and talking with tongues,"[9] according to David Smith, a Scottish Presbyterian, professor, lecturer, and writer. He quotes Bruey relative to the Huguenots of the Cevennes:

> The most striking instances of the gift of tongues in modern times are 'the little prophets of Cevennes' at the close of the seventeenth century and the Irvingites early in the nineteenth; and it is remarkable that these exhibited respectively the phenomenon of the Day of Pentecost as portrayed in the Book of Acts and the ecstasies which convulsed the Corinthian Church. . . . they preached and ex-

---

[9] David Smith, *The Life and Letters of St. Paul* (New York: Harper & Brothers, [n.d.]), p. 299.

horted, not in the Romance patois of their native mountains, but in good French.[10]

The Welsh nonconformist Matthew Henry (1662-1714), who pastored a Presbyterian church for twenty-five years, writes relative to tongues:

> *They began to speak with other tongues,* besides their native language, though they had never learned any other. They spoke not matters of common conversation, but the word of God, and the praises of his name, *as the Spirit gave them utterance* . . . apophthegms, substantial and weighty sayings . . . It is probable that it was not only one that was enabled to speak one language, and another . . . but that every one was enabled to speak divers languages, as he would have occasion to use them. . . . They did not speak here a word of another tongue, or stammer out some broken sentences, but spoke it as readily, properly, and elegantly, as if it had been their mother-tongue; for whatever was produced by miracle was the best of the kind. . . . Now this was . . . a very great miracle . . . They had not only never learned these languages, but had never learned any foreign tongue . . . They were neither scholars nor travellers.[11]

Commenting on the infilling at Cornelius' house, Matthew Henry clearly recognizes the accompaning speaking in tongues by asserting:

> Peter could not give the Holy Ghost, yet the Holy Ghost being given along with the word of Peter, by this it appeared he was sent of God. . . . The Holy Ghost fell upon those that were neither circumcised nor baptized . . . But, observe, when they spoke in tongues, they *magnified God*, they spoke of Christ and the benefits of redemption, which Peter had been preaching . . .[12]

Referring to the reception of the Holy Ghost at Ephesus, Matthew Henry explains:

> *The Holy Ghost came upon them* in a surprising over-

---

[10] *Ibid.,* citing Bruey, *Histoire du Fanatisme,* I, pp. 148 ff.

[11] Matthew Henry, *Commentary on the Whole Bible* (New York: Fleming H. Revell Company, 1935), VI, 16.

[12] *Ibid.,* p. 137.

powering manner, and *they spoke with tongues and prophesied,* as the apostles did and the first Gentile converts.[13]

This period differed very little from the sixteenth century period, because the spiritual climate for the most part was unchanged. The church was still more occupied with surviving persecution than preaching and propagating the gospel.

III. THE EIGHTEENTH CENTURY

The eighteenth century produced several outstanding Bible scholars and Christian leaders. Some of them were mightily used of the Spirit and expressed their belief in the deep things of God. Baumgarten, Clarke, and Wesley are well-known men of this period.

John Wesley (1703-1791), the great preacher and founder of Methodism defines tongues as, *a sign to unbelievers* "to engage their attention, and convince them the message is of God."[14]

It is not intended to prove that Wesley spoke in tongues himself, but it is evident that he had more than a passing interest in the subject. The content of his correspondence indicates his favorable attitude toward glossolalia. He says in a letter to a friend, the Reverend Dr. Middleton:

> I must observe an historical mistake which occurs toward the bottom of your next page. Since the Reformation, you say: "This gift [tongues] has never once been heard of, or pretended to, by the Romanist themselves." (Page 122.) But has it been pretended to (whether justly or not) by no others, though not by the Romanist? Has it "never once been heard of" since that time? Sir, your memory fails you again . . . It has been heard of more than once, no farther off than the valleys of Dauphiny [France].[15]

---

[13] *Ibid.,* p. 245.

[14] John Wesley *et. al., One Volume New Testament Commentary* (Grand Rapids: Baker Book House, 1958), 1 Corinthians XIV: 22.

[15] Taken from *The Works of John Wesley,* published by Zondervan, used by permission. Vol. X, pp. 55, 56.

The Camisards of France, during the eighteenth century, held their religious meetings at night in secluded places. Prophecies and tongues speaking were common. Despite the aid given by the state to the ecclesiastical efforts to stamp out the advance of the Camisards, it is reported that ecstatic phenomena increased. In religious services, trances were common.

Jacob Baumgarten (1706-1757), a German theologian and teacher, describes the Spirit-possessed individual:

> The Christians, in consequence of having received the gift of the Spirit, spake *with other tongues* . . . This expression might, possibly, convey no other sense than that "the tongues of the disciples were essentially changed by the operation of the Spirit, and now became the organs of the Holy Ghost, whereas they had formerly been the organs of flesh."[16]

Adam Clarke (1762-1832), the Wesleyan preacher, commentator, and theologian who established Methodism on the Shetland Islands, commenting on the subject of tongues wrote:

> At the building of *Babel* the *language* of the people was *confounded;* and, in consequence of this, they became scattered over the face of the earth . . . the gift of various languages was given to the apostles, that the scattered nations might be *gathered.* . . .
> As the Spirit gave them utterance . . . seems to imply such utterance as proceeded from immediate inspiration, and included oracular communications.
> *Every man heard them speak in his own language.* . . .
> *Are not all these—Galileans?* Persons who know no other dialect, save that of their own country. Persons wholly uneducated, and, consequently, naturally ignorant of those languages which they now speak so fluently. . . . the *gift of tongues* was actually given to the *apostles,* we have the fullest proof; as we find particular ordinances laid down by those very apostles for the regulation of the exercise of this gift.[17]

---

[16] John Peter Lange (ed.), *Commentary on the Holy Scriptures: Acts* (Grand Rapids: Zondervan Publishing House, [n.d.]), p. 29, quoting Baumgarten.
[17] Adam Clarke, *Commentary on the Holy Bible* (Nashville: Abingdon-Cokesbury Press, [n.d.]), V, 693, 694.

The eighteenth century closed with revival soon to follow in England and America.

IV. THE NINETEENTH CENTURY

A review of the happenings during the "Great Revival of 1800" (1797-1803) *is profitable in the light of its probable relationship to the Pentecostal revival of today.* This revival was the result, to a large extent, of the first camp meetings of the nineteenth century. The most outstanding one was conducted in July, 1800, in the state of Kentucky. The impetus of these meetings created one of the most extraordinary religious awakenings recorded in American history. Both criticism and applause came from the people, press, and pulpit.

Crowds of 20,000 to 25,000[18] gathered at Cane Ridge, Logan County, Kentucky. (Presbyterians, Baptists, and Methodists were engulfed in this movement.) Usually, several preaching stands were set up. "Testimony" time was the order of the day, and often as many as three hundred laymen would be testifying. The shouts of "Amen!" and "Hallelujah!" were heard as preacher after preacher would drive home a point. One witness compared the sound to the "roar of Niagara;" another called James McGrealy, a Presbyterian preacher, a "veritable son of thunder."

William Burke, a Methodist preacher, says, ". . . under the word of God, hundreds fell prostrate on the ground before him, and lay in agonies of distress, with a sinner occasionally jumping to his feet to give vent to 'shouts of triumph.' " When William Burke could find no stand from which to preach, he climbed up a fallen tree to a height of fifteen feet above the ground while a "brother Methodist tied an umbrella to a pole and held it over his head while he spoke."[19]

James B. Finley, the son of a Presbyterian minister, who

---

18 Bernard A. Weisberger, *They Gathered at the River* (Boston: Little, Brown and Company, 1958), p. 31. Copyright © 1958, by Bernard A. Weisberger.
19 *Ibid.*, p. 32, quoting Burke.

later was to become a Methodist preacher, went to Cane Ridge, as many others, out of sheer curiosity. While attending the meetings he became conscious "that his heart was thundering. His knees became jellylike, and, sitting down on a log, he looked wide-eyed as five hundred people collapsed with 'shrieks and shouts that rent the very heavens' under the spell of an exhorter." He fled to the woods, where he spent a night in fear because of sins upon his conscience. He returned to the meeting; then he went back to the woods where upon falling to his knees, "he gave a shout and fell prostrate." He was put to bed, and "When he awoke, he had a sudden feeling of release, and he went on home, uncontrollably laughing, weeping and shouting most of the way."[20]

During this revival period, people shouted, exhorted with "all possible ecstasy"; "trances" were common, the "mourners" bench was filled with penitent sinners, and often "the floor was covered with the slain." Several writers present undeniable evidence that the Spirit often took control of the believers. They would laugh, sing, fall down and remain prostrate, shout, dance, jerk, and some purportedly saw visions.

While it is not definitely stated that there was tongues speaking in these meetings, certain religious exercises indicate that such was the case. Some of the manifestations were similar to those frequently seen in Pentecostal meetings; and, in Bernard A. Weisberger's description of these meetings, he says:

> Even if there had been only these things—the shouts, the wagons, the murmurous, plastic crowds, surging in the half darkness under the rain-beaten branches, Cane Ridge would have burned itself for life into the memories of men who were there. But stranger things were said to have happened; (the power of the Lord was shown as it was when cloven tongues of fire sat upon the apostles\ and amid a rushing, mighty wind, they spoke to an untoward generation of Parthians, Medes and Elamites, each in his own tongue. For at Cane Ridge, many men testified to the physical

---

[20] *Ibid.*, pp. 33, 34.

power of the Holy Spirit's baptism, which unstrung the knees and melted, with fervent heat, the hearts of the worshipers.[21]

It is certainly implied and many strongly believe that tongues speaking was in evidence during these revival services.

Not only did the spirit of revival come to America, but on the British Isles, in both Scotland and England, Edward Irving (1792-1834), a Scotch Presbyterian, and his followers, were recipients of a special visitation. Mary Campbell, dying with consumption, was instantly healed and "suddenly she received the gift of tongues and 'broke forth in loud, ecstatic utterances.' "[22] This occurred in March of 1830. Simultaneously, James and George Macdonald received the gift of healing. While they were praying for their sister, "she prayed for the Baptism of the Spirit. Her request was granted; her weakness was forgotten, and for several hours she poured forth her soul in praise, prayer, and exhortation."[23]

Thomas Erskine, a saintly and wise man, visited the Macdonalds for six weeks. He wrote:

'Whilst I see nothing in Scripture against the reappearance, or rather the continuance, of miraculous gifts in the Church . . . I see a great deal of internal evidence in the west country to prove their genuine miraculous character, especially in the speaking with tongues. . . . After witnessing what I have witnessed among these people, I cannot think of any person decidedly condemning them as imposters, without a feeling of great alarm. It is certainly not a thing to be lightly or rashly believed, but neither is it a thing to be lightly or rashly rejected. I believe that it is of God.'[24]

A London solicitor, upon investigating the phenomenon wrote, " 'that their organs of speech are made use of by the Spirit of God.' "[25]

Erskine says of the tongues he heard in the meetings: " 'The

---

[21] *Ibid.*, p. 32. Italics ours.
[22] David Smith, *op. cit.*, p. 300.
[23] *Ibid.*, p. 300.
[24] *Ibid.*, p. 301, quoting Erskine, *Letters,* pp. 182 ff.
[25] *Ibid.*, quoting Erskine, p. 186.

languages are distinct, well-inflected, well-compacted languages . . . they are composed of words of various length, with
the natural variety, and yet (possessing that commonness of
character which marks them to be one distinct language.'[26]
Without question, Erskine was so profoundly impressed by the
revival of spiritual gifts in his own day that he recognized it
as indubitably a divine operation. Irving's church received the
real impact of the Holy Ghost revival in 1831. It would be enlightening to note that before this real outpouring, there was a
craving for the gifts of the Spirit. The news of isolated cases of
the infilling was commonly known: the stage was set, interest
was great, even to the extent that on the last day of the last
Albury Conference in July, 1830, it was proposed and agreed:

> "That it is our duty to pray for the revival of the gifts
> manifested in the primitive Church,—healing, miracles,
> prophecy, kinds of tongues and interpretations of tongues,
> and that a responsibility lies on us to inquire into the
> state of those gifts . . . said to be now present in the west
> of Scotland."[27]

Thousands of people, not a few of high estate, flocked to
hear Irving's messages. Many spoke in tongues in his meetings.
Irving wrote to a friend, " 'Every Wednesday night I am
preaching to thousands "the Baptism with the Holy Ghost"
. . . pray diligently that Satan may not be able to put this
light out!' "[28]

Due to severe criticism from some circles, of Irving and his
movement, and since reference has been made to him, it is
logical to give reason for projecting him. The Scottish historian, biographer, and essayist, Thomas Carlyle (1795-1881),
who from school days remained a constant friend to Irving yet
was unsympathetic to tongues speaking and other miracles
connected with the Irvingite movement, wrote:

---

[26] *Ibid.*, pp. 301, 302, quoting Erskine, p. 186.
[27] Andrew Landale Drummond, *Edward Irving and His Circle* (London:
James Clarke & Company, Ltd., 1934), p. 135.
[28] *Ibid.*, p. 159, quoting Irving.

"But for Irving, I had never known what the communion of man with man means. He was the freest, brotherliest, bravest human soul mine ever came in contact with: I call him, on the whole, the best man I have ever, after trial enough, found in the world, or now hope to find."[29]

F. D. Maurice, a fellow disciple with Irving under Coleridge, said of Irving: "In spite of enormous prejudice against him, I was forced and am now more than ever forced to reverence and love him."[30] —> transformation

Dr. John Hunter in commemorating, "the men who did most for the widening of religious thought in Scotland during the first half of the nineteenth century," in a series of stained glass windows installed in Trinity Congregational Church, Glasgow (1908), included F. D. Maurice, McLeod Campbell, Erskine of Linlathen, A. J. Scott, Irving and Carlyle.[31] In view of the memorials given above by both contemporaries and admirers after the demise of Irving, it is concluded that reference to him and his work is justifiable.

Irving tells of a "Gifted Person" who described his inmost experience of the Tongues:

"When I am praying in my native tongue, however fixed my soul be upon God, and Him alone, I am conscious of other thoughts and desires, *which the very words I use force in before me.* I am like a man holding straight forward to his home full in view, who, though he diverge neither to the right hand nor to the left, is ever solicited by many well-known objects on every hand of him.

"But the moment I am visited with the Spirit, and carried out to God in a tongue which I know not, it is as if a deep covering of snow had fallen on all the country round, and I saw nothing but the object of my desire and the road which leadeth to it. I am more conscious than ever of the presence of God. He and He alone is in my soul. *I am filled with some form of the mind of God,* be it joy or grief, desire, love, pity, compassion or indignation; and I am *made* to utter it in words which are full of *power* over my

[29] *Ibid.,* pp. 276, 277, quoting Carlyle.
[30] *Ibid.,* p. 276, quoting Maurice.
[31] *Ibid.*

> spirit, but not being accessible to my understanding, my de-
> votion is not interrupted by *association or suggestions from
> the visible or intellectual world*: I feel myself, as it were,
> shut in with God into His own pavilion, and hidden close
> from the invasions of the world, the devil, and the flesh."[32]

The role of Methodist circuit riders, their emotional preaching, the ever-present "mourners" bench, the ecstatic praying,
the "testimony meetings," "trances," and revivalism in general,
naturally influenced preachers and theological writers. Their
works will follow. It is obvious that the nineteenth century
Biblical commentators both in America and Europe felt the
impact of revival, and many wrote accordingly. Their comments upon the subject of glossolalia are of particular interest to us.

Meyers (1772-1849) points out, and Schultz agrees, ". . .
the tongue, set in motion involuntarily . . . by the power of the
Holy Spirit, spoke apparently of its own accord. It was not the
person, but the *tongue* itself which spoke . . ."[33] Delitzsch says
when one was under the influence of the Spirit . . . "its posses-
sor was perpetually master of himself . . . to which may be
added, that he was in no communion with the outward world,
but wholly absorbed in communion with God."[34]

Frederick Louis Godet (1812-1900), a Swiss professor of
theology, holds that the "mystery" referred to by Paul implies
that the matter was "secret to other men." He further says,

> What the speaker in a tongue says remains between God
> and him, and is a mystery to the hearers . . . then it
> is the spirit of the glossolalete himself, who is carried
> away in ecstasy, and in a manner raised for the time
> above the exercise of the understanding . . . the state
> of the glossolalete was that of ineffable conversation with
> God . . .
>
> .   .   .   .
>
> From his intimate communion with God, the glossolalete
> derives a blessing which, even though it is not transformed

---

[32] *Ibid.*, pp. 161, 162.
[33] Lange, *op. cit.*, *Corinthians*, p. 299, citing Meyer.
[34] *Ibid.*, p. 300, citing *Delitzsch*, pp. 317 ff.

into precise notions by the exercise of understanding, makes itself felt as a power in the depths of his soul.[35]

Drs. Godet, Fausset, Plumptre, Buttrick, G. Campbell Morgan, and Kling concur with Spence and Exell that tongues speaking is that media through which (God uses a surrendered life to transport the Spirit-filled person into a direct communion with God. Godet expresses himself by saying: "Paul seems to compare it, xiii. 1, [the gift of speaking in tongues] to the language of angels" in which the newly-filled soul, enraptured by the experience, was "lifted" and expressed itself in "extra ordinary language of which we can no longer form an idea."[36]

Dr. Godet further elaborates:

"he speaks mysteries." . . . which remain a secret to men, so long as God does not reveal them; it refers to the secrets of a man in relation to other men. What the speaker in a tongue says remains between God and him, and is a mystery to the hearers.[37]

Samuel Macauley Jackson classifies tongues speaking as, "God's spirit which speaks within us, and when we know not how to pray, the Spirit makes intercession with unutterable groanings (Romans viii: 26), and this God understands (verse 27)."[38]

Dr. Arthur Charles Hervey, Church of England bishop of Bath and Wells, writer of exposition and homiletics of *The Acts of the Apostles,* a volume in *The Pulpit Commentary* (1880), enriches the subject by presenting such vivid descriptions as these which follow:

The only room for doubt is whether the speakers spoke in these divers languages, or the hearers heard in them though the speakers spoke in only one tongue. But not to mention

---

[35] Frederick Godet, *Commentary on the Epistle of St. Paul to the Corinthians.* Published by Zondervan Publishing House, used by permission, Vol. II, pp. 266, 268.

[36] *Ibid.,* pp. 203, 204.

[37] *Ibid.,* p. 266.

[38] Schaff-Herzog, *op. cit.,* p. 37.

that this is far more difficult to imagine, and transfers the miracle from those who had the Holy Spirit to those who had it not, it is against the plain language of the text, which tells us that "they began to speak with other tongues," and that "every man heard them speaking in his own language." "Speaking," said they, "in our own tongues the mighty works of God." There may, indeed, have been something ecstatic besides in these utterances, . . . The narrative before us does not hint at any after use of the gift of tongues for missionary purposes . . . nowhere . . . is the gift of tongues spoken of in connection with preaching to foreign nations . . .

. . . .

We conclude that the "tongues" were sometimes "tongues of men," foreign languages unknown to the speakers, and of course unintelligible to the hearers unless any were present, as was the case of the day of Pentecost, who knew the language; and sometimes languages not of earth but of heaven, "tongues of angels." . . . It may also not improbably have been used occasionally, as it was on the day of Pentecost, to convey doctrine, knowledge, or exhortation, to foreign people; but there is no distinct evidence that this was the case.[39]

Professor of theology at Marburg, the German Irvingite, Heinrich Wilhelm Josias Thiersch (1817-1885) applies "the term tongues *of men* to the various tongues spoken by the apostles on the Day of Pentecost, and tongues *of angels* to the gift of tongues as it flourished at Corinth."[40]

J. C. Lambert gives his condition for the use of tongues in the church:

If . . . the gift of tongues was such has been described, the gift of interpretation would consist in turning what seemed a meaningless utterance into words easy to be understood (v. 9). The interpretation might be given by the speaker in tongues himself (vv. 5, 13) after his mood of ecstasy was over, as he translated his exalted experiences and broken cries into plain intelligible language. Or, if he lacked the

---

[39] H. D. M. Spence and Joseph S. Exell (eds.), *The Pulpit Commentary:* (Grand Rapids: Wm. B. Eerdmans Publishing Company, 1950), XVIII, 49, 50.
[40] Godet, *op. cit.*, pp. 235, 236, citing Thiersch.

power of self-interpretation, the task might be undertaken by another possessed of this special gift (vv. 27, 28).[41]

The Reverend David Brown, referring to the apostolic out-pouring, clearly points out:

> Real, living languages, as is plain from what follows. The thing uttered, probably the same by all, was "the wonderful works of God," perhaps in the inspired words of the Old Testament evangelical hymns; though it is next to certain that the speakers themselves understood nothing of what they uttered.[42]

He continues his comments on Acts 10:44, 45.

> *While he yet spake, the Holy Ghost fell*—by visible and audible manifestation (v. 46). *They of the circumcision . . . heard them speak with tongues and magnify God.* As on the day of Pentecost it was no empty miracle, no mere speaking of foreign languages, but utterances of "the wonderful works of God" in tongues to them unknown. . . .[43]

This author explicitly and fundamentally identifies "tongues" in their historical place at the Jerusalem outpouring.

The Reverend E. H. Plumptre (1821-1891), a preacher, lecturer, and hymnist of the Church of England, catalogues tongues speaking as an ecstatic exercise:

> The utterance of the "tongue" is presented to us as entirely unconnected with the work of teaching. It is not a means of instruction. It does not edify any beyond the man who speaks. . . . He may utter prayers, or praises, or benedictions. . . . Those who speak with tongues do well, for the most part, to confine their utterance to the solitude of their own chamber, or to the presence of friends who share their rapture.[44]

---

[41] *The International Standard Bible Encyclopaedia*, James Orr, gen. ed. (Grand Rapids: Wm. B. Eerdmans Publishing Company, 1952), V, 2844.

[42] Robert Jamieson, A. R. Fausset, and David Brown, *Commentary on the Whole Bible*, Vols. I and II (Grand Rapids: Zondervan Publishing House, [n.d.]), II, 187.

[43] *Ibid.*, p. 187.

[44] Charles John Ellicott (ed.), *Ellicott's Commentary on the Whole Bible* (Grand Rapids: Zondervan Publishing House, 1877), Vol. VII, p. 7.

Dr. Plumptre speaks in the present tense, even though he calls for care and warns of excesses; yet, he recognizes the gift in operation. In fact, during the time of his ministry, there were many who spoke in tongues in England, France, and possibly America, the Irvingites being the most numerous. He declares, "it is a 'sign to them that believe not,' *i.e.*, it startles them, attracts their notice, impresses them with the thought that they stand face to face with a superhuman power."[45] It would seem utterly impossible to fulfill the above in the solitude of their own chamber. The latter is advisable without question, but this divine manifestation is not limited to a closet experience but may lift up a person or congregation to a sublime spiritual state where both the individual and the church are edified. Dr. Plumptre urges, "If it was not right or expedient to check the utterances of the tongues altogether, St. Paul at least thought it necessary to prescribe rules for its exercises . . ."[46] The exercise of order in God's house is expedient. Therefore, in this we have grounds for agreement. It is evident that this man of God carefully evaluated this marvelous gift by concluding:

> The utterances of the disciples are described in words which convey the idea of rapturous praise. They speak the "mighty works," or better, as in Luke 1:49, the *great things* of God. Doxologies, benedictions, adoration, in forms that transcended the common level of speech, and rose, like the Magnificat, into the region of poetry; this is what the word suggests to us. . . . St. Paul . . . contrasts the "being drunk with wine" with "being filled with the Spirit," and immediately passes on, as though that were the natural result, to add "speaking to yourselves in psalms and hymns and spiritual songs."[47]

Plumptre reiterates, "*In the spirit he speaketh mysteries.* The utterances come, not from his mind, but from his spirit, stirred by the Holy Spirit; and he speaks mysteries unintelligible to

---

[45] *Ibid.*, p. 7.
[46] *Ibid.*, p. 7.
[47] *Ibid.*, p. 8.

others."[48] "It is here implied that speaking in a tongue was, as regards an individual, an acceptable mode of worship."[49] "They communed with God by the speaking with tongues . . ."[50]

The speaking in tongues is of value not only to the individual but also to the whole congregation. In order for the Church to receive edification when a message is given in tongues, the same should be interpreted by either the speaker or someone else who receives the message given by divine inspiration. "The teacher of religious truth to others, who thereby builds up the whole edifice of the body of Christ, is a greater one than he who is himself benefited by being possessed by profound but uncommunicable emotion."[51]

Dr. Plumptre shows the relative value of interpreting in its relationship to speaking in tongues:

> The gift of interpreting might therefore belong to the same person who had the gift of tongues: and if he had this power of articulating for the benefit of others the emotion which he incoherently expresses in reverie, then the gift of tongues was useful to the Church at large, and so was as valuable as prophecy.[52]

Plumptre interprets that Paul encouraged the Corinthians to seek to "excel" to the edifying of the church or congregation; he writes, ". . . the gift is to be sought so that it may edify others . . . they are to seek this gift [tongues] for the benefit of others, and so they will themselves, by serving others, abound yet more and more . . . The gift of interpretation would make the gift of tongues useful for the edifying of the Church."[53] In all probability, Plumptre, a contemporary with Irving, had familiarized himself with the latter's meetings. He says, "Tongues were useful to arrest the atten-

48 *Ibid.,* p. 340.
49 *Ibid.,* p. 342.
50 *Ibid.,* p. 340.
51 *Ibid.,* p. 341.
52 *Ibid.*
53 *Ibid.,* p. 342.

sign to them

tion of unbelievers, and, if rightly used, to arouse their convictions; but prophecy is in the highest sense useful for believers."[54] A feeling of awe, remorse, and conviction oftentimes
is observed among sinners in the congregation when a saintly person speaks a divine language, known only to God.

Conybeare (1815-1857), also a Church of England writer, agrees with Plumptre by recognizing that interpretation of
tongues was a subsidiary gift to be exercised concurrently when
the gift of tongues was in operation. He says, relative to the
interpretation of tongues: ". . . by which the ecstatic utterance
of the former [tongue speaking] might be rendered available
for general edification."[55]

Richard Belward Rackham says of tongues:

> . . . for 'speaking in tongues' or 'glossolaly' continued
> long in the church, and it ranked among the *charismata*
> or spiritual gifts . . . Glossolaly was in the main un-
> intelligible . . . But glossolaly was emphatically a speaking
> *in the spirit* as distinct from speaking *with the intelligence*,
> and to be understood by others the tongue had to be in-
> terpreted. In one way it might edify others, but chiefly the
> unbelievers, that is as being an evident sign of a divine
> presence within. . . .
> The individual may be in 'ecstasy,' i.e., entirely absorbed
> in his spiritual being or in spiritual things, so as to be for
> practical purposes 'out of the body' and 'in the spirit.'
> Sometimes the spiritual energy may manifest itself in
> ecstatic speech or utterance—that is what we understand
> by 'speaking with tongues.'[56]

Writes Dr. A. B. Macdonald, a Scotch Presbyterian minister:

> Its [the Spirit's] most striking manifestation at first was
> "speaking in tongues," the power of ecstatic utterance in an
> unintelligible speech; and both those seized by this power
> and those who saw and heard its manifestations were con-
> vinced that some Power from a higher world had broken

---

[54] *Ibid.*, p. 343.

[55] W. J. Conybeare and J. S. Howson, *The Life and Epistles of Saint Paul*
(Hartford, Connecticut: The S. S. Scranton Company, 1920), p. 375.

[56] Richard Belward Rackham (ed.), *The Acts of Apostles* (in *Westminster
Commentaries Series*, ed. Walter Lock. Fourteenth edition; London: Methuen
& Co., Ltd., 1951), pp. 19, 20.

into their lives, endowing them with capacities of utterance.
. . . People who hitherto had seemed to be nothing out of
common suddenly became capable of impassioned prayer
and speech, or of lofty moods in which they were manifestly holding converse with the Unseen.[57]

Dr. Macdonald recognized the influence that affected fishermen, and custom collectors, men not normally educated and
certainly not endowed with natural oratorical ability. These
"suddenly"—not through study—were capacitated. They communed with the "Unseen" and were able, as never before, to
speak freely and with boldness. This characterizes many present-day Pentecostals whose ministry has attracted thousands to
the surprise of theologically prepared ministers who with difficulty serve a much smaller congregation.

Henry J. Ripley, professor of sacred rhetoric and pastoral
duties in the Newton Theological Institution, states:

Various conjectures have been formed in regard to the gift
of tongues, particularly by those writers who are not willing to acknowledge it as a miraculous endowment by the
Holy Spirit. Some have contended that "speaking with other
tongues" was only an uttering of indistinct or inarticulate
sounds; of course, that no intelligible human language was
employed. Others have supposed that the lively use of obsolete, foreign, or unusual words was intended by the expression *other tongues;* others, again, that the speakers, in
an excited state of mind, united Hebrew modes of expression with Greek or Latin words; or, that they spoke under
the influence of an extraordinary enthusiasm, in a highly
oratorical or poetic style, with uncommon warmth and eloquence. If, however, we lay aside all conjecture, and
examine the subject just as it is presented in the Scripture, we cannot doubt that, however unable we are to enter
into particular explanations, the sacred writers regarded this
matter as a miraculous one, and placed it among the extraordinary miraculous gifts of the Spirit. This appears evident both from the book of Acts (2:4; 10:44-46; 19:6),
and from 1 Cor. chapter 14. Nor can we reasonably
doubt that the persons spoke a real language . . . and with

---

[57] Myer Pearlman, *Knowing the Doctrines of the Bible* (Springfield, Mo.:
The Gospel Publishing House, 1937), pp. 314, 315, quoting Macdonald.

much emotion to pour forth prayers and praises to God.
. . . the Holy Spirit miraculously bestowed on the apostles,
and on many of the first disciples, the power to use foreign
languages which they had never learned . . .

. . . .

It seems to have been the language of praise for those wonderful blessings, and of prayer for their continuance and
diffusion, that the multitude heard.[58]

Richard Charles Henry Lenski (1864-1936)—German-born
Lutheran teacher, editor, and pastor—asks:

Why tongues and why like fire? May we say that these
tongues point to the speaking with tongues? When the heart
overflows with grace and power, the tongue is kindled into
utterance. . . . Like the noise, the tongues were a supernatural, heavenly manifestation . . .

. . . .

The sound and the visible tongues were external, but this
miraculous speaking was a personal act due to the inward
presence of the Spirit. In Mark 16:17, Jesus promised this
gift: "they shall speak with new tongues." . . . Every word
of these strange languages was an immediate gift of the
Spirit. The rare verb describes the utterance as being made
in an exalted manner. . . .

. . . .

The gift of tongues is one of the proofs for divine Inspiration.
The Spirit who put the words of strange language into the
mouths of disciples wherewith to speak the great things of
God had no trouble in attending to the words of the holy
writers, so that they recorded what He desired and in the
way He desired it.[59]

Marcus Dods, evaluating Paul's letters, comments on the
gifts in the church:

Paul delighted to survey the variety of endowment and
faculty which appeared in the Church. Wisdom, knowledge, faith, power to work miracles, extraordinary gifts of
exhortation or prophecy and also of speaking in unknown
tongues, capacity for managing affairs and general help-

[58] Henry J. Ripley, *Ripley's Notes on the Acts* (Boston: Gould, Kendall,
and Lincoln, 1844), pp. 22, 26.
[59] R. C. H. Lenski, *Interpretation of the Acts of the Apostles* (Columbus,
Ohio: The Wartburg Press, 1944), pp. 59, 61, 62.

fulness—these and other gifts were the efflorescence of the new life.[60]

Nicoll vividly pictures the interpretation of tongues which God used in the Early Church and still uses today:

> . . . sometimes there was present a person in the same key of feeling whose spirit vibrated to the note struck by the speaker, and who was able to render his inarticulate sounds into intelligible speech. For as music can only be interpreted by one who has a feeling for music, and as the inarticulate language of tears, or sighs, or groans can be comprehended by a sympathetic soul, so tongues could be interpreted by those whose spiritual state corresponded to that of the gifted person.[61]

Heinrich August Wilhelm Meyer (1800-1873), a German Lutheran theologian, in describing speaking in a foreign tongue without learning it, says:

> . . . an outburst of prayer in petition, praise, and thanksgiving, as was so ecstatic that in connection with it in the speaker's own conscious intellectual activity was suspended, while the tongue did not serve as the instrument of the utterance of self-active reflection, but, independently of it, was involuntarily set in motion by the Holy Spirit, by whom the man in his deepest nature was seized and borne away.[62]

Abraham Kuyper (1837-1920), professor of systematic theology in the University of Amsterdam, evaluates tongues speaking:

> . . . it is noteworthy that in 1 Cor. XIV. 1-33 the apostle gives special attention to this extraordinary sign, showing that then it was quite ordinary.
>
> .   .   .   .
>
> . . . the speaking with tongues had an edifying effect upon the speaker himself; but it was an edification not under-

---

60 W. Robertson Nicoll (ed.), *The Expositor's Bible* (Grand Rapids: Wm. B. Eerdmans Publishing Company, 1940), V, 687.

61 *Ibid.*, V, 694.

62 *The Peoples Bible Encyclopedia* (Chicago: The Peoples Publication Society, 1921), p. 1117.

stood, the effect of an unknown operation in the soul.

. . . .

According to St. Paul's interesting information, the miracle of tongues consisted in this, that the vocal organs produced sounds not by a working of the mind, but by an operation of the Holy Spirit upon those organs.[63]

Charles Gerok and G. V. Lechler portray with graphic word pictures the ecstacy of the believer upon receipt of the gift:

> The disciples could not repress the joyful emotions awakened by the power of that divine life which was poured into their souls, and all began to speak. They now speak with other tongues! They received new tongues, enkindled, not from below, but from above, by heavenly fire, and with these they gave praise to God . . .
>
> . . . .
>
> *We do hear them speak in our tongues* . . . scarcely a doubt can remain respecting the meaning of the present passage: it describes the speaking of the disciples *in different languages and dialects* . . . which when rationally interpreted, can only mean that while one disciple spoke in one dialect, another employed a different one, so that every foreigner could hear his own dialect spoken . . . that these natives of Galilee should express themselves in many vernacular dialects or languages . . . was an event that amazed and confounded the hearers.[64]

Philip Schaff records the marvelous advent of the Spirit and the accompanying phenomena:

> The church of the new covenant was ushered into existence with startling signs which filled the spectators with wonder and fear . . .
>
> . . . .
>
> . . . the communication of the Holy Spirit was not confined to the Twelve. It extended to the brethren of the Lord, the mother of Jesus, the pious women who had attended His ministry, and the whole brotherhood of a hundred and twenty souls who were assembled in that chamber. They

---

[63] Abraham Kuyper, *The Work of the Holy Spirit* (Grand Rapids: Wm. B. Eerdmans Publishing Company, 1941), pp. 134, 136.

[64] Lange, *Acts, op. cit.*, pp. 31, 34.

were "all" filled with the Spirit, and all spoke with tongues; and Peter saw in the event the promised outpouring of the Spirit upon "all flesh," sons and daughters, young men and old men, servants, and handmaidens.[65]

The Church was a new institution, coming into existence that day. A new force was to guide and comfort her. As evidence that the Holy Ghost had come, miraculous things happened. Let Schaff describe them:

> The mysterious gift of tongues, or glossolalia, appears for the first time, but became with other extraordinary gifts of the Spirit, *a frequent phenomenon in the apostolic churches* [italics ours] . . . The supernatural experience of the disciples broke through the confines of ordinary speech and burst out in ecstatic language of praise and thanksgiving to God . . . It was the Spirit himself who gave them utterance and played on their tongues, as on new tuned harps, unearthly melodies of praise. The glossolalia was here, as in all cases where it is mentioned, an act of worship and adoration, not an act of teaching and instruction, which followed afterwards in the sermon of Peter. It was the first *Te Deum* of the new-born church. It expressed itself in unusual, poetic, dithyrambic style and with a peculiar musical intonation . . . the Pentecostal glossolalia was the same as that in the household of Cornelius in Caesarea after his conversion, which may be called a Gentile Pentecost, as that of the twelve disciples of John the Baptist at Ephesus . . . and as that in the Christian congregation at Corinth.
> . . . at its first appearance the speaking with tongues differed in its effect upon the hearers by coming home to them at once *in their own mother-tongues;* while at Corinth it required an interpretation to be understood.[66]

With the comments of Schaff, what better conclusion to this area of thinking could be given? He places one in the arena with a ringside seat to this great event—the birth of the Church, the fulfilling of Christ's prophecy: ". . . I will build my church; and the gates of hell shall not prevail against it." (Matthew 16:18).

---

[65] Philip Schaff, *History of the Christian Church* (Grand Rapids: Wm. B. Eerdmans Publishing Company, 1955), I, 228-230.
[66] *Ibid.,* pp. 230, 231.

To conclude the study of the nineteenth century, Godet gives a concise, yet Biblically supported, picture:

> I can only therefore regard the gift of tongues as the expression, in a language spontaneously created by the Holy Spirit, of the new views and of the profound and lively emotions of the human soul set free for the first time from the feeling of condemnation, and enjoying the ineffable sweetness of the relation of sonship to God. And as the influence of the Holy Spirit takes possession of the whole soul and every one of its natural powers, to make it its organ, it also took possession of the gift of speech, transfiguring it, so to speak, to give utterance to emotions which no natural tongue could express.[67]

At the close of the last century frequent reports of tongues speaking were recorded in Kentucky, Tennessee, and North Carolina. But with the beginning of this twentieth century, almost simultaneously in Topeka, Kansas; Azusa Street in Los Angeles; Corpus Christi, Texas; in Korea, Sweden, Chile, and South Africa people of all walks of life became interested in a deeper walk with God. In each of these places the Pentecostal phenomenon was manifested. The "latter rain" without doubt had begun. This period was ushered in as the result of renewed consecration in resistance against spiritual decadence, formalism, and materialism in the "nominal" churches. As for the last sixty years, time and space would not permit accounts to be given of the great outpourings witnessed around the world. It is doubtful that there is a country in the world that does not have Pentecostal people with the Pentecostal experience who speak with other tongues as the Spirit gives the utterance.

V. THE TWENTIETH CENTURY

The first half of this century has been a period of change. Industry, international relations and commerce, standards of living and labor, ideals and ethical morals have all been af-

---

[67] Godet, op. cit., p. 320.

fected by this twentieth-century revolution. For more than half a century political, sociological, economic, and religious forces have brought to bear pressures which have changed the maps of the world, affected the whereabouts and the way man lives, given him comforts never known before, and brought him to a place of little reliance upon the Creator. Twentieth-century churches are generally prosperous. The ministry ordinarily is well provided for. The Church is at "ease in Zion." This period presents different interpretations about sin, morality, a future life, and religion as a whole.

The Pentecostalists have provided the need of the hour. Their growth attests to God's blessings upon them. Before the century was ushered in, scattered showers of the Pentecostal outpouring were felt in various places of the world. The full "rain" that would water the spiritually dry land started in the first decade and has continued unabated until this very day. Revivals at home and abroad bring together thousands of people. The miraculous claims the attention of the hungry masses. Characteristic of these "campaigns" in India, South Africa, New York City, Los Angeles, Chile, Korea, Guatemala and around the world are the great crowds wanting salvation, healing, and a filling of the Holy-Ghost baptism with the initial evidence of speaking in tongues. Millions have been divinely blessed and are witnesses to, and participants of, the Pentecostal phenomenon of glossolalia.

Theologians, commentators, and religious editors, of many faiths, through their writings have contributed to the desire for more knowledge about spiritual things in this space and atomic age. These men have inspired others to "search the Scriptures," and in so searching these have found satisfying experiences from the Word of God.

The Reverend Dr. Thomas Whitelaw proffers that the real reason for tongues at Pentecost was to enable the disciple, being "supernaturally excited" to speak languages which were understood by the hearers. He remarks:

The gift itself was "the power of speaking in foreign languages."

. . . The disciples, thus supernaturally excited, spoke the wonderful works of God in dialects which men from all lands heard and understood . . .

Every man . . . heard one at least in the apostolic company preaching in his own tongue.
It is obvious that the tongues of Pentecost were not mere unintelligible gibberish, ecstatic or frenzied utterances, "sound and fury signifying nothing," but distinct, articulate, and reasonable speech which could be followed and understood.[68]

F. F. Bruce in *The New Bible Commentary*, asserts relative to the apostolic experience:

> Suddenly they were seized by the Holy Spirit from heaven, while visible and audible signs accompanied the effusion of the promised heavenly Gift . . . more impressive was the outburst of *glossolalia*, speaking with tongues, as the disciples were heard praising God in languages and dialects diverse from their native Galilean Aramaic, but recognizable by visitors to the feast as those which some of them spoke. . . . The Galilean dialect was so distinctive and difficult for non-Galileans to follow that the disciples' release from the peculiarities of their local speech and their sudden capacity for speaking in tongues understood by the motley crowds then in Jerusalem could not fail to be remarked.[69]

In *A Commentary on the Holy Bible*, edited by the Reverend J. R. Dummelow of Queen's College, Cambridge, it is projected that:

> One who has the gift of tongues speaks only to God; he does not communicate to others the mysterious truths of which he is conscious; he cultivates his own spiritual life.
>
> . . . what is suggested to us is that the utterances of those who have received this gift are a sign to attract the at-

---

[68] *The Preacher's Complete Homiletic Commentary* (New York: Funk and Wagnalls Company, [n.d.]), XXVI, *Acts*, p. 51, quoting G. T. Stokes; pp. 53, 55.
[69] Francis Davidson, A. M. Stibbs, and E. J. Kevan (eds.), *The New Bible Commentary* (Grand Rapids: Wm. B. Eerdmans Publishing Company, 1953), p. 902.

tention of unbelievers and warn them of the presence of
the Spirit; whereas, on the other hand prophecy makes its
appeal rather to believers.[70]

Among modern writers there is a school of thought which
classifies tongues speaking primarily as ecstatic speech. Peloubet, Gray, Adams, Clarke, Ripley, Martin Dibelius and G. C.
Morgan, to one degree or another, make this identification.

G. Campbell Morgan though not always favorable to glossolalia defines the gift of tongues:

> When we inquire what this gift was, we have first to re-
> member that the Greek word here used, *glossa*, referred in
> Greek thought and literature to words that were either
> obsolete or incomprehensible, and the word was always used
> to describe a certain form of speech which was born of
> great ecstasy, the speech that was the result of catching
> up of the spiritual or mental side of the nature, and carry-
> ing it away into some region of dream and vision, but al-
> ways of delight and of ecstasy. . . . and there is no doubt
> that this is exactly what is meant here, in the gift of
> tongues. If the gift of tongues fell upon anyone, it bore
> them up into a realm of vision and light and glory and
> joy and ecstasy, and they poured out that which described
> things they saw.[71]

Commenting upon the Pentecostal advent, Morgan says:

> . . . they . . . heard with absolute distinctness . . . In many
> tongues and dialects, with perfect distinctness this chanting,
> this ecstatic utterance of the newly baptized company
> . . . broke upon the astonishing and listening ear of that
> assembled multitude . . . All the reference in Acts, Co-
> rinthians, and Ephesians, show that the exercise of tongues
> consisted of ecstatic utterance. These people were not
> preaching, they were praising; they were not indulging in
> set discourse, they were pouring out the rapture that filled
> their souls.[72]

Morgan wrote at the beginning of this century. He admits

---

[70] John R. Dummelow (ed.), *A Commentary on the Holy Bible* (New York:
The Macmillan Co., 1941), p. 915.
[71] G. Campbell Morgan, *The Corinthian Letters of Paul* (London & Edinburgh: Fleming H. Revell Co., 1946), p. 169.
[72] Morgan, *The Acts of the Apostles, op. cit.*, pp. 37, 38.

the "signs" were "material" yet "spiritual," and that "they were needed at the commencement." Has the whole world felt the impact of that Pentecostal morn? If the same phenomenon produces the same results today, then why negate the benefits, or what is worse, why declare its cessation?

> . . . these signs of the day of Pentecost were initial, and produced no final result. The gift of tongues exercised in the midst of the multitudes, to the astonishment of the multitude, and probably to the astonishment of the disciples, also, brought nothing to a conclusion. . . . It needed prophecy to complete it. It created the opportunity for prophecy . . . All this was initial; and it was incomplete. It was . . . a sign, to arrest the attention of Jerusalem.[73]

How can a man of the repute of Morgan say that "these signs produced no final result," yet continue to admit, "it created the opportunity for prophecy?" That which is creative definitely produces results. If signs brought the people together at Pentecost, no evidence has been produced that they will not do the same today. The fact has been attested to in many parts of the world in our own day.

Morgan becomes vague, and at times he even questions the use of glossolalia in the church; but note his contributions in support of the phenomenon:

> "What meaneth this?" . . . It was a threefold impression. First, amazement; second, perplexity; third, criticism. What was this amazement? It was mental arrest; not yet illumination. They did not know the meaning of what they heard and saw; but they wondered. Out of wonder worship is born. Where wonder ceases worship ceases. Wonder is not worship, but it is the first movement toward worship. For a moment, Jerusalem was compelled to turn from other interest, to attend to this matter. . . . For a brief hour or two at least, men left the schools, and the disputations, and the quarrellings, forgot their differences, and united in common amazement . . . The amazement was mental arrest, a compulsion laid upon the men of a city, to

---

[73] *Ibid.*, p. 40.

turn from all other matters, in wonder.

. . . .

What is this? Look and listen. Look at the glory in the eyes.
Listen to the abandonment in the voice. Mark the pul-
sating passion of these people. To some of them . . . They
were drunk!
They were nearer the truth than they knew, but they were
exactly as far from it as hell is from heaven.

, ...

Amazement, perplexity, criticism; these were the effects
produced by the tongues . . .
If these impressions are not produced, it is because the
Church is not Spirit-filled. Is the Church of God amazing
the city, perplexing the city, making the city criticize? The
trouble too often is that the world is not at all amazed, not
at all perplexed, not at all critical; because there is nothing
to amaze, to perplex, to criticize. The work of the Church
is to be Spirit-filled, and amaze the city, and perplex the
city, and make the city listen. Are we doing it?[74]

Dr. Morgan presents provocative projections that should
cause the church to rethink its theology, reshape its worship,
rechart its course, and get in step with the true Pentecostal pattern of apostolic times. And he continues his excellent
observation of the Pentecostal experience by describing a
church endowed with Pentecostal experiences and manifestations. His description is worthy of even an old-line Pentecostal.
He says,

They knew that the river of God had come by the way of
the altar, and they were in the full flood tide of its healing
and life-giving waters. . . .
Did they know they were speaking in other tongues?
One cannot be at all sure that they did. . . . They praised
with a new inspiration, they poured out their songs, and
lo, Parthians, Medes, and Elamites, sojourners from Rome,
people from Mesopotamia, men of all dialects, listened; and
they heard the songs in their own languages, with perfect
accuracy and distinctness. The Resurrection was the first
note, in their singing, as it came to be the first note in
apostolic preaching. One could almost wish that one could

---

[74] *Ibid.,* pp. 38-40, 42.

have listened to that first chanting of the Church, in which
singers set forth the mighty works of God.[75]

Morgan lets one see the people of God at Pentecost in "the
full flood tide of the healing and life-giving waters" of "the
river of God" and then lines up the saints of all subsequent
time on the river bank to dry out in the heat of polemical,
nonessential squabblings, and cold Laodicean formalism. As
others, he sees but does not plunge into the stream. He recognized the possibility that, "someone may get it, may receive
the gift of tongues," and he elaborates further by saying, "The
crowds were arrested because they heard . . . 'the wonderful
works of God.' That was the peculiar gift. *I am not going to
say it is never bestowed today.* It was common in the early
days of the Church, that gift of worship in tongues, which
were ecstatic utterances."[76] In addition, he emphatically says,
"There is no doubt that at the very beginning it [tongue
speaking] was a sign to the outsider."[77] Reverend W. K.
Lowther Clarke pictures the use of tongues and other spiritual
gifts in the Early Church in such a way that one can easily
identify the similarity between those apostolic services and services of our own day where there is recognition of the Spirit. The
same results are frequently evident. He comments thus, ". . .
spiritual excitement, accompanied by ecstasy . . . marked the
gatherings of Christians in these early days."[78] Clarke, in his
comparison, shows a well-defined difference in the tongues
speaking as related by Luke and Paul: "The essential difference was that the former, however, ecstatic in origin, was intelligible. The latter was often unintelligible to the speaker."[79]

In support of ecstatic speaking he says further:

> "Speaking with tongues," ecstatic utterance, is abundantly
> testified in all ages . . . If I Cor. 14:6-11 is treated as
> a later interpretation, difficulties are removed and noth-

---

[75] *Ibid.*, p. 38.
[76] Morgan, *1 Corinthians, op. cit.*, p. 153. Italics ours.
[77] *Ibid.*, p. 170.
[78] W. K. Lowther Clarke, *op. cit.*, p. 845.
[79] *Ibid.*, p. 846.

ing more than ordinary ecstatic speaking is meant, such was common in early Israel and was a natural accompaniment of a revival of prophecy.[80]

Lowther Clarke amplifies the projections of the above by saying, "The true use of tongues is as a sign of divine presence, to impress outsiders, who would not understand prophesying. If the quotation is to be pressed, the meaning is that tongues are a sign to unbelievers, who close their ears to God's message, so that it works for their condemnation."[81] Dr. Lewis Sperry Chafer (1871-1925), internationally-known teacher, points out, in his work *Systematic Theology*, directions for the use of tongues:

a. Tongues must be addressed to God (1 Cor. 4:2, 28).

b. The utterance must be in prayer (1 Cor. 14:14).

c. The element of thanksgiving must be present (1 Cor. 14:15-17).

d. Tongues can be understood only by interpretation (1 Cor. 14:2, 5, 6).

e. One must interpret—the complementary gift—if there is to be any use of the tongues gift (1 Cor. 14:28). . . .[82]

The speaking in tongues—among other benefits both personal and for the whole church—is also a divine provision for personal edification. Henry J. Foster commenting upon Paul's emphasis of "understanding" writes:

. . . within even the holy place of the "understanding," there is another, most sacred spot, where not even the natural man, of understanding and intellect cultured to their highest of capacity, may tread. It is the Holy of Holies of manhood, the "spirit"; the inmost shrine, where God Who "is a Spirit" dwells and reveals Himself in glory, and where the spiritual man holds a fellowship with God, of worship on the one side, and of revelation and blessing on the other, which is a holy secret between them.

---

[80] *Ibid.,* p. 800.

[81] *Ibid.*

[82] Lewis Sperry Chafer, *Systematic Theology: Doctrinal Summarization* (Dallas: Dallas Seminary Press, 1948), VII, 304, 305.

> In that innermost secrecy, in the holy privacy of the Holy
> of Holies, the man "*speaking in a tongue*" is for the time
> closeted with God. (In a holy outpouring of prayer and
> praise, and even of song, he is a high priest standing be-
> fore God within the central shrine of His personality.) The
> bystanders in the assembly may hear his voice, as it were
> through the thick, dulling veil of the physical organs, but
> their ear catches nothing of the sense of the ecstaic words of
> holy communion between him and God.[83]

It would be difficult to portray in a better way a child of
God in spiritual communion with his heavenly father. What
a vivid description! What eloquent language! "In the innermost
secrecy, in the holy privacy of the Holy of Holies, the man
speaking in tongues is for the time closeted with God."

President Arnold Theodore Olson of the Evangelical Free
Church of America writes in *This We Believe:*

> Believing as we do in the presence and power of the Holy
> Spirit we must accept the possibility and probability of spir-
> itual manifestations. But each and all of these must be in
> accord with the Word of God, whether they be tongues,
> renewals, revivals, or infillings. To deny the possibility of
> the Holy Spirit speaking through a believer in an "unknown
> tongue" would be to limit the power of the third Person of
> the Godhead.[84]

John Short, writing in the *Interpreter's Bible,* edited by
George Arthur Buttrick, clearly classifies tongues speaking
or glossolalia as articulate sounds. He writes: "Luke's meaning
is quite plain: under the stress of spiritual emotion these men
spoke intelligibly in foreign tongues and were understood by
those standing around who spoke the same language."[85] However, when he discusses the phenomenon at Corinth, he identifies the exercise as "ecstatic utterances": ". . . these ecstatic

---

[83] *The Preacher's Complete Homiletic Commentary: Corinthians, op. cit.,* p.
309.

[84] Arnold Theodore Olson, *This We Believe* (Minneapolis: Free Church
Publication, 1961), p. 228.

[85] *The Interpreter's Bible* (Nashville: The Abingdon-Cokesbury Press, 1953),
X, 155, quoting F. J. Foakes Jackson, *The Acts of the Apostles* (London:
Hodder and Stoughton, 1931; "The Moffatt New Testament Commentary"),
p. 11.

utterances were treasured by the early church as signifying
the presence and power of the Spirit in the midst of believers.
Ecstatic utterances were probably regarded as a kind of divine
frenzy, and therefore of superhuman origin."[86]

Short says of the speaking in tongues:

> . . . it was a manifestation of the emotional enthusiasm
> engendered by the new faith: it was a sign of spiritual fer-
> vor. As such it was apt to be contagious. A near ap-
> proach to it is seen in great revivalist gatherings, where
> emotion can sweep across a vast audience like a breeze
> rippling over a field of ripening corn. *Speaking in tongues,*
> *as in certain instances of the same phenomenon in our own*
> *times* [Italics ours], might take the form of an unintelligible
> monologue, which was conceived to be inspired by the in-
> dwelling Spirit of God. Or it might take the form of ejacu-
> lations and ecstatic utterances, some of which were in-
> telligible . . . There is no need, following Paul's courteous
> and understanding example, to treat such manifestations
> with disdain . . . the manifestation was not confined to
> the less well-educated or less intelligent members of the
> community.[87]

G. H. C. Macgregor in the volume on Acts declares:

> . . . glossolalia quite clearly means the outpouring of in-
> articulate sounds under the stress of an overpowering re-
> ligious emotion, *a phenomenon to which there are many*
> *parallels in the history of all religious revivals down to our*
> *own day* [Italics ours]. It was evidently regarded as a supreme
> proof of possession by the divine Spirit and as such was
> earnestly coveted.[88]

Clarence Tucker Craig emphasizes: ". . . by *tongues* Paul
means speech directed toward God and caused by the Spirit."[89]

F. F. Bruce, a distinguished English scholar and professor
of Biblical history, recognizes in glossolalia ecstatic manifestation. His comparison of the present-day church to the Early
Church is most certainly applicable to a great segment of the
twentieth-century body of believers, but by no means is repre-

---

86 *Ibid.,* X, 155.
87 *Ibid.,* p. 196.
88 *Ibid.,* IX, 37.
89 *Ibid.,* X, 197.

sentative of all present-day Christians. There is still a "super-natural" force at work in God's Church:

> Speaking with tongues, or *glossolalia* (to give the phenomenon its Greek name), is not an unparalleled manifestation. Not only are the speaker's words partially or completely beyond his conscious control, but they are uttered in a language of which he has no command in normal circumstances . . .[90]
> The phenomenon of glossolalia has appeared in many forms. The context here implies that the disciples' words made good sense to those who understood the various languages or dialects, but were unintelligible to others. . . . The disciples, suddenly delivered from the peculiarities of their Galilean speech, praised God and rehearsed His mighty works in such a way that each hearer recognized with surprise his own native language or dialect. . . . The effect of the Pentecostal glossolalia was better understanding on the part of the hearers; this does not appear to have been so at Corinth, *nor is it so in many circles where the gift of tongues is cultivated nowadays* [italics ours]. The test as to whether this or any other form of utterance represents the Holy Spirit's activity is this: Does it edify the hearer? Does it help him to become a Christian, or to be a better Christian than he already is?[91]

Bruce fairly recognizes the present existence of the same apostolic phenomenon and treads softly where others have condemned without basis.

Unknown tongues and languages are to be taken into consideration as two distinct spiritual manifestations. Dr. D. Edmond Hiebert, commenting on "The Gift of Tongues" relates that:

> Modern commentators generally hold that the Corinthian tongues were not identical with the Pentecostal tongues, but were ecstatic outbursts of prayer and praise in which the utterances often became abnormal and incoherent and the connection with the speaker's own conscious intellectual ac-

---

[90] Frederick F. Bruce, *Commentary on the Book of the Acts* (Vol. V of *The New International Commentary on the New Testament*, ed. Ned B. Stonehouse. Grand Rapids: Wm. B. Eerdmans Publishing Company, 1954), pp. 56, 57.
[91] Frederick F. Bruce, *The Acts of the Apostles* (Grand Rapids: Wm. B. Eerdmans Publishing Company, 1960), p. 82.

tivity was suspended. It is held that the utterances were-incomprehensible to the speaker as well as to the audience. . . .[92]

Howard Carter, an Assemblies of God preacher of England, aptly declares:

> . . . we teach that . . . speaking with other tongues the articulation is a supernatural manifestation of the indwelling Holy Spirit . . . this gift is the power to speak supernaturally by the Holy Spirit in a language not known to the one possessing the gift . . . it (tongues) is almost last in the list of spiritual gifts, and is the least of the gifts of inspiration. We do not want to find fault with the designation, which is often used in a disparaging way, but we shall at least expect the least gift to be the one in greatest evidence. It should, therefore, be the possession of all God's people. If we do not possess the least gift, how can we expect the greater.[93]

It is often quoted that tongues and interpretation of tongues were listed last among the spiritual gifts with which the Early Church was endowed. This would not alter the fact of their existence or indicate that they were of less importance among the spiritual gifts bestowed upon the Church. Why should the younger children, who would likely be listed last, be of lower esteem in any family? Just because "faith" is mentioned midway of the characteristics of the fruit of the Spirit and "temperance" last does not necessarily imply that either of them is inferior to "joy" or "gentleness."

VI. SUMMATION

In all fairness to several eminent writers of the period in question who have been quoted as favorable to the phenomenon of glossolalia at Jerusalem and Corinth, it must be acknowledged that some of these men erroneously, yet with-

---

[92] *The Zondervan Pictorial Bible Dictionary,* Merrill C. Tenney ed. (Grand Rapids: Zondervan Publishing House, 1963), p. 860.

[93] Howard Carter, *Questions and Answers on Spiritual Gifts* (London: Assemblies of God Publishing House, 1955), p. 118.

did it really cease?

out doubt sincerely, believe that tongues ceased after the times of the early apostolic church. This work, as well as many others, has disproved this point of view. A close observer will notice the weakness of the objections presented by great men whose favorable comments relative to the "early rain" conflict with the questions raised relative to the "latter rain."

Dr. Plumptre, who has been quoted in this work, carefully declares, "From the indwelling Spirit of God resulted certain marvelous 'gifts,' some of which ceased with the apostolic age—some of which seem to have lingered for centuries, even to our own day—declaring themselves intermittently in times of profound religious awakening."[94] He admits that Paul, "does not undervalue that gift [tongues speaking], the misuse and exaggeration of which he is censuring; he possesses it himself in a remarkable degree."[95]

Charles R. Erdman declares, "The gifts granted to the Corinthian church were many and varied, yet they all came from one divine Source and all were designed for the common good of believers."[96] He continues to describe the experience at Corinth which has contrasting characteristics: ". . . the gift of tongues . . . was not identical with the manifestation on the Day of Pentecost. It probably did not consist in the ability to speak in known languages, but rather was 'an overpowering influence of profound emotion,' which enabled one 'to pray, sing, or give thanks in an ecstatic language unintelligible to every one who did not share the emotion.' "[97]

diff at Pentecost

John Short stresses that, "Speaking with tongues had no future at all. . . . Hence, in the nature of the case, speaking with tongues was bound to vanish from the regular life and witness of the church. It has *largely* done so . . ."[98] The qualified

---

[94] Ellicott, *op. cit.*, p. 335.
[95] *Ibid.*, p. 342.
[96] From *The Epistle of Paul to the Corinthians* by Charles R. Erdman. Copyright 1928 by Charles R. Erdman. Copyright renewed 1956 by Charles R. Erdman. The Westminster Press. Used by permission, p. 108.
[97] *Ibid.*, p. 110.
[98] *The Interpreter's Bible, op. cit.*, X, 187. Italics ours.

statement is indicative of recognition that glossolalia continues.
William Smith, who may be classified as unsympathetic, indicates that after the initial appearance of glossolalia at Pentecost, tongues gradually disappeared. After the succeeding
age "within the Church we lose *nearly all traces* [italics ours]
of them."[99] He too, as Short, admits the presence of the phenomenon of tongues "within the church."

G. Campbell Morgan says that "while it was a definite gift,
Paul did say . . . that 'tongues shall cease.' " Yet, he too says,
"someone may get it, may receive the gift of tongues." "Ever
and anon in the history of the Christian Church we have had
a recrudescence of it . . ."[100] Morgan is particularly careful
in his criticism of the "Tongues Movement" of the United
States and of London.

Erdman questions the presence of the gift of tongues in the
modern church by stating: "The gift of tongues is coveted
and even claimed by many members of the modern Church.
Whether this claim is true or false is a question of fact to be
established upon evidence."[101]

The Pentecostals ask, "Upon what evidence?" If it's Biblical
evidence, there is sufficient. If it's experiential evidence, the
words of those professing the experience must be accepted.
If not theirs, whose? If it's historical evidence, there is an
abundance of it available to those who seek it. At the very
least the Pentecostals have the same evidence as the apostles.

Alexander Maclaren, who lived over one hundred years ago,
a prolific English Baptist writer, although admitting a transient
element in the Pentecostal experience of tongues, says relative
to ". . . whether there be prophecies they shall fail; whether
there be tongues, they shall cease":

> that has been misunderstood as if it amounted to a declara-
> tion that the miraculous gifts in the Early Church were in-

---

[99] Wm. Smith, *Bible Dictionary* (Chicago, Ill.: The John C. Winston Co.,
1884), p. 710.
[100] Morgan, *The Corinthian Letters of Paul, op. cit.,* pp. 170, 171.
[101] From *The First Epistle of Paul to the Corinthians,* Erdman, *op. cit.,* p. 126.

tended to be of brief duration . . . it is not what Paul means here. The cessation to which he refers is their cessation in the light of the perfect Future . .   .   .

.   .   .   .

What will drop away? Paul answers, "prophecies, tongues knowledge." Now these three were all extraordinary gifts belonging to the present phase of the Christian life. But inasmuch as these gifts were the heightening of natural capacities and faculties, it is perfectly legitimate to enlarge the declaration and to use these three words in their widest signification. So understood, they come to this, that all our present modes of apprehension and of utterance are transient, and will be left behind. . . . the knowledge, the mode of apprehension belonging to the present, will pass —because here it is indirect, and there it will be immediate. . . . Modes of utterance will cease. With new experiences will come new methods of communication. . . . "Tongues shall cease"; and the modes of utterances that belonged to earth, and all that holds of them, will drop away, and be of no more use.[102]

There is no question about tongues ceasing at the same time that knowledge, prophesying, and preaching will cease. None of these, as we know them, will be needed any more in the new life. Erdman further attests:

There may be too much religious fervor and excitement in some religious gatherings, but surely not in many; and most churches need to pray earnestly for a new moving and inspiration of the Holy Spirit in order that the hearts of the worshipers may know something of the passion, the joy, the rapture, the exultation, the triumphant hope, which was the common experience of the early Christians even in Corinth.[103]

Godet well defines tongues speaking as a glorious spiritual experience:

Such manifestations therefore give evidence of a real faculty latent in the depths of the human soul, which a profound religious awakening may call into exercise at any time un-

[102] Maclaren, *Exposition of the Holy Scriptures, op. cit.,* **XIII,** 187-189.
[103] Erdman, *op. cit.,* 1928 edition, p. 131.

der fixed conditions, and the creative action of which may yet in our day produce effects similar to those of the first days of the church. We were not wrong, therefore, in maintaining the possibility of the reappearance of gifts during the whole course of the present economy.[104]

He also comments:

I can only therefore regard the gift of tongues as the expression, in a language spontaneously created by the Holy Spirit, as of the new views and of the profound and lively emotions of the human souls set free for the first time from the feeling of condemnation and enjoying the affable sweetness of the relation of sonship to God. And as the influence of the Holy Spirit takes possession of the whole soul and every one of its natural powers, to make it its organ, it also took possession of the gift of speech transfiguring it, so to speak, to give utterance to emotions which no natural tongue could express.[105]

Harold Horton, a Pentecostal, most eloquently describes the blessedness of the Pentecostal experience:

The Gift of Tongues sinks a well into the dumb profundities of the rejoicing spirit, liberating a jet of long-pent ecstasy that gladdens the heart of God and man. Blessed fountain of ineffable coherence, of inexpressable eloquence! Have you never in the presence of Jesus felt inarticulate on the very verge of eloquence? This heavenly Gift will loose the spirit's tongue and burst upon the speechless heart with utterance transcending sages' imaginings or angel rhapsodies. Have you never wept to think how helpless your words are to express emotion in the presence of Him whom your soul loveth? Other tongues alone can give you utterance equal to the holy task. Other tongues will give you the Names for Jesus that even revelation has not vouchsafed. Other tongues will capture the escaping thought, the elusive expression, the inarticulate longing, lending worthy and soul-satisfying utterance to profoundest gratitude and worship.[106]

It would appear that the majority of Biblical scholars agree

---

104 Godet, *op. cit.*, p. 321.
105 *Ibid.*, p. 320.
106 Harold Horton, *Gifts of the Spirit* (Clapham Junction London: Northcote Printing Works, 1954), pp. 152, 153.

that the disciples spoke in known languages at Pentecost, and that they were clearly understood by peoples of various other lands and tongues; whereas glossolalia at Corinth was speech unknown to man, directed to God.

The glory revealed that Pentecostal day brought together the multitudes. God was praised and magnified in many tongues. Men, women and children—three thousand of them—were receptive to the message delivered under the divine move of the Holy Ghost. The Spirit had come, as was promised by Christ.

Luke was present and was filled with the experience. He wrote what he saw and felt. History was being made. The Church was born that day. Glory, wonder, and ecstasy filled the upper room, the hallways, and poured out into the street. People looked from their windows, as the crowd moved down the narrow corridor-like streets and followed the newly-filled disciples into the marketplaces, the street stalls, and homes. The people were amazed as the awe-inspiring effects of the advent brought wonder. The Holy Ghost, the Comforter, had come. Men shouted from the housetops. The temples were filled. Marvelous and great things were happening. Humble Galileans were anointed and spoke under the control of the Spirit the "mighty works of God." Men and women made altars at their bedsides, at the grinding mills, and at the public washing places. The stone steps of the houses lining the streets became altars of prayer. Revival to the things of God, recognition of the resurrection of Christ, salvation through the Healer so recently crucified, were the order of the day.

What was seen, felt, and heard that day was conveyed to almost every part of the known world, because "they heard them in their own tongues." The message is the same; the miraculous is still evident in the Church of God; only the time and places have changed. The limited confines of Jerusalem have been exchanged for "all the world."

Thus we conclude this study on glossolalia from the Reformation until the twentieth century. It is the opinion of the writer that sufficient historical testimony on tongues speaking has been presented to prove it was believed and practiced during this period. Although it is not an exhaustive compilation, it is a reasonable resumé of recorded evidence which shows what was believed, witnessed, and experienced. It should be clear from the testimony given that *many believed* that the scriptural account of the Baptism of the Holy Ghost was a miraculous enduement of spiritual power accompanied by tongues speaking; that *others witnessed tongues speaking* though they themselves were not possessors of the experience; and that others *actually received the Pentecostal blessing* and spoke in tongues as the Spirit gave the utterance.

These testimonies from the pages of history are proof of the immutability of God's Word that declares, "I will pour out my Spirit upon all flesh) . ." and ". . . the promise is unto you, and to your children, and to all that are afar off, even as many as the Lord our God shall call."[107]

---

[107] Joel 2:28; Acts 2:17; Acts 2:39.

Glossolalia
In Contemporary Times

Ray H. Hughes

Ray H. Hughes is President of Lee College, Cleveland, Tennessee. Prior to this appointment he served in other important positions in his church. including state overseer, National Radio Speaker, and National Sunday School and Youth Director. He has served on the National Sunday School and Youth Board, as Chairman of the Evangelism Committee, and is presently serving his eighth year on the Executive Council. He holds the Bachelor of Arts degree from Tennessee Wesleyan College and Master of Science and Doctor of Education degrees from the University of Tennessee. Lee College conferred on him the Doctor of Letters degree. He has authored five books: What Is Pentecost?, Religion on Fire, The Order of Future Events, The Outpouring of the Spirit, *and* Planning for Sunday School Progress. *His travels in deputational work have taken him into fifty-five countries.*

Ray H. Hughes

Glossolalia
In Contemporary Times

The streets of Jerusalem were filled with people on their way to Mount Zion. The day was May 21, 1961. Jews were chanting Old Testament Scriptures in their Israeli tongue, and the atmosphere was charged with expectancy. What could all this excitement mean? It was the Day of Pentecost, and like the Apostle Paul, who "hasted, if it were possible for him, to be at Jerusalem the Day of Pentecost" (Acts 20:16), these had come with great enthusiasm.

Not only was there excitement among the Jews on that Sunday morning of May, but the hearts of three thousand delegates who were present in Jerusalem for the Sixth World Pentecostal Conference burned within them as they also turned their feet toward Mount Zion. One can understand very readily why the Jews were enthusiastic, but why were these Gentiles from many nations under heaven present? There was a quizzical look upon the faces of the Jews as the convention delegates mingled among them and passed them by. They looked upon them as if to say in words echoing from centuries past, "What meaneth this?"

What did it mean? It was a milestone in the fulfillment of the prophecy: "I will pour out of my Spirit upon all flesh" (Acts 2:17).

143

People from many nations had made their pilgrimage, not to commemorate a feast of the Hebrew law but to focus attention upon the fact that it was here that the Holy Ghost was sent down from heaven almost two thousand years ago. This is sometimes called "the founding miracle of the Church." These people were present, not for reflection only—for they did not look upon Pentecost as a memorial—but as witnesses to the entire world that they were samples of twentieth-century believers who had discovered the fact that the Holy Spirit baptism with the evidence of glossolalia, or speaking with tongues, is the heritage of believers today.

In addition to those believers who were present for this great holy convocation, the eyes of Christians from many denominations all over the world were focused upon this event. *Christianity Today,* an evangelical publication, reported:

> When viewed in retrospect, Pentecost weekend of May 21 probably will be associated with a religious spectacle in Jerusalem unparalleled almost certainly since New Testament times. In historic proceedings climaxed on Pentecost Sunday, more than three thousand delegates to the sixth Pentecostal World Conference participated in what is believed to have been the largest meeting of any kind ever held in the Holy Land. Appropriately enough, the three-day meeting came on the edge of what its followers the world over regard as a twentieth-century revival of Pentecostalism in general and glossolalia in particular.[1]

Spanning twenty centuries, the experience still abides. The experience of Pentecost was not a once-for-all sign of the birth of the Church, but an experience to be possessed by believers in all ages.

This fact was pointed up by an event which took place on that day in May. A delegate, hungry of heart for a deeper experience in Christ, arose early Pentecost morning and made the trek up Mount Zion to the traditional site of the "upper

---

[1] Carl F. H. Henry, "Pentecostal Meeting Makes Holy Land History," *Christianity Today,* V. No. 17 (May 22, 1961), 25. Copyright 1961 by *Christianity Today;* used by permission.

room,"[2] the place of the original outpouring. There, in spirit, he joined the 120 believers of the first century by receiving the Pentecostal baptism and speaking with tongues. Surrounded by dead ritual, and unnoticed by the crowd, this man witnessed a live, vital experience which many believers claim to be obsolete or nonexistent. As always, God again validated His promise:

> . . . ye shall receive the gift of the Holy Ghost. For the promise is unto you, and to your children, and to all that are afar off, even as many as the Lord our God shall call (Acts 2:38, 39).

This man, not a Jew but one of those afar off (a Gentile), received the promise of the Father. "For all the promises of God in him are yea, and in him Amen. . ." (2 Corinthians 1:20).

I. PENTECOST IN PROPHECY

Many centuries prior to the outpouring of Pentecost, the prophets foretold the events of the new epoch and the place of the advent of the Spirit. Isaiah, Ezekiel, Joel, and Zechariah joined hands in Pentecostal chorus and announced the dawning of a new day.

Couched in terms which hid the full meaning from the people of his day, Isaiah said, "Until the spirit be poured upon us from on high, and the wilderness be a fruitful field, and the fruitful field be counted for a forest" (Isaiah 32:15). Jesus later used a portion of this terminology in His charge to His disciples, "tarry . . . until ye be endued with power *from on high*" (Luke 24:49; italics ours).

Ezekiel, in the promise to restore God's people, spoke of another day: "Then will I sprinkle clean water upon you . . . And I will put my spirit within you . . ." (Ezekiel 36:25, 27).

---

[2] Acts 1:13.

Twenty-four generations before Pentecost, Joel, looking through the eyes of God, said, with full assurance:

prophecy of what was to come... (margin note)

> And it shall come to pass afterward, that I will pour out my spirit upon all flesh; and your sons and your daughters shall prophesy, your old men shall dream dreams, your young men shall see visions: And also upon the servants and upon the handmaids in those days will I pour out my spirit. And I will shew wonders in the heavens and in the earth, blood, and fire, and pillars of smoke. The sun shall be turned into darkness, and the moon into blood, before the great and the terrible day of the Lord come (Joel 2:28-31).

In these scriptures Joel gave a picture of the operation of the Spirit from the Day of Pentecost until the rapture of the Church, after which God's judgments will be poured out upon the earth. Notice that *all* flesh—sons, daughters, old men, young men, servants, handmaids—were told to live in anticipation of the Spirit during this new era.

Both Joel and Zechariah pointed out the location of this prophetical event. The Holy Ghost was to be poured out on Mount Zion in Jerusalem (Joel 2:23-32, Zechariah 12:10). By shadow and prophecy, the Old Testament is replete with promises of the advent of the Spirit.

repeated 4 times... (margin note)

The last of the prophets of the old order, John the Baptizer, heralded the message of a new and added experience which would be made possible through Christ. Four times the Gospels repeat his prophetic promise: ". . . he shall baptize you with the Holy Ghost, and with fire" (Matthew 3:11); ". . . he shall baptize you with the Holy Ghost" (Mark 1:8); ". . . he shall baptize you with the Holy Ghost and with fire" (Luke 3:16); ". . . the same is he which baptizeth with the Holy Ghost" (John 1:33). These references dealt with a Baptism yet to be and not as yet experienced or bestowed at that particular time. The announcement was prophetic.

After John the Baptizer—the link between the Old and New Testaments—came Jesus, witnessing to the message of John and prophesying of the coming of the Spirit: "For John truly

promise of Christ, the waiting disciples received *another Comforter,* the Holy Ghost. This was "as good news from a far country." This was evidence that Jesus Christ was at the right hand of Majesty on High, making intercession for His people.

What did all of this really mean to the church? Let us reverently try to understand what happened on the Day of Pentecost. Just ten days prior to this time Christ had ascended, and now He was exalted at the right hand of the Father. He had left His disciples with a promise that the Spirit would come to aid them in their witness. He had impressed upon them that although they were His disciples, followers, and believers, there was a need for a new power and strength to make them witness bearers. It was His desire that they should become equipped witnesses. So then, this coming of the Spirit meant, for the disciples, equipment for service and adequacy for vocation. It was an enduement of power from on high to aid in the tremendous task of the evangelization of the world. Without the coming of the Holy Ghost, the message of Christ in all probability would have died within the confines of Palestine; but the coming of the Holy Ghost meant that this message would be taken to the uttermost part of the earth.

> Had no Pentecost followed the ascension, the story of Calvary and the resurrection would probably have long since been forgotten, or at best would have only found a place among the mysterious records of a remote era in which the later generations could have felt little special interest.[7]
>
> Every view of Pentecost is incomplete which does not connect it with the great work which our Saviour came to earth to accomplish.[8]

ONLY THE GENESIS

The Day of Pentecost was not the apex, the summit, nor the

---

[7] J. M. Thoburn, *The Church of Pentecost* (New York: Methodist Publishing House, 1899), p. 32.
[8] *Ibid.,* p. 31.

[handwritten margin note: Pentecost only beginning of]

conclusion of this experience. It was the beginning. Peter testified in his memorable sermon, "this is [the beginning of] what was spoken through the prophet Joel" (Acts 2:16, *Amplified New Testament).* Christ calls the coming of the Spirit a beginning for the disciples.[9] Peter again testified to the fact that the Day of Pentecost was the beginning of the age of the Spirit: "The Holy Ghost fell on them, as on us at the beginning" (Acts 11:15).

The advent of the Spirit took place about A.D. 30. The period of time covered by the book of Acts is approximately thirty-three years, during which time the Holy Spirit was poured out upon the first-century church. But this experience did not end with the book of Acts. (It is interesting to note that the book of Acts has no benediction or complimentary close.) The Apostle Paul was left in his own hired house, preaching the kingdom of God; and Pentecost went marching on.

III. PENTECOST THROUGH THE CENTURIES

[handwritten margin note: HS work doesn't stop op to]

The experience of the Baptism of the Holy Ghost with the evidence of speaking with other tongues was not confined to the Day of Pentecost nor to the first-century church.

The phenomenon of "speaking with tongues as the Spirit gives utterance" (Acts 2:1-13) has appeared in all ages of the church.[10]

> That this phenomenon [glossolalia] is by no means restricted to early Christianity is universally recognized. It was common in the Christian movement as late as Tertullian and Irenaeus . . . In later years it appeared again, and has been the seemingly inevitable consequence of all extended seasons of "revival."[11]

---

[9] Luke 24:47.

[10] Lefferts Loetscher, *Twentieth Century Encyclopedia of Religious Knowledge* (Grand Rapids: Baker Book House, 1955), II, p. 1118.

[11] Madeleine Miller and J. Lane Miller, *Harper's Bible Dictionary* (New York: Harper & Brothers, 1952), p. 768.

something new (handwritten note in left margin)

The historical accounts of the occurrence of glossolalia from patristic times to the present would be interesting to review, but space is limited and the main burden of this presentation is to give the *contemporary* picture of Pentecost.

IV. TWENTIETH CENTURY OUTPOURING

Only a cursory glance has been taken at the Biblical and historical background of Pentecost. Detailed investigation would clearly substantiate that this experience called "glossolalia" has weathered the storms of the centuries and has come down to this day to be manifested in all of its glory. In fact, the church has often been challenged, and the challenge is repeated by H. Orton Wiley, the Church of the Nazarene theologian, that the gifts of the Spirit "did not cease with the apostles, but are available to the Church in every age."[12]

This truth became more than a challenge to the Church of God. It became a *reality* to her founders in 1896, at Camp Creek, North Carolina. Around the turn of the century there were isolated revivals of Pentecost throughout the United States. For many people, the year 1906 was a red-letter year, for in that year the Pentecostal revival came to Azusa Street in Los Angeles and received widespread attention.

It is reported, however, that in the United States about a thousand people had received the Baptism in the Holy Ghost prior to 1906. In the Middle West, in Topeka, Kansas (1901); in the foothills of the Unicoi Mountains in North Carolina (1896);[13] in Texas (1902);[14] and in other places, the outpouring of the Spirit had been experienced among holiness groups.

From this time on, the revival spread throughout the United

---

[12] H. Orton Wiley, *Christian Theology* (Kansas City: Beacon Hill Press, 1952), II, p. 321.
[13] Charles W. Conn, *Like a Mighty Army* (Cleveland, Tenn.: Church of God Publishing House, 1955), p. 25.
[14] Marcus Bach, "Whether There Be Tongues," *Christian Herald*, LXXXVII, (May, 1964), p. 11.

States and other countries in the world like a prairie fire. God was again visiting His people.

EYEWITNESS REPORTS

The writer has witnessed the Holy Spirit outpouring in evangelistic campaigns and camp meetings throughout the world. During an evangelistic campaign in Detroit, Michigan, in 1942, one of the worshipers spoke with tongues. While the people waited for the interpretation, a robust young man came from the back of the church and very hastily made his way to the altar. In conversation with him after the meeting, it was discovered that the young man was of German descent. He said that the lady, speaking in his native tongue, had invited him forward. Upon inquiry, it was discovered that the woman did not know the German language. The Holy Spirit had spoken to this young man through this anointed vessel.

In 1947 the writer was in Shawnee, Oklahoma, attending a camp meeting. In one of the services the Spirit moved with a message in other tongues, and although there was no interpretation, one gentleman in the congregation seemed to be filled with exceptional joy. After the service it was learned that the man was a Mexican. He asked the writer, "Do you speak Spanish?" The reply was "No." He said, "In your message today, you said in my language, 'The table of the Lord is set. Eat, O my friends!' "

A similar experience occurred in 1948 during a visit to the island of Haiti. The churches were packed to capacity. On one occasion at Poste Marchand, the message was on the Baptism of the Holy Ghost, pointing up the availability of the experience in these last days. The writer paused in his message, turned his head heavenward and asked God to pour out the Spirit again as He did on the Day of Pentecost. Almost immediately, people began to speak in other tongues all through the congregation. Soon they made their way to the platform and testified to having received the Holy Ghost baptism. Their testimonies were something like this: "While I sat in the congregation and the evangelist asked God to send an outpouring of the Spirit, I began to speak in a language I had never learned." That night thirteen gave testimony to receiving the Holy Spirit.

Another great outpouring occurred during the spring of 1962 when the student body and faculty of Lee College, Cleveland, Tennessee, were observing Spiritual Emphasis Week. At the very outset of this meeting, the entire campus seemed to sense a divine move of Almighty God. The singing of the campus choir was fraught with power, and hearts were melted as the people waited before the Lord. Day by day the services mounted higher and higher, until on the sixth night there was a spontaneous overflow of the Holy Spirit upon the audience. It seemed that each student who entered the door of the chapel became visibly aware of the presence of the Spirit. All set form of worship was laid aside and without singing or preaching the service continued until well after midnight. There were confessions of sins, definite calls to full-time Christian service, and many other visible results. Many were filled with the Holy Ghost, according to Acts 2:4, and spoke with other tongues as the Spirit gave them utterance.

On October 15, 1965, the writer received a letter from Esdras Betancourt, one of the instructors of the Church of God Bible College in Switzerland. He wrote:

> I have often heard of Christians who have had the experience of listening to another Christian speak in their native tongue as the Holy Ghost gave them utterance. I found myself last July in the Germany Camp Meeting, and could not fully understand their language. I prayed asking God to let me hear someone speak in my native tongue, Spanish. I had forgotten my request when two days later I heard a familiar sound. As I listened closely, I found it to be Spanish. A lady was uttering in Spanish a very familiar form of praise, one which I very often use myself: "Santo, Santo, Santo," and "Gracias, Padre amado" which translated means, "Holy, Holy, Holy," and "Thank you, my beloved Father." It was so clear and normal that I was sure the lady was of Spanish orgin; but through an interpreter

baptized with water; but ye shall be baptized with the Holy Ghost not many days hence" (Acts 1:5).

Throughout the ministry of the Lord Jesus Christ, He spoke often of the Holy Ghost. In fact, in His opening sermon He said, "The Spirit of the Lord is upon me, because he hath anointed me to preach . . ." (Luke 4:18). He taught that the salvation of all men depended on the work of the Holy Ghost.[3] This was a cardinal point in the teaching of Jesus Christ. He taught dependence upon the Spirit and not upon the flesh: "It is the spirit that quickeneth; the flesh profiteth nothing" (John 6:63). He taught that speaking against the Holy Ghost constitutes blasphemy: "The blasphemy against the Holy Ghost shall not be forgiven . . . whosoever speaketh against the Holy Ghost, it shall not be forgiven him . . ." (Matthew 12: 31, 32). He taught us to ask for the Holy Spirit, and by our asking we shall receive.[4] He commanded His disciples to wait for the Holy Ghost baptism,[5] and He urged upon them to take, to receive, or accept the Holy Ghost.[6] The Lord assured His disciples that the Holy Ghost would be present for emergencies; He would be their strengthener in conflicts and their advocate in time of trouble: "For the Holy Ghost shall teach you in the same hour what ye ought to say" (Luke 12:12).

During the closing hours of our Lord's life upon earth, His words were focused upon the ministry of the Holy Spirit, and they form the climax of all that He told His disciples; for it was through the Holy Spirit that they would be prepared for the tasks that were before them.

II. THE FIRST PENTECOST

THE DAY OF PENTECOST

The Day of Pentecost was fully come! In answer to the

---

3 John 3:5.
4 Luke 11:11-13.
5 Acts 1:4.
6 John 20:22.

I found that she had absolutely no knowledge of Spanish. This thought comforts me that while Christ is at the right hand of the Father interceding for me, the Holy Ghost is in my heart praising and glorifying God.[15]

RAPID GROWTH

During the first half of the twentieth century, Pentecost grew very rapidly. Churches sprang up everywhere. During the last decade, the Pentecostal revival has accelerated. The eyes of the world are focused upon the Pentecostals; and the humble group of people, who for many years had gone unnoticed, have been thrust into prominence because of the vitality and the virility of their religion in these decadent and destitute times. America is experiencing one of the strangest revolutions in the history of any nation. This is an unusual day of spiritual upheavel. The Spirit has fallen afresh upon the people of God. Until this decade, hardly was the speaking of other tongues mentioned in polite church circles; but now it is common to see such headlines as, "Churches Look Closely at Gift of Tongues,"[16] or some other similar title.

The Reverend Henry P. Van Dusen, the retired president of Union Theological Seminary in New York, says:

> The Pentecostal movement is nothing less than a revolution comparable in importance to the establishment of the original apostolic church and to the Protestant Reformation.[17]

It is having revolutionary effect upon entire countries. Sir Kenneth Grubb, writing in *Frontier*, tells of the fascinating development of Pentecostal churches in Brazil.

> The modern evangelical scene in Brazil has provided new features. Among these is the fascinating development of the Pentecostal Churches. There are Pentecostal congregations

---

[15] Personal correspondence with the writer, October 15, 1965.
[16] Dan L. Thrapp, "Churches Look Closely at 'Gift of Tongues'," *Los Angeles Times*, March 17, 1963, p. 6.
[17] Lee E. Dirks, "The Pentecostals: Speaking in Other Tongues," National Observer Newsbook, *Religion in Action* (Silver Springs: Newsbook, 1965), p. 169.

which bring together on Sunday over 5,000 people, and do it with astonishing regularity.[18]

The Church of England newspaper, speaking of the Pentecostals, says:

> The growth of this movement in many parts of the world in recent years has certainly been phenomenal. In such a comparatively small country as Finland, there are reported to be 40,000 Pentecostalists, while in Sweden they number approximately 100,000. From almost every part of the world come reports of new Pentecostal churches being established.[19]

A Catholic journal, *The Catholic Church and American Life*, July, 1959, posed the question, "Can the church hold New York's Puerto Ricans?" The growth of the Pentecostals among the Catholic-oriented Puerto Ricans has given the Catholic Church no little concern. This was the same concern that religious leaders had concerning Pentecost in the first century: "they doubted of them whereunto this would grow" (Acts 5:24).

Frank Farrell said:

> Ecumenical leaders have shown increasing interest in the Pentecostal movement, known as the fastest growing segment of Protestantism in the Western Hemisphere, where approximately one of every three Latin American Protestants is Pentecostal.[20]

PENTECOST IN THE HISTORIC CHURCHES

For many years the members of the historic church have quoted the statement of the apostles' creed: "I believe in the Holy Ghost." In most cases, this is not true experientially. They only give intellectual assent to the Holy Ghost. Dr. Van Dusen, in speaking of the historic church, labels the Holy

---

[18] "Millions Read About Revival of Speaking in Tongues," *Pentecost*, No. 54 (December 1960 to February 1961), p. 2, quoting Grubb.

[19] *Ibid.*

[20] Frank Farrell, "The Outburst of Tongues: The New Penetration," *Christianity Today*, VII (September 13, 1963), 3. Copyright 1963 by *Christianity Today*; used by permission.

Spirit as "the neglected 'step-child' of traditional Protestant theology."[21] However, the picture seems to be changing in some historic churches. "Nearly all of the major denominations have been affected by what is called the charismatic revival, Episcopalians and Lutherans preeminently so."[22]

> Speaking in tongues, widely publicized in 1960 when first reported among Episcopalians, has now quietly infiltrated every major Protestant denomination. Once the province largely of the unlettered and the unsophisticated, it now flourishes also among the debonair and the highly educated.[23]

"Speaking in tongues," observes *The Living Church*, an independent Episcopal weekly,

> . . . is no longer a phenomenon of some odd sect across the street. It is in our midst, and it is being practiced by clergy and laity who have stature and good reputation in the Church . . . Its widespread introduction would jar against our esthetic sense and some of our more strongly entrenched preconceptions. But we know that we are members of a Church which definitely needs jarring . . . if God has chosen this time to dynamite what Bishop Sterling of Montana has called "Episcopalian respectabilianism," we know of no more terrifyingly, effective explosive.[24]

The sociologists have long since classified Pentecostals among the lower class of society. Speaking with tongues has been classified by them "as a phenomenon which appears almost exclusively among the underprivileged groups in society."[25] One wonders what explanation the modern sociologists will give for this new classification of Pentecostals, since it is evident that the Spirit is being received by the affluent and poor, the high church and the low church, the intellectuals

---

[21] "The Challenge of the 'Sects'," *Pentecost*, No. 47 (March, 1959), p. 3, quoting Henry P. Van Dusen, *Christianity and Crisis.*

[22] Farrell, *loc. cit.*

[23] Dirks, *loc. cit.*

[24] "Speaking in Tongues," *Time*, LXXVI (August 15, 1960), p. 55, quoting *The Living Church* (July 17, 1960).

[25] John Thomas Nichol, "Pentecostalism" (unpublished Doctoral dissertation, Boston, Massachusetts, 1965), p. 9.

and the unlettered, the elite and the uncouth, constituting what Joel called "all flesh." In the outpouring of the Spirit, social classification is not considered, for the Holy Spirit is no respecter of persons. He does not require that a vessel be gold, silver, ceramic, ornate, nor attractive; His requirement is that the vessel be clean.

> . . . today Bible scholars, theologians, ministers, and laymen are scrutinizing the New Testament passages dealing with these occurrences. Not many months ago these same people showed relatively little interest in the subject despite a half-century of aggressive promotion on the part of the Pentecostal movement. For the movement was outside the historic, mainline denominations. Now it is within, and clergy and laity have been driven to a probing of the Scriptures and church history for answers to questions and explanations of the phenomena pressed hard upon them by fellow ministers and parishioners. And assessments are about as varied as the phenomena.[26]

Many ministers and laymen of the historic churches are aware of a need in the church which prepares the way for inquiry and quest of the power of God. Billy Graham stressed the need for the Holy Spirit at a meeting of the ministerium in Sacramento, California:

> In the main denominations, we have looked a bit askance at our brethren from the Pentecostal churches because of their emphasis on the doctrine of the Holy Spirit, but I believe the time has come to give the Holy Spirit His rightful place in our churches. We need to learn once again what it means to be baptized with the Holy Spirit. I know that we can rationalize, and immediately 10,000 theological questions arise, and we try to figure it all out; but I want to tell you that we need to accept—we need to get something. Give it any terminology you want, but we do not have the same dynamic power the early church had; they had the filling of the Holy Spirit.[27]

The Bishop of Montana, Chandler Sterling, told the Episcopal Diocese of Oregon that "they too often were a hiding place for

---

[26] Farrell, *loc. cit.*
[27] *The Full Gospel Business Men's Voice,* January, 1961.

theological bones—all dried out, with no nourishment in them." The Bishop also stated that he was "convinced another Pentecost is coming, and it's already started. If the people would just get 'the organization church' out of the spotlight."[28]

In a report to the American Lutheran Church District Conventions, President Frederick A. Schiotz said they were " 'receiving reports from many parts of the church concerning experiences in faith healing and "speaking in tongues." ' Dr. Schiotz also reported that a sub-committee of the commission had been appointed 'to study these reported "manifestations of the Holy Spirit's power." ' "[29]

Testimonies from the historic churches.

> One man wrote: ". . . the fire of the Holy Spirit is mighty disturbing. And I'm disturbed! As I have gone through this, Scripture really comes alive and the hymns of the church shout out at me, but so does the world, and believe me, I feel caught right between the two. It is one thing to be an administrator of an organization or even to be a pastor who can 'give some advice and talk to people about Christ,' but it is quite another thing when one really begins to find the Spirit at work as he seems to be in recent months."
>
> From a letter of a Lutheran Free Church pastor we quote: "In 1954 I experienced the presence of the Holy Spirit and speaking in tongues, with a definite enrichment of my own spiritual life, a deepening understanding of God's Word, and a new confidence to pray for others. While my testimony has been met with considerable unbelief, perhaps doubt is a better word, nevertheless, I am increasingly confident that the infilling, or baptism, or whichever term you use, of the Holy Spirit is a scriptural, personal experience which the Lord promises to every believer. This personal experience of the Holy Spirit does not detract, but greatly adds to our precious Luther heritage of Word and Sacrament."
>
> Another pastor writes: "I want to say that I . . . and

---

[28] "Bishop Jolts Arid Church," *Portland Oregonian,* April 12, 1961.
[29] Lewis Holm, "Speaking in Tongues," *Lutheran Standard,* II, (September 11, 1962), p. 3.

my wife plus a number in our church have entered into these experiences. It has been almost four years since the first time I experienced 'speaking in tongues' which brought me into a new awareness of Jesus and a new form of praise to God which has been so precious to me. The individual gifts of the Spirit in 1 Corinthians 12 and the ministry gifts in the last part of the chapter have been ministered through us as simple channels for which we only and always glorify Jesus! The experience of the baptism with the Holy Spirit is only a door—it leads one into a greater and closer walk with God in our service for him . . ."

One writer commented on the rapid growth of this phenomenon: "It may interest you to note that within a diameter of 25 miles there are three Lutheran pastors and three Methodist pastors besides the many, many others in the denominational churches far and wide who minister through the gifts of the Spirit including the 'speaking in tongues.' It is quite evident in our day that God is trying to reveal to us that 'Pentecost' is not a denomination—it is an experience."[30]

Some of the newspapers in the Minneapolis-St. Paul area ran headline accounts of the manifestation of the Spirit in the Lutheran and other denominational churches of that area. The newspapers pointed up that attendances had increased, physical healings had been documented, conversions had mounted, and that the inevitable charismata had been reported.[31] Some put forth an effort to discredit this spiritual renewal among whom were psychiatrists and denominational leaders.

Mr. Vernon M. Blikstad reports concerning these attempts to discredit the movement:

But among Lutherans and other churches in the Great Plain states, the upper Midwest, this was like trying to persuade a new convert that Jesus Christ was a mythical figure. They have seen; they believed like the first apostles. Many Lutherans came out of their traditional isolation and with unembarrassed excitement began to share with other Protestants the great things God is doing.[32]

---

30 Ibid., pp. 3, 4.
31 Vernon M. Blikstad, "Spiritual Renaissance," Christian Life, XXVI (May, 1964), p. 31.
32 Ibid.

There are 350 Lutheran churches within a ten-mile radius of Minneapolis. This area has often been called the garden spot of evangelical Christianity, but something new has happened to these people, and this area has now become the point of dissemination of the good news of the manifestation of the Holy Spirit in this day.[33]

> Actually, the gifts of the Spirit have been exercised on the Lutheran-oriented campus of the Bethany Fellowship Missionary Training Center since 1956. Its consecrated student body of over 100, a faculty and staff of 25 led by Rev. T. A. Hegre, Rev. Harold J. Brokke, Evangelist Leonard Ravenhill, and Rev. Jack Winters have fanned out into the area as well as across the U.S. and the world with the message of the Holy Spirit's ministry. Simultaneously with this, other Lutheran groups began to experience a moving of the Holy Spirit.[34]

> Hungry Lutherans, belonging to large congregations (one over 10,000 members) are finding fellowship they have never known before. The moving of the Holy Spirit has alone qualmed their fears of communism. Neo-orthodoxy, and liberal theological trends have gone down the drain as new faith has swept into their Lutheran churches. This fellowship is upsetting the trend towards a non-evangelical church service.

> Even if you do not believe in "speaking in tongues" you must admit the charismatic revival has stirred a new hunger for reality in religion. We can have new confidence that if men choose to quench the Spirit and mutilate the gospel in some areas, God will raise up His witness to be carried out in other places by other men.[35]

An ordained minister made the following observation:

> "Whatever the old-new phenomenon of worshipping the Lord in other languages means, it is amazing that it should break out among staid Episcopalians, stolid Lutherans and conservative Presbyterians."[36]

Objections from the Historic Churches. While we have

---

33 *Ibid.*
34 *Ibid.*
35 *Ibid.*, p. 33.
36 *Ibid.*

given testimonies pointing out the acceptance of this experience, we are also aware of the objections raised by some Christian onlookers who have not received this experience.

Pentecostalists do not deny the fact that there have been spiritual excesses and fleshly extravagances among those who profess the operation of the spiritual gifts. By the same token, there are many who profess other religious experiences who do not measure up to the requirements. This does not, however, negate the experience. While some may err, countless thousands bear witness to the true testimony.

Dr. Schiotz, in giving appraisal of 1 Corinthians 12:14, said:

> "The weight of the entire three chapters (1 Corinthians 12-14) is to downgrade the importance of 'speaking with tongues'."[37]

It is true that the Apostle Paul is dealing with the negative aspect of speaking in tongues in 1 Corinthians 14. However, it should be pointed out that not one time did he deprecate the gift of tongues, but simply the misuse of the gift. He had no quarrel with the gift of tongues, but with the abuse. The abuse, or imperfections, in the exercise of the gift can be attributed to the fallibility of man and not to imperfection of the gift.

Although the Apostle Paul dealt with the negative aspect of tongues, he did not deemphasize, nor did he downgrade, the gift. Instead, he took advantage of this occasion to defend its place in the church and the life of the believer. Interspersed among the corrective and regulatory statements are words of encouragement for the right use of tongues. It should be noted that no less than eleven times he defended the purpose and place of tongues in the church and the life of the believer.[38] Even a cursory glance at these scriptures reveals that the apostle favored the gift and was urging the Corinthians not to quench the gift because of the misuse of tongues.

---

[37] Holm, *loc. cit.*, p. 5.
[38] See 1 Cor. 14:2, 4, 5, 14, 15, 17, 18, 21, 22, 27, 39.

Some who would disparage or play down speaking in tongues have made the observation that in Paul's taxonomy of the gifts, speaking with tongues is listed last. By the same token, love would be the least gift according to the listing in 1 Corinthians 13:13, "And now abideth faith, hope, charity." The position of charity in these scriptures has nothing to do with Paul's appraisal of its importance. The greatness of a gift is determined by its edification to the church and individual and not by its location in a passage of Scripture.

Studies by the Historic Churches. Several denominations among the historic churches have appointed commissions to study tongues and their operation in today's church. A special commission on tongues reported in 1960 to the Episcopal Bishop of Chicago. The following are five recommendations which were made at the conclusion of this study:

"We recommend that provision be made:

(a) that the exercise of 'spiritual speaking' shall in no way intrude itself into the regular worship and work of the church so as to disturb the order and peace thereof;

(b) that those who engage in this activity avoid occasion for giving offense to the church either by exalting themselves or by suggesting that others seek this gift as a mark of spiritual superiority;

(c) that the exercise of this gift be guarded with vigilance so as to protect both the faithful and the weak from the dangers of irrationality and emotional excess;

(d) that the persons who experience this gift consult regularly with their pastors;

(e) that groups of people who exercise this gift under the auspices of any minister of the church shall, through such minister, report regularly to the bishop of their activities."[39]

Very briefly, let us consider the recommendations of this commission. At the best, this first statement suggests an attitude of tolerance so long as speaking with tongues does not become a part of their regular worship. This statement suggests that speaking in tongues is an appendage and not a vital

---

[39] *Ibid.*, p. 15.

part of the church worship. This attitude has resulted in a dual operation within the church community—one liturgical and the other apostolic or Pentecostal in nature. This system might operate smoothly for a limited period of time under some circumstances, but, by and large, division will arise which will necessitate a decision of rejection or acceptance of glossolalia. History will verify this.

This was evident at Van Nuys Episcopal Church when the Reverend Dennis Bennett received the Baptism of the Holy Ghost.[40] Division resulted which gave rise to the Blessed Trinity Society. The existence of this fellowship automatically forms an inner circle within the historic churches. The *Trinity* magazine, which is a publication of this society makes an appeal to those within the historic churches to receive the fullness of the Spirit.

Lee Dirks says:

> The new tongue speakers differ in several ways from the old-line Pentecostals. They have no interest in splitting off to form new churches, but try instead to make tongue speaking an added dimension of the Christian experience in mainstream churches.[41]

One should not be too critical of this intention on the part of those with their newfound experience, because it is possible that some of them will effect revival in their churches; however, the opposite will be the case in most circumstances.

The early disciples endeavored to remain with the worshipers of the synagogue, attending the synagogue on the Sabbath and a gathering of the charismatics on the first day of the week and daily in meetings from house to house. Their religious convictions and expressions were suppressed to the extent that an exodus from the synagogue worship, as far as participation was concerned, became a necessity. A case in point is the opposition that Paul received in Corinth, which caused him to leave the synagogue and "entered into a certain man's house,

---

[40] "Rector and a Rumpus," *Newsweek*, LXI (July 4, 1960), p. 77.
[41] Dirks, *op. cit.*, p. 172.

named Justus, one that worshipped God, whose house joined hard to the synagogue" (Acts 18:7).

When Peter and John had been persecuted because of their charismatic actions in the healing of the lame man, "being let go, they went to their *own* company," (Acts 4:23; italics ours). The fellowship of faith welded these early believers together, thus creating another group of worshipers of like precious faith. It should be pointed out that dual standards of worship cannot long exist in a church. One will triumph over the other, or one will succumb to the other.

The second recommendation, that no offense be given by exaltation of self, or an expression of spiritual superiority, would meet with full acceptance by old-line Pentecostalists. In 1 Corinthians 13, the apostle emphasizes the place of love in the operation of the gifts. This chapter does not suggest that love is to supplant the gifts but to dominate the operation of the gifts. Tongues without love spell self-aggrandizement and spiritual superiority, but love itself guarantees the proper attitude toward gifts in this respect (1 Corinthians 13:1-5).

The third statement is reasonable. This is nothing more than what the apostle desired in 1 Corinthians 14. It is expected of all good shepherds that they should keep Biblical order in the operation of the gifts, and for that part, in all exercises of worship. This point would not be objectionable to old-line Pentecostals.

In the fourth and fifth statements, which are similar in nature, the attitude of the pastor or bishop would determine how these restrictions would be received. If the purpose of this regulation is to smother or play down the operation of the gifts, the parishioners or ministers involved would soon look for a more amenable climate in which to express their newfound experience.

PENTECOST AND THE NEW OUTPOURING

This outpouring in the historic churches has many labels

such as "Spiritual Renaissance," "The New Penetration," "Spiritual Renewal," "Charismatic Renewal," "Neo-Pentecostalism," and others.

Contrary to the thinking of many, this is not a new revival. The twentieth-century outpouring did not begin in 1956 or 1960. For Pentecostals it is but an added surge of what they have enjoyed since the turn of the century. God forbid that any man or group of men would dare take the glory of revival which belongs to God alone, but it might be well for those who are now experiencing this wonderful gift—and we rejoice with them—to be made aware of the source of their Pentecostal heritage.

At the turn of the century, God visited many of the members of the historic churches, and they accepted the Holy Ghost baptism. Many of these Pentecostals, like John Wesley, had no desire to leave their formal complacent churches. They hoped that all of the members would be awakened to their need of revival. But the denominations, in their complacency, or in their rejection, forced the Pentecostals to create groups wherein there could be the free exercise of the Holy Spirit.

Donald Gee, of Great Britain, says:

> After all allowances have been made for the admitted fanaticism and extremes of those zealous early Pentecostals, it still has to be said that the responsibility for the creation of yet another group of denominations (the "Pentecostals") rested squarely on the shoulders of the older churches that rejected them, demanded the resignation of missionaries who testified to their new-found Blessing, and did not hesitate to publish the literature stating that the Pentecostal Movement was of satanic inspiration.[42]

For many of the historic churches, the beginning of their introduction to the charismatic renewal was the outpouring in Van Nuys in 1960. But how did the Reverend Dennis Bennett

---

[42] Donald Gee, "Don't Spill the Wine," *Pentecost*, No. 61 (September-November, 1962), p. 17.

come in contact with this experience?[43] Was it not that two
Episcopal members had been attending a prayer meeting in the
home of old-line Pentecostals and received the experience and
returned to their church with such renewed zeal and commit-
ment until he was attracted to the experience?

The Reverend Harald Bredesen, the pastor of the First Reformed Church of Mount Vernon, New York, and the chairman of the Board of Directors of the Blessed Trinity Society,
testifies that God filled him with the Holy Ghost at a Pentecostal camp meeting in Green Lane, Pennsylvania.[44]

It was through T. L. Osborn, an old-line Pentecostal, that the
Dutch Reformed Church in Holland was moved by a mighty
revival of Pentecost. Osborn addressed crowds up to 100,000
in attendance, the largest in Holland's history. Because of the
impact that the ministry of spiritual gifts made upon the
Dutch Reformed Church, an official pastoral letter, entitled
"The Church and the Pentecostal Groups," was circulated by
the synod of the Dutch Reformed Church stating:

> We cannot say that in our times there is less need of these
> gifts than in the beginning of the church. Are we opposed
> by less strong demon powers than in that time? Is hea-
> thenism of the present day less aggressive than that of the
> time of the apostles?[45]

This is but a sample of the heritage of this new penetration.

All of us should be reminded that for years Pentecost was
relegated to store buildings, tents, temporary churches across
the tracks and in the undesirable sections of the cities; but
through the weary nights and toilsome days, the pioneers of
the faith labored and travailed until once again God is knocking
at the door of Protestantism to restore its protest and firm up
its foundation. It is the belief of many that this is the last

---

[43] "Speaking in Tongues," Time, loc. cit.
[44] Harald Bredesen, "The Foolish Things," Trinity, II (Trinitytide, 1962), p. 3.
[45] Harald Bredesen, "Return to the Charismata," (tract) Mount Vernon,
N.Y., [n.d.].

move of God's Spirit before the coming of Christ, and in this move He is calling out a people for His name.

The happenings of this present day should humble the hearts of all who have been privileged to come in contact with this glorious experience. Whatever the difficulties, much patience and wisdom should be exercised lest the Spirit should be grieved with our proceedings.

ACTIONS AND REACTIONS

The historic churchmen have observed this spiritual renaissance with mixed emotions. Some, like Bishop Pike, the Episcopal bishop of California, advised his clergy against participation in services where speaking with tongues was promoted and gave them the following direction: " 'Exert no pressure in any form' to induce tongue speaking in any person. The practice, he declared, is 'heresy in embryo.' "[46]

Some have labeled it heresy; others, remembering the exodus of the Pentecostal members from the historic churches just after the turn of the century, have adopted a more tolerant attitude.

> The official position of the Episcopal Church within any given geographical area seems to depend largely on the viewpoint of the bishop. These positions range from outright acceptance, through casual tolerance to violent opposition. It depends upon the particular bishop's interpretation of what is *meant* as against what is specifically stated in the New Testament.[47]

The action and reaction of non-Pentecostals is given in a nutshell by Frank Farrell:

> James A. Pike, Episcopal Bishop of California, confronts the practice in the Bay Area to the accompaniment of front-page headlines in San Francisco newspapers; a journal relates that in the entire state of Montana, only one American Lutheran pastor has not received the experience of speaking

---

[46] Dirks, *op. cit.*, p. 174.
[47] D. D. Stone, "The Speaking in Tongues and the Episcopal Church," *Trinity Magazine*, I (Eastertide, 1962), p. 9.

with tongues; Dr. Francis E. Whiting, director of the Department of Evangelism and Spiritual Life of the Michigan Baptist Convention (American Baptist) speaks in support of present charismatic works of the Spirit at a Northern Baptist Seminary evangelism conference, declaring the choice is Pentecost or holocaust; a Minneapolis Evangelical Free Church splits over the issue; a United Presbyterian minister who wishes to ask youth to repent and receive the Holy Spirit at the First North American Reformed and Presbyterian Youth Assembly is stopped by a church officer before he reaches the Purdue University stage and is escorted out by a campus policeman; members of the Inter-Varsity Christian Fellowship at Yale speak in tongues, as does also a Roman Catholic student, a daily communicant at St. Thomas More chapel; and echoes of the penetration come from evangelical institutions and organizations such as Fuller Seminary, Wheaton College, Westmont College, Navigators, and Wycliffe Bible Translators.[48]

Unfortunately the strongest attacks against Pentecostalists have come from those closest to them—the fundamentalists, some holiness groups, or the evangelical Christians. It could be that the Pentecostalists are the greatest threat to the existence of these churches, since basically their doctrine is the same, with the exception of the Pentecostal experience; or it could be sectarian pride that produces the existing antagonism. Because a number of fundamentalists have realized a need for going one step further, and that is the step from Calvary to Pentecost, Pentecostalists have been charged with proselyting and troublemaking. The answer to this change is simply that which Peter gave as his defense: "Forasmuch then as God gave them the like gift as he did unto us, who believed on the Lord Jesus Christ; what was I, that I could withstand God?" (Acts 11:17). When God chooses to bring a soul into deeper fellowship and greater power with Him, the church cannot deny Him this privilege.

It cannot be denied that speaking in tongues is a divisive factor in many churches, but has this not been the case in all

---

[48] Farrell, *loc. cit.,* pp. 3, 4.

ages when men have made full commitments to the cause of Christ. Did Christ bring unity among the religionists in His day, or was He a divisive factor? He said, "Suppose ye that I am come to give peace on the earth? I tell you, Nay; but rather division" (Luke 12:51). The message of Christ divided homes when only a portion of the family would believe on Him. When people are expelled from or leave cold historic churches or fundamental churches, whichever the case may be, because they have received a spiritual renewal, it is unfair to label Pentecostal churches as sheep stealers. *They have not stolen one from Christ; they have only encouraged a deeper walk with Him.* Pentecostalists do not deny that confusion arises in many quarters because of the charismatic renewal, but this is no indication that the spiritual renewal is wrong. It is true that God is not the author of confusion, but of peace; but as Elijah troubled Israel, so does a move of God upset the equilibrium of an established order. The sleepy, satisfied saints are disturbed. The confusion is not caused by the spiritual renewal, but by those who refuse to obey the Spirit. Wherever the Early Church went, there was disturbance because "they went forth, and preached every where, the Lord working with them, and confirming the word with signs following" (Mark 16:20). As the early disciples could not avoid the unfortunate confusion and divisiveness brought about because of the rejection of their message, so is it impossible to avoid such in this day.

J. B. Phillips describes the modern church as being fat and short of breath through prosperity and muscle-bound with over-organization.[49] It is no wonder that this church rebels when it is called upon for spiritual exercise.

Errors of the New Penetration

One should use extreme caution in dealing with corrective

---

[49] J. B. Phillips, *The Young Church in Action* (New York: Macmillan Company, 1955), p. vii.

measures concerning things of the Spirit lest the wheat should be rooted up with the tares or lest Satan should take advantage for an occasion to blaspheme. In times of spiritual revolution, excesses and error are inevitable. It must be realized that some will see in this move of God an opportunity for self-advantage as did Simon the Sorcerer (Acts 8:18, 19). Therefore much discretion, wisdom, and Biblical instruction are necessary to protect the revival against error. Teaching and understanding are essential cornerstones for this revival if it is to continue untainted.

The term *Pentecostal* is so widely used until it now embraces some practices and doctrines which true Pentecostals would never condone or endorse. Donald Gee says:

> Quite reputable writers use it [the term *Pentecostal*] without any discrimination. We who are standing and struggling within the Movement for a clean, sane, and scriptural Pentecostal testimony often blush with shame at even nominal association with certain things laid at its door.[50]

Thus it behooves us to point up the errors as a warning and a defense lest some stumble unnecessarily. It is not with a feeling of spiritual supremacy nor with superiority that the writer points out these errors, but with a deep concern for the continuance for this revival along scriptural lines. The equipment for world evangelization has been rediscovered, and the opportunity must not be prostituted through error.

Some of the prominent errors of the present charismatic renewal are:

1. *Teaching that the Holy Spirit is received by faith alone.* To be sure, everything we receive from God must be received by faith.[51] But faith alone is not sufficient. The temple (body) must be prepared for the reception of the Spirit.[52]

---

[50] Donald Gee, "Critics and Criticism," *Pentecost*, No. 35 (March, 1956), p. 17.

[51] Hebrews 11:6; Mark 11:24; Matthew 21:22; James 1:6.

[52] 1 Corinthians 3:17; 6:19.

2. *The absence of "holiness."* Pentecost without holiness is fanaticism. Calvary is the fountainhead of true Pentecost. Where there is an attempt at the exercise of glossolalia separate and apart from holiness, nothing but carnality, disaster, and shipwreck can result. This vital emphasis is being grossly neglected among some of the new adherents of glossolalia.

> This new movement has leaped over the boundaries that formerly contained its predecessor, the holiness-tongues movement, and is taking on a character of its own. In this respect it resembles the English language, which has ceased to be confined to England and has spread over the earth. In each place where it takes root, it develops features that pain the purist or teacher of the Queen's English. So with this new movement. It now appears to be quite at home among church adherents who feel under no obligation to give serious heed to "holiness" restrictions, for example, on the use of tobacco and alcohol or going to the movies.[53]

It is well to make an observation at this point that this error does not prevail among all the neo-Pentecostalists. The Reverend Dennis Bennett makes the statement:

> Perhaps the most universal result is that people begin to recognize as sin things that did not appear as such to them previously. Through this new awareness of sin and through subsequent repentance and confession of it, their lives begin to change. By the power of the Sanctifier Himself, they become transformed and truly new creatures in Christ Jesus. Old habits, resentments, and fears drop away as if by magic, and the fruit of the Spirit begins to manifest itself through these children who have been filled with the Spirit of God.[54]

The bodies of Christians are not taverns but temples. We are admonished not to defile the temple.[55] The reception of the Spirit is on the premise of a clean heart and faith.[56] One must

---

[53] Raymond Frame, "Something Unusual," *His*, XXIV (December, 1963), p. 18. Reprinted by permission from *His*, student magazine of Inter-Varsity Christian Fellowship, © 1963.

[54] Jean Stone, "What Is Happening Today in the Episcopal Church?" *Christian Life*, XXIII (November, 1961), p. 40.

[55] 1 Corinthians 3:17.

[56] Acts 15:8.

repent[57] and obey.[58] There is no shortcut or bargain-counter experience available.

3. *Repeating syllables as a preparatory exercise.* This practice is totally unbiblical. To mouth certain syllables as "pump priming operation" is unnecessary. The Bible clearly teaches: ". . . the Spirit gave them utterance" (Acts 2:4). In some services, those desiring to be baptized with the Holy Ghost are told to make noises during the laying on of hands. But the Holy Spirit does not need this type of human intervention. The speaker in tongues is not passive; however, he does not form the words of his own accord. He speaks only as the Spirit gives the utterance.

4. *The inbreathing of the Spirit.* The scriptures used to substantiate this so-called method of receiving the Baptism of the Holy Ghost are ". . . open thy mouth wide, and I will fill it" (Psalm 81:10) and a translation of John 20:22, "Jesus inbreathed and said to them, receive ye the Holy Ghost." These scriptures are interpreted to mean that it is possible to breathe God's Holy Spirit into one's being to the extent that the body becomes full of the Spirit, thus resulting in speaking with other tongues. It takes but a passing glance at these scriptures for one to determine readily that they are not couched in this context. They do not mean that one, by breathing, can inhale the Holy Spirit of God. The inhaling or exhaling of one's physical breath has nothing to do with the reception of the Holy Spirit.

5. *The operation of the Spirit at will.* There is a tendency among the neo-Pentecostalists to use the gifts of the Spirit instead of yielding themselves to be used by the Spirit to minister through the gifts. One person, in relating his experience, said:

> ". . . the 'gift of tongues' is mine. I can speak in tongues
> at any time. I am in control of the gift and its steward

---

[57] Acts 2:38.
[58] Acts 5:32.

so to speak. . . . It is a tongue which is mine just like
my command of the English language."[59]

Kelsey says that "glossolalia is the product of 'no neurosis,
no psychosis, no seizure and no hypnosis. A person can turn
speaking in tongues on and off like a faucet.' "[60]

The Spirit does not operate at the behest of the individual,
but as He (the Holy Spirit) wills. Tongues are a purposeful
gift and are not given to be manipulated according to the fancies
of men, nor to satisfy the curiosity of men. The source of
tongues is the Holy Spirit. Tongues come not from men, but
from God. Man is merely the vehicle for the transmission of
the divine message or communication. In recent years there
has been a great flare for the spectacular in religious circles.
Therefore, there is a danger of pursuing spiritual gifts merely
for the glory of man or display. Any religious exercise that
exalts the individual over Christ grieves the Spirit. In the presence of Christ, all other personalities must decrease. Beware
of speaking in tongues for tongues sake and not for Christ's
sake!

A flag of warning must be raised at this point: Those who
speak to satisfy the curiosity of unbelievers or to subject the
language to the study of linguists, border on exhibitionism.
Speaking with tongues is a hallowed, holy, sacred exercise and
should be regarded with all reverence. Christ was not willing
to satisfy Satan by proving his Sonship through a miracle. He
could have turned the stones into bread, for it was He who
made the stones. He did not use His miracle-working power
to satisfy the whims and fancies of men. Herod, when he called
for Christ, thought that he would see some miracle, but His

---

[59] From *Tongue Speaking*, by Morton T. Kelsey. Copyright © 1964 by
Morton T. Kelsey. Reprinted by permission of Doubleday & Company, Inc.,
p. 133.

[60] McCandlish Phillips, "And There Appeared to Them Tongues of Fire,"
Saturday Evening Post (May 16, 1964), p. 39, quoting Kelsey.

Morton Kelsey has done a splendid work on "Tongue Speaking" and is to be
commended for his extensive research in this area; however, it should be noted
that he speaks as an observer and not as one who possesses this gift.

miracles were reserved for the needs and emergencies of humanity.

Any religious exercise which focuses the attention upon the individual and tends to exalt man bears investigation. The true Holy Spirit seeks to draw attention to Jesus, and anything which does not glorify, testify of Christ, or point people to Christ is not in harmony with the Scriptures. This was the purpose of the Holy Spirit's advent—to glorify Christ and to witness of Him.

Curious persons often ask those who make a claim of glossolalia to give them a sample of the speaking. No doubt, some honest-hearted people desiring to prove or defend their new-found experience have fallen into this trap and made a sincere effort to satisfy the request. In rare instances, the Spirit could come upon one allowing him to speak the language of the inquirer (should he be of foreign descent) in order to convince him of Christ. This is remotely possible. On the other hand, it is possible for persons who have spoken with tongues or who have heard others speak with tongues to memorize some of the phrases and repeat them under their own power. Such speaking is a pseudo-glossolalia, which is not prompted by the Holy Ghost and, therefore, has no meaning. Speaking with tongues has meaning only as the Spirit gives the utterance.

6. *The impartation of spiritual gifts.* The spiritual gifts, including the gift of tongues, are given to man severally as He (the Spirit) wills.[61] *They are not imparted by man.* God, according to His sovereign will, distributes the gifts to whomsoever He desires. The scripture, "For I long to see you, that I may impart unto you some spiritual gift, to the end that ye may be established" (Romans 1:11), is not dealing with the nine spiritual gifts. Gift, in this particular passage of Scripture, merely means "blessing."

When one understands that there is a Baptism in the Holy Ghost which is accompanied by speaking with other tongues

---

[61] 1 Corinthians 12:11.

as the initial evidence, which is the will of God for all to receive, and that there is also a "gift of tongues" given only as God wills and to whom He wills, then he will be able to understand what is meant by the scripture, "do all speak with tongues?" (1 Corinthians 12:30). The answer is definitely, No, all do not speak with tongues as a *gift* for the edification of the body of Christ. There is a distinct difference between the speaking with other tongues which evidences the Baptism with the Holy Ghost, and the *gift of tongues* which is one of the nine spiritual gifts. All believers may have the Baptism of the Holy Ghost and speak with tongues according to the promise of God. This is God's will for all.[62] On the other hand, all may not possess the gift of tongues as one of the nine spiritual gifts.

The act of laying on of hands is to invoke God's blessing and does not mean that the person exercising this right has some supernatural power in his hand which he imparts to others. No one can receive the Holy Ghost by laying on of hands until he is prepared. The criterion for reception does not rest in powerful hands, but in a purified, yielded heart.

At all times there must be a balance between the experience of glossolalia and the Word of God. No visions or revelations supersede God's Word, regardless of how ecstatic, zealous, or enthusiastic one may appear to be. The Word is the authority, for holy men of old spake as they were moved by the Holy Ghost. Therefore, the Holy Spirit's operation must be according to His pattern—the Word.

7. *Speaking with tongues, a psychological phenomenon.* The charge that glossolalia is a psychological phenomenon was made by Bishop Pike in his pastoral letter warning against the practice of glossolalia in the California diocese. He said, "Glossolalia is a psychological phenomenon which has been known over many, many centuries, quite apart from any parti-

---

[62] Acts 2:39.

cular religious orientation; in more extreme forms it is associated with schizophrenia.[63] To deny that glossolalia provides a psychological release would be to admit that one knows little about the nature of man. Tears of repentance, confession of sins, and other religious exercises provide a cathartic effect, because the whole man is affected by true religion. But to say that glossolalia is a psychological phenomenon and is not Christian in its origin is to confess an absence of a vital experience and a lack of knowledge in Biblical interpretation.

GLOSSOLALIA AND RESEARCH

Man has gained a great deal of skill in research methods and has startled the world with some of his findings. Psychologists and researchists have endeavored to apply the same methods of research to the glossolalic experience. These researchists begin with data accumulated; they set up assumptions, and endeavor to prove them by data analysis and by logic. Many phases of a true religion defy logic. The Bible does not try to prove there is a God, but it assumes as much, saying, "The fool hath said in his heart, There is no God" (Psalm 14:1). For no man, by searching, can find out God. This does not mean that we cannot know some things about God, that we cannot observe and come up with some conclusions; but we all must go back to the fact that man receives truth by faith. Faith must precede reason, while at the same time it is not without reason. Flesh and blood cannot reveal God, but the Father who is in Heaven reveals Himself.

Speaking with tongues is a spiritual phenomenon. Therefore, the Holy Ghost, a Biblical and spiritual experience, is not researchable by modern methods. To be sure, one can do historical and descriptive research, and even some experimental research, but one must receive (experience) the Spirit in order to discern His operation. For the Apostle Paul has said in 1 Corinthians 2:14, "the natural man receiveth not the things

---

[63] Phillips, *loc. cit.,* p. 39, citing Bishop Pike.

of the Spirit of God: for they are foolishness unto him: neither can he know them, because they are spiritually discerned."

Until recent years, Pentecostals were considered by most people to be a group of neurotic, abnormal, religious zealots to be pitied or looked upon with tolerance so long as they did not interfere with the status quo or upset the equilibrium of the religious community. Possibly the passiveness of professional researchers could be attributed to the general attitude of the lack of importance of the subject, because value judgments enter in to the material or subject to be researched.

In recent months, research in this area has come to the fore. Presently there is a special psychological and linguistic study being conducted at the Lutheran Medical Center under a small federal grant. The purpose of this study will be to determine possible differences in personalities between those who practice glossolalia and those who do not who are members of the same congregations. There is also a search to determine possible similarities of speaking with tongues with any of the known languages of the world.

Another recent study is that done by Dr. Stanley C. Plog, a psychologist at the University of California, who questioned more than 350 Pentecostalists in forty separate denominations. His deduction was that he found the movement as a whole to be "a reaction to mass society, a reaffirmation of the individual and his importance."[64]

It might be of interest to Bishop Pike to learn that Dr. Plog says that he has yet to find a schizophrenic tongue speaker.

There are other significant research studies now underway which further point up the fact that glossolalia is receiving a hearing in these last days.

When the last research has been done and man can hypothesize no further, it will be said, The half hath not been told, for only "the Spirit searcheth the deep things of God."[65]

---

[64] Phillips, loc. cit., p. 32.
[65] 1 Corinthians 2:10-12.

V. CONCLUSION

As we draw near to the termination of this age, there seems to be an intensification of the work of the Holy Spirit. It must be that God is calling out a people for His name to prepare them for His soon return.

> Be patient therefore, brethren, unto the coming of the Lord. Behold, the husbandman waiteth for the precious fruit of the earth, and hath long patience for it, until he receive the early and latter rain (James 5:7).

While there is grave apostasy on one hand, there is a hungering for the Spirit in the hearts of believers on the other hand. This hunger is being met by an outpouring of God's Spirit. The Holy Spirit has leaped out of its humble Pentecostal setting, over denominational barriers, and is overriding plan and program, ritual and ceremony, to satisfy longing hearts.

Joel's prophecy—"I will pour out my spirit upon all flesh"— is being fulfilled before our eyes. This wonderful power which was given to assist the Church in facing the challenge to witness to the uttermost part of the earth (Acts 1:8) must not be limited to first-century Christians. The outpouring at Pentecost was not a mere memorial for the Church to keep in her memory and to haunt the believers in their powerlessness. It was the beginning of an outpouring which has continued through the ages and is still available today. Christ commissioned the Church to make disciples of all nations, and He has sent the Spirit to accompany believers in the task of carrying out His great commission. For this reason, the Baptism of the Holy Ghost cannot be considered as an optional or inconsequential experience.

In the shadow of the return of Christ, believers throughout all Christendom should arise and appropriate the power which is provided through the Baptism of the Holy Spirit.

Glossolalia:
Its Value to the Church

James A. Cross

James A. Cross is the State Overseer of the Church of God in Florida. He served eight years in the two highest positions in his church: Assistant General Overseer and General Overseer. He is a member of the Executive Council. He served as Chairman of the Pentecostal Fellowship of North America and as a member of the Advisory Board of the World Pentecostal Fellowship. His duties as a leader in his church and among other evangelicals have taken him into fifty-five countries around the world. He is a graduate of Lee College and has done additional work at Temple University and the University of Chattanooga. For several years he has contributed sermons and articles to the Church of God Evangel, and he presently writes a regular feature for the Evangel, entitled "Answers From the Word." He has written two books, The Glorious Gospel and Healing in the Church.

James A. Cross

Glossolalia:
Its Value to the Church

I. ESTABLISHING THE PREMISE

Caesarea Philippi was the setting chosen by Jesus, our Lord, to make the proclamation that would change the world: "upon this rock I will build my church; and the gates of hell shall not prevail against it."[1]

The disciples were electrified by the pronouncement. As Jesus continued speaking, His words jolted them into a realization that this process of building a church involved them. Grave and serious responsibilities would devolve upon their shoulders. They consoled themselves in the knowledge that no matter how heavy their accountabilities, the One to whom they were answerable would be with them to aid, guide, and strengthen them.

Their solace was changed to dismay as they continued listening to the Master's teachings. They were chilled with apprehension when Jesus revealed to them His approaching sufferings and death on Calvary. It was unthinkable that the Christ should be killed and that they would be left alone without Him. It was unreasonable for the founder of the Church to be taken away, leaving them to struggle with the problems

[1] Matthew 16:18.

181

of an infant church in a hostile world. The Lord warned Peter and the other disciples, however, that He would be leaving them. He told them that He must be crucified, buried, and raised. "It is expedient for you that I go away,"[2] Jesus later explained.

If Jesus left them, in what condition would this leave the infant church and their leaders? To whom could they go for guidance? Who would teach them doctrine? Who would offer them comfort in their hours of distress?

THE PROMISE

Anticipating their distress and anxiety, Jesus said, "And I will pray the Father, and he shall give you another Comforter, that he may abide with you for ever" (John 14:16). "But the Comforter, which is the Holy Ghost, whom the Father will send in my name, he shall teach you all things, and bring all things to your remembrance, whatsoever I have said unto you" (John 14:26). "Howbeit, when he, the Spirit of truth is come, he will guide you into all truth" (John 16:13).

In these words Jesus clearly sets forth the value of the Holy Ghost to the Church. This was true not only for the Early Church, but also for succeeding ages to come: *that he may abide with you forever*—[3] giving comfort, direction, teaching, reproving the world of sin, and glorifying God the Father.

The sorrow that filled the hearts of the disciples was turned to gladness at His resurrection. After showing Himself alive by many infallible proofs, the time for His return to the Father and heaven drew near. He led His followers out to Bethany and reminded them of the promised Comforter. They were commanded to tarry in Jerusalem and to "wait for the promise of the Father" (Acts 1:4). "Behold, I send the promise of my Father upon you: but tarry ye in the city of Jerusalem, until ye be endued with power from on high" (Luke 24:49);

---

[2] John 16:7.
[3] John 14:16.

"ye shall be baptized with the Holy Ghost not many days hence" (Acts 1:5). "These signs shall follow them that believe . . . they shall speak with new tongues . . ." (Mark 16:17).

THE INITIAL OUTPOURING

The Biblical account of the outpouring of the Holy Ghost is recorded in Acts 2:1-4:

> And when the day of Pentecost was fully come, they were all with one accord in one place. And suddenly there came a sound from heaven as of a rushing mighty wind, and it filled all the house where they were sitting. And there appeared unto them cloven tongues like as of fire, and it sat upon each of them. And they were all filled with the Holy Ghost, and began to speak with other tongues, as the Spirit gave them utterance.

It is quite evident that this event marks the opening of a new era. From henceforth many would have identical experiences in all ages. This is evident in Joel's prophecy quoted by Peter, "I will pour out of my spirit upon *all* flesh" (Acts 2:17, 18), and again in Acts 2:39, "For the promise is unto you, and to your children, and to all that are afar off, even as many as the Lord our God shall call."

John M. Versteeg, in his book *Perpetuating Pentecost,* made the following statement: "The one thing we dislike to concede is that glossolalia may have been a part of Pentecost."[4] This statement was spoken against glossolalia rather than in support of the fact. This does not make it any less valid. The irrefutable evidence is that speaking in tongues is inseparably connected with the baptism or filling with the Holy Ghost. Acts 2:4, Acts 10:44-47, Acts 19:1-6—all substantiate this fact. The account in Acts 8:14-19 implies that the Samaritans spoke with tongues when they received the Holy Ghost: "When Simon *saw* that . . . the Holy Ghost was given." Adam Clarke, in his commentary on this scripture said, "It was the *miraculous*

---

[4] John M. Versteeg, *Perpetuating Pentecost* (Chicago: Willet, Clark, & Colby, 1930), p. 17.

gifts of the Spirit which were thus communicated: the speaking with different tongues."[5]

When Peter preached on the Day of Pentecost, his language was precisely chosen. When quoting Joel, Peter did not indicate that this initial outpouring would be the complete fulfillment as such, but "this is that" which was promised by Joel and it would occur over and over again as God poured out the Holy Ghost on all flesh. "Repent, and be baptized . . . and ye shall receive the gift of the Holy Ghost," he exhorted (Acts 2:38).

In verse 33 Peter said, ". . . and having received of the Father, the promise of the Holy Ghost, he hath shed forth this, which ye now *see* and *hear*." The multitude *saw* the powerful effects of the Holy Ghost in manifestations and *heard* the disciples speak in other tongues. This was the promise of the Father. This was the enduement and the endowment. The promise "ye shall be baptized with the Holy Ghost," in chapter 1, is now the outpouring in chapter 2, evidenced by the Spirit's utterance.

THE WITNESS OF THE SPIRIT

Jesus said of the Holy Ghost, "Howbeit when he, the Spirit of truth, is come, he will guide you into all truth: for he shall not speak of himself; but whatsoever he shall hear, that shall he speak" (John 16:13); and "he shall testify of me" (John 15:26). "And we are his witnesses of these things; and so is also the Holy Ghost" (Acts 5:32). ". . . the Holy Ghost witnesseth in every city, saying . . ." (Acts 20:23). It would be impossible to speak, to testify, or to witness without speaking. In 1 Timothy 4:1 Paul declares: "Now the Spirit speaketh expressly." "As they ministered to the Lord and fasted, the Holy Ghost said . . ." (Acts 13:2). Seven times in the book of Revelation (2:7, 2:11, 2:17, 2:29, 3:6, 3:13, 3:22)

---

[5] Adam Clarke, *Commentary on the Holy Bible* (Nashville: Abingdon-Cokesbury Press), V, p. 74.

it is recorded, "He that hath an ear, let him hear what the Spirit saith unto the churches." From these Biblical statements we must concede that the Holy Ghost does speak, and that the channel through which He speaks is human lips that have been yielded to God. He, the Spirit, dwells in us, and as the Spirit gives utterance, speech in other tongues is heard; thus, the Spirit speaks.

THE DISPENSATION OF THE HOLY GHOST

This is the dispensation of the Holy Ghost. In this dispensation the Spirit speaks to man. When God dealt directly with man, He spoke to man. When Christ was on earth, He spoke with man. "God, who at sundry times and in divers manners spake in time past unto the fathers by the prophets, Hath in these last days spoken unto us by his Son, whom he hath appointed heir of all things, by whom also he made the worlds" (Hebrews 1:1, 2). In like manner the Holy Ghost speaks in this age to man from His temple: "Know ye not that ye are the temple of God, and that the Spirit of God dwelleth in you?" (1 Corinthians 3:16). "For with stammering lips and another tongue will he speak to this people" (Isaiah 28:11).

The overwhelming evidence from these scriptures cited is sufficient ground for pointing out that glossolalia is connected in thought and in action with the person and the work of the Holy Ghost.

The Comforter. Jesus spoke of "another Comforter" in John 14:16. *Another* means "of the same kind or effect." While Jesus was here in this world, He spoke to men, guided them, directed them, and taught them. He also comforted them and revealed things to come. While on earth, Jesus convicted men of sin, and of righteousness, and of judgment. Since Christ promised another Comforter, it is reasonable to suppose that this Comforter, who was coming in the place of Jesus, would perform the same type of work that Christ performed while here in this world. Of the Holy Ghost, Christ said, "I tell you the truth; It is expedient for you that I go away: for if I go not away, the Comforter will not come unto you; but if I depart, I will send him unto you. And when he is come, he will reprove the world of sin, and of righteousness, and of judgment" (John 16:7, 8); "when he, the Spirit of truth, is come, he will guide you into all truth: for he shall not speak of himself; but whatsoever he shall hear, *that shall he speak:* and he will shew you things to come. He shall glorify me: for he shall receive of mine, and shall shew it unto you" (John 16:13, 14; italics ours). "But the *Comforter, which is the Holy Ghost,* whom the Father will send in my name, he shall teach you all things, and bring all things to your remembrance, whatsoever I have said unto you" (John 14:26; italics ours).

The Holy Ghost is the promised Comforter; and His work, direction, help, and activities are inseparably connected with speaking—that is, with glossolalia. It is upon this predication that this study, "Glossolalia: Its Value to the Church," is herein set forth.

II. VALUE TO THE FIRST-CENTURY CHURCH

ATTRACTING AND CONVERTING

The value of the Holy Ghost and speaking in tongues was demonstrated in this infant church. The believers were few in number, unnoticed, and even disdained; but this new experience attracted attention and gave opportunity to witness to the resurrection of Jesus Christ. One hundred and twenty, speaking in tongues as the Spirit gave utterance, stirred Jerusalem. At least fifteen different languages and dialects were fluently spoken by people not learned in these languages. An amazed multitude gathered. Peter used the occasion to preach a sermon. The Holy Ghost convicted hearts of sin, as our Lord had promised: "when he is come he will reprove the world of sin, and of righteousness, and of judgment" (John 16:8). "Now when they heard this, they were pricked in their heart, and said unto Peter and to the rest of the apostles, Men and brethren, what shall we do?" (Acts 2:37). Explicit instruction was given, and, as a result, three thousand souls were saved and added to the church. Here is clear evidence of the value of the Holy Ghost in the work of evangelism.

Just a short time later, following the healing of the lame man at the Temple gate the Holy Ghost again aided this work of evangelism. Acts 4:4 records that five thousand were saved. The work continued to grow until they no longer numbered converts, but simply said, "And believers were the more added to the Lord, multitudes both of men and women" (Acts 5:14).

The Holy Spirit did not confine His activity to attracting multitudes and converting great numbers. He also proved his value in personal soulwinning. Philip was in a great revival when the Lord pointed out a lone individual who needed salvation. Leaving the great revival, Philip, following directions, went toward Gaza. There he found an Ethiopian sitting in a chariot reading from Isaiah's prophecy. "Then the Spirit said unto Philip, Go near, and join thyself to this chariot" (Acts 8:28). The result of Holy Spirit guidance was the salvation of the eunuch.

The growth and spread of the Church was causing the devil great concern. Here was a Church: small, its ministers unlearned and unrenowned, with very little finances, having no printing presses, and without magnificent church buildings, yet literally turning the world upside down. In an effort to halt the victorious march of the Church, the devil launched persecution against it. The saints were scattered. Instead of putting out the fire, persecution fanned these live coals until they burst forth in flaming fagots. Instead of deterring the ministers, persecution made ministers out of the members. "Therefore they that were scattered abroad went everywhere preaching the word" (Acts 8:4).

INSTRUCTING AND DEFENDING

Christ warned His followers of times when they would be

brought before religious leaders, magistrates, and powers. On such occasions, He assured them, there was no need for anxiety or apprehension about an adequate defense, "For the Holy Ghost shall teach you in that same hour what ye ought to say" (Luke 12:12).

When Stephen was brought before the council and false testimony was given against him, it is recorded that the council, "saw his face as it had been the face of an angel" (Acts 6:15). He was full of the Holy Ghost as he gave his defense, and it could be said on this occasion, as it was when he was in the synagogue, "they were not able to resist the wisdom and the spirit by which he spake" (Acts 6:10).

Annas the high priest, Caiaphas, John, Alexander, kindred of the high priest, rulers, elders, and scribes—an imposing array of religious dignitaries—had summoned Peter to answer about his religious activities. It was a delicate situation that demanded extreme caution. Provision for this occasion had been made: "Then Peter, filled with the Holy Ghost, said . . ." (Acts 4:8). The defense rested. The Sanhedrin "marvelled" (v. 13). The decision was given. God was glorified, and His followers were again "filled with the Holy Ghost and spoke the word of God with boldness" (v. 31).

CALLING AND QUALIFYING

The Early Church recognized the value of having proper and qualified missionaries and workers to fulfill the great commission. The question was, Who were proper workers, and who was to designate the criteria for determining qualifications? The problem of selection and qualifications was solved by the Holy Ghost: "As they ministered to the Lord, and fasted, the Holy Ghost said, Separate me Barnabas and Saul for the work whereunto I have called them. And when they had fasted and prayed, and laid their hands on them, they sent them away. So they, being sent forth by the Holy Ghost, departed . . ." (Acts 13:2-4). Any missions board could have objected and demurred over such a choice, but under these circumstances they could not afford to do so: the Holy Ghost had spoken. "The Holy Ghost said . . ." and that was satisfactory to the Church. Subsequent records of the mighty work wrought by these Spirit-filled men should banish any doubt of the wisdom and value of deferring to the Holy Ghost in His selection and direction of the missionary workers of the Early Church.

DIRECTING AND EXTENDING

Not only was the value of the Holy Ghost proved in the selection of ministers, but also in His direction as to the specific place where these chosen men should exercise their ministry.

Peter was directed of the Holy Ghost to preach in Caesarea to the Gentiles. Peter would never have done this of his own volition. The "Spirit said unto him . . . go with them doubting nothing . . ." (Acts 10:19, 20). Note again the scripture, "The Spirit said. . . ." The results of obeying the direction of the Spirit are satisfying and dramatic: Peter preached, and the Holy Ghost fell on the Gentiles just as He had on the Jews. A new chapter was written in the history of the Church. A new door was opened for the preaching of the gospel. A new people was included in the mighty outpouring of the Holy Ghost. The Church realized anew every day the value of the Holy Ghost to this important task of preaching the gospel to every people and nation.

INTERVENING AND RESTRAINING

Paul had outlined his missionary itinerary. As he made his determined rounds, the Scripture records: "so were the churches established in the faith, and increased in number daily" (Acts 16:5). Surely God had directed when the missionary tour was set up. But changes in plans and schedules came suddenly and abruptly: They were "forbidden of the

Holy Ghost to preach the word in Asia" (Acts 16:6). Paul then decided to go into Bithynia.

G. A. McLaughlin, in his *Commentary on the Acts of the Apostles,* said,

> They now attempted to go into Bithynia, another country of Asia Minor, but were forbidden by the Holy Ghost. It does not tell how they were forbidden. It might have been by some special providence or by direct communication. Then they went into Mysia and tried to go into Bithynia and the Spirit suffered them not. No doubt they were perplexed, as one sometimes is, at the strange leading of the Spirit; but it was all for the divine glory in having the gospel carried into Europe as they were now in Asia. God never makes mistakes. He leads just right, although we cannot see it at the time. But everything will be cleared and made plain in due time. Paul was made to understand the mind of the Spirit and the only real point of rational interest—he obeyed. And to everyone cherishing this same obedient spirit, the mind of God will in some assured way be made known. Why their proposed movements were thus divinely hedged around on every side save the sea, is clearly intimated in the summon that so soon followed to cross the sea and enter into Europe. So plainly it appeared that the gospel's first marked entrance into Europe was definitely directed by the Lord.
> Paul himself could hardly have known how significant his advent into Europe was. He had thus far been led by the Spirit. He knew not why, or how, but now he is directly informed of his mission and duty. God does not keep his workmen always in the dark. He lets them know at the right time his purposes. The churches at Thessalonica and Galatia were the result of his crossing over to Europe and the church universal has the two epistles to the Corinthians, the two to the Thessalonians and that to the Galatians as the result.[6]

While Paul was in Troas, the Holy Ghost plainly revealed to him that God wanted a church in Macedonia. Paul, being led of the Spirit, made his way to Philippi, Macedonia, to preach. Following the Spirit's direction resulted in the salvation of souls and the establishment of a new church.

---

[6] G. A. McLaughlin, *Commentary on the Acts of the Apostles* (Chicago: Christian Witness Co., 1915), pp. 177, 178.

PRESERVING AND UNITING

Perhaps it was inevitable for differences to arise among the ministers and leaders over policies and doctrine of the Early Church. Peter was charged with a breach of tradition for going to Cornelius' home to preach the gospel. They contended that Peter ate and associated with uncircumcised Gentiles. In that tense hour the Holy Spirit gave the exact words to Peter. After his defense it is recorded, "When they heard these things, they held their peace, and glorified God, saying, Then hath God also to the Gentiles granted repentance unto life" (Acts 11:18). Thus the Holy Ghost guided them through stormy waters into safe passage.

It seemed as if the Early Church would be rent in twain over differences in doctrine. Some preached grace plus law. Others preached grace apart from the law. Sides were chosen and battle lines formed. A council was called at Jerusalem to discuss the issue. The debate was intense, and the future of the church wavered in the balances. In this hour of supreme trial for the church, the Holy Spirit breathed upon the assemblage, cooling feverish anxieties and comforting distressed souls. "It seemed good to the Holy Ghost, and to us . . ." (Acts 15:28) was the decision. A crisis was averted and the unity of the saints preserved and "they rejoiced for the consolation" (v. 31). The blessedness and value of the unifying power of the Holy Ghost was demonstrated to the Early Church. This lesson was not forgotten; and through the years, even down to this modern day, the blessed influence of the Holy Ghost has safeguarded and led the Church.

COMFORTING AND ESTABLISHING

The Early Church was not without persecution. In the midst of harrassment, persecutions, beatings, imprisonments, and dispersions, this young church bravely hoisted high her banners. When it seemed impossible to advance, and weariness was ready to overcome them, it is refreshing to read, "Then had the churches rest throughout all Judaea and Galilee and Samaria, and were edified; and walking in the fear of the Lord, and in the comfort of the Holy Ghost, were multiplied" (Acts 9:31). Oh, the blessedness of such an experience: Walking in the comfort of the Holy Ghost and enjoying growth at the same time! Let the devil rage and do his utmost to disturb; the Comforter has come and is performing His office work.

III. VALUE TO THE TWENTIETH-CENTURY CHURCH

Many readers of the book of Acts have rejoiced at the acts of the Holy Ghost in apostolic days and sighed for bygone days. Others not only have been exhilarated by reading these things, but through the years also have personally experienced and boldly proclaimed that the experience of Pentecost is for men in all ages. They have laid hold on the promise of God that "the promise is unto . . . as many as the Lord our God shall call" (Acts 2:39), and have experienced a mighty baptism of the Holy Ghost and have spoken in tongues "as the Spirit gave them utterance" (Acts 2:4).

Among those in recent times who believed that the promise of the Holy Ghost was to every believer was a lay member belonging to the Christian Union, the church which later changed its name to the Church of God. This member, William F. Bryant, was a leading man of the community and conducted Sunday school and regular prayer meetings. During the time of these meetings in 1896, the Holy Ghost began to fall on the earnest seekers who tarried before God. "One after another fell under the power of God, and soon quite a number were speaking in other tongues as the Spirit gave them utterance."[7]

---

[7] L. Howard Juillerat, "Brief History of the Church of God," Book of Minutes (Cleveland, Tennessee: Church of God Publishing House, 1922), p. 11.

L. Howard Juillerat, an early preacher in the Church of God, wrote of this outpouring in 1918 in writings published in 1922. In recording the meetings conducted by William F. Bryant, Juillerat said, "Men, women and children received the Holy Ghost and spoke in other tongues under the power of the mighty Spirit of God."[8]

Charles W. Conn interviewed persons who were present at these meetings in 1896 and who shared in or witnessed these phenomena. In recording this occurrence in the history of the Church of God, *Like a Mighty Army,* he wrote, "Soon others began to have similar ecstatic experiences and, regardless of the place, time, or circumstances contingent to the experience, one manifestation was uniform in all; they spoke in tongues, or languages, unknown to those who listened in wonder and hope."[9] "So parallel were the Biblical accounts to the experience of these people that recognition of what had happened became crystal clear. A new outpouring of the Holy Ghost had occurred upon the earth."[10]

God is no respector of place or people when He bestows His blessings. It is doubtful that many of those humble people knew or would ever hear of Los Angeles and the events that occurred on Azusa Street ten years later. They only knew that on them also was poured out the gift of the Holy Ghost. For they heard them speak with tongues and magnify God.

Donald Gee, in the magazine *Pentecost,* wrote, "We usually regard what happened on Azusa Street, Los Angeles, in April 1906, as the beginning of the Pentecostal Revival," but goes on to say that there had been previous outpourings of the Holy Ghost in the United States and other lands. "It is computed that upwards of a thousand people had spoken

---

8 *Ibid.*
9 Charles W. Conn, *Like a Mighty Army* (Cleveland, Tennessee: Church of God Publishing House, 1955), p. 11.
10 *Ibid.,* p. 25.

with tongues on receiving the baptism in the Spirit before the fire fell in Los Angeles."[11]

REVIVAL

The Holy Ghost revival of 1896, which began in Cherokee County, North Carolina, continued in glory and power. The record of this revival states, "It is estimated that more than one hundred persons really received the baptism with the Holy Ghost and spoke in tongues as the evidence during that revival."[12]

It is significant to note in reporting this revival the recurring phrase, "speaking in other tongues as the Spirit gave them utterance," "received the Holy Ghost and spoke in other tongues," and "spoke in tongues as the evidence." This was and is the Biblical pattern. The Church of God recognized this, and speaking in tongues as the initial evidence of the Baptism of the Holy Ghost has been one of her prominent teachings to this present day. While this truth was preached by Church of God ministers, and all of them were Holy Ghost baptized men, it was not until 1910 that this teaching was stated in writing. The *Church of God Evangel*, in the summer of 1910, printed a list of our teachings, and among them was "The speaking in tongues as the evidence of the Baptism with the Holy Ghost. John 15:26, Acts 2:4, Acts 10:44-46, Acts 19:1-7."[13] Since the revival of 1896, hundreds of thousands have received the Holy Ghost in our churches and have spoken with other tongues as the Spirit has given utterance.

GROWTH

It was pointed out earlier that the Holy Ghost was of great value in the evangelization of the world and the growth of the

---

[11] Donald Gee, "Do 'Tongues' Matter," *Pentecost*, No. 49 (September, 1958), p. 17.

[12] Juillerat, *op. cit.*, pp. 12, 13.

[13] "Teaching," *Church of God Evangel*, I (August 15, 1910).

church. The record of our own organization reveals that very little progress was made until the Holy Ghost fell. "For ten years this servant of God [pastor Spurling] prayed, wept and continued his ministry against much opposition and under peculiar difficulties, before seeing much fruit of his labor."[14] Conn, in *Like a Mighty Army*, points out that there was little immediate success and no material gains made in this young church: "After ten years of almost fruitless labor the revival that had been so yearned for came so abruptly and in such an unexpected way that the entire hill country was shaken."[15] The fire fell. The latter rain about which Joel had prophesied[16] was falling. Great throngs of people flocked to the schoolhouse. Hundreds were saved and baptized with the Holy Ghost. Many miraculous healings occurred during this Holy Ghost outpouring.

Evangelization and the spreading of the gospel in the homeland and abroad gained impetus as the holy fire of the Spirit blazed brightly. The countryside, towns, and cities witnessed soul-stirring revivals in brush arbors, tents, storefront churches and wherever a church building could be secured or built. Conviction seized the hearts of men and women until they fell prostrate under God's holy power, or bowed at a mourners' bench. They cried out as of old, "Men and brethren, what shall we do?" These meetings were characterized by congregational singing, many people offering prayer in concert, exultant shouts of praise to God, and unbounded joy. In many cases the minister lacked formal education. He, like Amos, was no prophet, nor the son of a prophet, "but the Lord took me . . . and said unto me, Go, prophesy. . . ."[17] Filled with the Holy Ghost and a message from God and His Word, he went forth to declare these truths and to thunder against sin, worldliness, and unconcern. These sons of thunder, these flames

---

[14] Juillerat, *op. cit.*, p. 10.
[15] Conn, *op. cit.*, p. 16.
[16] Joel 2:23.
[17] Amos 7:14, 15.

of fire, were instruments God used to spread this Pentecostal message far and near until it has gone around the world.

WORLD OUTREACH

At the sixth Annual Assembly of the Church of God the report from the general overseer's office disclosed the fact that the church had a total of fifty-eight duly organized churches. The mission outreach consisted of two churches in the Bahama Islands. Fifty-four years later the report from the general overseer's office revealed a total of 3,679 organized churches in the United States and Canada, and a missions outreach into 69 countries with 3,140 organized churches and an additional 1,513 mission and preaching stations.

This is a report from only one Pentecostal church organization. Add to this the reports of all Pentecostal churches and the results are staggering. Gordon F. Atter in the chapter "Pentecostal Statistics" writes, "In view of the fact that almost always only adults are listed, and then only those who are active members, it is certain that there are well over 10,000,000 Pentecostal believers in the world today. In addition there are many adherents."[18]

Morton Kelsey states, "One of the most interesting phenomena has been the tremendous growth of the churches which stress speaking in tongues, the Pentecostal churches. While the more conventional established churches have barely kept pace with the population explosion in the United States, these fundamentalistic and enthusiastic groups have skyrocketed in membership to seventh place, and have sprung up in every city throughout the country."[19]

In an article entitled "Outburst of Tongues," Frank Farrell has the following to say: "Ecumenical leaders have shown increasing interest in the Pentecostal movement, known as the

---

[18] Gordon F. Atter, *The Third Force* (Peterborough, Ont.: The College Press, 1962), p. 226.

[19] From *Tongue Speaking*, by Morton T. Kelsey. Copyright © 1964 by Morton T. Kelsey. Reprinted by permission of Doubleday & Company, Inc., p. 5.

fastest-growing segment of Protestantism in the Western Hemisphere, where approximately one in every three Latin American Protestants is Pentecostal."[20] "Their virility, in recent years particularly, has aroused the wonder of the church world, and they form the largest segment of what has become known as the 'Third Force in Christendom.' "[21]

EMPOWERMENT

Why do these Pentecostal churches reflect such outstanding growth? There is only one answer: Men and women have been called of God from various walks of life, filled with the Holy Ghost, and anointed of God to preach His Word. In spite of privations, hardships, persecutions, and opposition by some established churches, they have been conscious of an impelling fire of God indwelling their souls, and have gone "everywhere preaching the word." Jesus demanded of the ministers in the Early Church, "tarry . . . until ye be endued with power from on high" (Luke 24:49). He promised: "ye shall be baptized with the Holy Ghost" (Acts 1:5), and "ye shall receive power, after that the Holy Ghost is come upon you" (Acts 1:8).

The great commission was delivered to the disciples by our Lord: "Go ye into all the world and preach the gospel to every creature."[22] "But ye shall receive power, after that the Holy Ghost is come upon you: and ye shall be witnesses unto me both in Jerusalem, and in all Judaea, and in Samaria, and unto the uttermost part of the earth."[23] This was Christ's command. Before they were to attempt this task, Jesus instructed the disciples to tarry until the power of the Holy Ghost came upon them. In this instruction it is clearly implied that without this enduement they were unequal to the task.

---

[20] Frank Farrell, "Outburst of Tongues: The New Penetration," *Christianity Today,* VII (September 13, 1963), p. 3. Copyright 1963 by *Christianity Today;* used by permission.
[21] *Ibid.,* p. 5.
[22] Mark 16:15.
[23] Acts 1:8.

This enduement, this power, was to come upon believers after the Holy Ghost baptism: "Ye shall receive power, *after* that the Holy Ghost is come upon you" (Acts 1:8). If the disciples needed this Spirit baptism to preach and witness, is it any less necessary for men of today? A. J. Gordon said, "No servant of Jehovah was deemed qualified for his ministry without this holy sanctifying touch laid upon him."[24] A. T. Pierson said, "We cannot afford to attempt the work appointed us without this same anointing," and "the one supreme qualification of Christ's witnesses is this: *that they be endued and endowed with power by the Holy Spirit.*"[25] A. B. Simpson wrote, "Without the Holy Ghost you are unequal to the journey of life; you are unfit for the service of the Master; you are unwarranted in attempting to preach the gospel or win a soul for Christ."[26]

Commenting on Luke 24:49, W. Clarkson wrote, "It is this which, if anything does, will make us strong also. What the Christian workman wants is the power which comes immediately from God, the inspiration of the Divine Spirit; in truth, the same bestowal as that which the apostles were now promised and afterwards received. . . . we need, as much as they did then, the illuminating, sanctifying, empowering influences of heaven—'God's Spirit in our hearts.' Without that, our most heroic efforts will fail; with it, our humblest endeavors will succeed."[27]

Notice the particular emphasis placed upon the necessity of being filled with the Spirit. The writers cited insist that the Holy Ghost baptism is a requisite for preaching and witnessing. This is the Biblical pattern and plan. No preacher

---

[24] A. J. Gordon, *The Ministry of the Spirit* (Philadelphia: American Baptist Publication Society, 1895), p. 88.

[25] A. T. Pierson, *The Acts of the Holy Spirit* (London: Morgan and Scott, [n.d.]), p. 21.

[26] A. B. Simpson, *The Holy Spirit*. By permission of Christian Publications, Inc., Harrisburg, Pennsylvania, p. 76.

[27] H. D. Spence and Joseph Exell (eds.), *The Pulpit Commentary* (Grand Rapids: Wm. B. Eerdmans Publishing Co., 1950), XVI, p. 297.

should attempt to do service for God without this special qualification. The vision of Christ which Paul received while on
the Damascus road, and while confined to the home of Judas,
was not enough to qualify him, nor for that matter was his
baptism in water. It required the Holy Ghost baptism with
the anointing and unction, being filled with the Holy Ghost,
to eminently qualify him for the God-called and appointed
task. That he was thus baptized is evident by his subsequent
preaching to others that they should be baptized with the Holy
Ghost, and by the fact that he said, "I thank my God, I speak
with tongues more than ye all" (1 Corinthians 14:18). "For
if I pray in an unknown tongue, my spirit prayeth . . . I
will pray with the spirit . . ." (1 Corinthians 14:14, 15).
"And my speech and my preaching was not with enticing
words of man's wisdom, but in demonstration of the Spirit and
of power" (1 Corinthians 2:4).

Wade H. Horton wrote concerning Acts 2:4: "Yes, when
the promised enduement came, they began to speak. Christ
had told them they would receive power to witness after the
Holy Ghost had come upon them (Acts 1:8). . . . Their
procedure should be a pattern for all time."[28]

This is the answer. Men have gone forth and "have
preached the gospel unto you with the Holy Ghost sent down
from heaven."[29] "For our gospel came not unto you in word
only, but also in power, and in the Holy Ghost and in much
assurance . . .";[30] "God also bearing them witness, both with
signs and wonders, and with divers miracles, and gifts of the
Holy Ghost."[31] Holy Ghost-baptized ministers, anointed and
filled with the fire of God, were impelled to declare the un-
searchable riches of Christ to a ruined world. As they
preached, whether with rude and halting speech for lack of

---

[28] Wade H. Horton, *Pentecost, Yesterday and Today* (Cleveland, Tenn.:
Pathway Press, 1964), p. 49.
[29] 1 Peter 1:12.
[30] 1 Thessalonians 1:5.
[31] Hebrews 2:4.

formal training, or with the precise speech and logical presentation of the educated, the Holy Ghost convicted and a mighty work was wrought.

GUIDANCE

The rapid growth of the Church of God and other Pentecostal movements has been at times imperiled by false teachers, erroneous doctrines promulgated by zealots not sufficiently instructed in Biblical truths, and by dissensions within their own ranks. On such occasions the Holy Spirit has always been present to exert His influence, guiding the Church to certain victory, preserving the purity of her doctrine and the unity of the saints.

The following three incidents are pointed out only to show that inestimable damage would have been inflicted on the Church if the Holy Ghost had not been present to save her in these situations.

In the early part of 1948 some Pentecostal preachers felt they had received a new revelation and were divinely inspired. They taught that the "latter rain" had really never fallen until they came along. They taught that the gifts of the spirit could be imparted by prophecy and by laying on of hands. They were against organization in the church, and labeled almost all other Pentecostals as cold and backslidden. Their belief was a strange admixture of truth and error. It seemed for a time that these teachings would divide the Pentecostal movement. Sincere men and women of God earnestly sought God in these hours, and by simple Bible teaching and Spirit direction, these errors were denounced and their effects largely annulled. The Pentecostal movement continued, victoriously advancing the cause of Christ.

When the Assemblies of God organization was only about two years old, its stability was threatened by a doctrinal issue referred to as "The New Issue"—the "Oneness" or "Jesus Only" doctrine. For a time it seemed to shake the foundations of this movement as some of its early ministers defected to this doctrine. A general session was convened in 1916 for a scriptural discussion of the issue. The Holy Ghost went before them. It is related that during the discussion a converted Jew was recognized by the moderator and given an opportunity to speak. He was an able defender, and his scriptural arguments were impressive. However, "one of the most extraordinary occurrences during the discussion was the breathtaking moment when someone began singing Reginald Heber's majestic hymn, 'Holy, Holy, Holy.' As one man, the audience arose, and even the anti-Trinitarians lifted up their hands in worship, and sang, 'God in three persons, blessed Trinity.' "[32] In that moment the trinitarian concept was sustained and it remains as one of their cardinal doctrines. Thus, the inestimable value of the Holy Ghost to the Church is dramatically demonstrated.

One of the historic doctrines of the Church of God is Sanctification. When differences of opinion arose as to whether it was an instantaneous definite work of grace, or a progressive work rather than instantaneous, the disputation became heated. It was decided that the intervening year between General Assemblies should be a time of study and prayer. When the Council of Ordained Ministers met the following year, the sessions were fraught with tension and controversy. When division seemed imminent, the general overseer advised that instead of arguing about the doctrine we go home and preach it and practice it before the world. The Holy Ghost spoke in tongues through one of the ministers and an interpretation was given. That settled the matter. All rejoiced in the moving of the Spirit, and once again the value of the Holy Ghost to the Church was majestically demonstrated.

INTERCESSION

The Holy Ghost proves its value to the Church in its prayers.

---

[32] Carl Brumback, *Suddenly . . . From Heaven* (Springfield, Mo.: Gospel Publishing House, 1961), pp. 208, 209.

Paul, in writing to the Corinthians, said, "For if I pray in an unknown tongue, my spirit prayeth . . . I will pray with the spirit . . ." (1 Corinthians 14:14, 15). To the Romans he wrote, "Likewise the Spirit also helpeth our infirmities: for we know not what we should pray for as we ought: but the Spirit itself maketh intercession for us with groanings which cannot be uttered. And he that searcheth the hearts knoweth what is the mind of the Spirit, because he maketh intercession for the saints according to the will of God" (Romans 8:26, 27).

When Herod was king, the Early Church was suffering persecution. Herod killed James, the brother of John, with the sword and had Peter arrested and imprisoned. Peter was placed under heavy guard and his fate was to be determined after Easter. The Church went to prayer, and Peter was delivered from prison by a great miracle.[33]

By order of the government of Haiti in 1941, every church and mission operated by the Church of God in Haiti was closed. Members were arrested and jailed because they sang Pentecostal songs and prayed in their own homes. Governments were appealed to and the State Department of the United States was asked to intervene in our behalf. For two years the churches remained closed. During that time our churches here at home were beseeching God, "with all prayer and supplication in the Spirit"[34] and "praying in the Holy Ghost."[35] In August of 1943 the churches were permitted to reopen and God's work moved ahead. As of 1964 we had in Haiti 182 churches, 230 missions, 12,620 members and over 40,000 adherents.[36] The Holy Ghost is of utmost value in the prayers of the Church.

Herman Lauster, a Church of God missionary in Germany, was conducting revivals in Krehwinkel, Stuttgart, and Kirchiem-

---

[33] Acts 12:1-17.
[34] Ephesians 6:18.
[35] Jude verse 20.
[36] *Minutes of the Fiftieth General Assembly of the Church of God* (Cleveland, Tenn.: Church of God Publishing House, 1964), p. 31.

Teck. When people began receiving the Holy Ghost and speaking in tongues, persecutions began and the Gestapo warned Herman Lauster to cease preaching. Despite these warnings, Lauster continued his preaching. On August 28, 1938, the Gestapo arrested him. He was incarcerated in Welsheim prison for seven months, expecting daily to be sent to Dachau, a notorious concentration camp where many thousands of prisoners were killed and cremated. The churches in Germany and America fasted, wept, and prayed. A special day, March 5, 1939, was set apart as a special day of fasting and prayer for Brother Lauster's release. Eleven days later he was released from prison. Intercession by the Holy Ghost for this saint of God was effectual, and the church learned anew the value of the Holy Ghost.

The following incident will further witness to the value of the Holy Ghost to the local church as the medium of prayer. In 1938, while the writer was pastoring the Church of God in Lake Worth, Florida, an amazing incident occurred. Paul H. Walker, field representative to the West Indies, was often away from home for weeks at a time. The headquarters out of which he worked was in Lake Worth. His family lived there and were regular attendants at the local Church of God. On one occasion when Reverend Walker was absent from his home for several weeks, his wife failed to receive any correspondence from him. This was very unusual in that he usually wrote frequently to keep his wife informed of his work and as to when he would be expected back in the states. Failure to hear from her husband for a number of weeks had given much concern to Mrs. Walker. She came to the parsonage one Saturday to talk with my wife.

The next morning, during our regular Sunday morning service, God especially visited the church with an outpouring of His Spirit. People were rejoicing in the Lord and a wonderful spirit of worship prevailed. During that service several persons spoke in tongues as the Spirit of God gave utterance, and a wonderful atmosphere continued as the writer stepped to the pulpit to address the congregation.

Before the text could be read, however, someone began weeping loudly. A member of the church, Mrs. Anna Fulwood, stood to her feet. With a voice charged with emotion and with deep sobs, Mrs. Fulwood said the Holy Ghost had impressed her that Reverend Walker was in need of prayer and was in danger at that present time. She asked me to call the congregation to prayer. Knowing the concern of Mrs. Walker, it disturbed me to hear this lady speak as she did. My fears were groundless, however, because the Holy Spirit knew what He was doing and this was His method of providing for the need in that particular hour.

The entire congregation was called to prayer in Reverend Walker's behalf. There was a great deal of groaning in the Spirit and speaking in tongues as concert prayer was made to God. Following a lengthy session of prayer, the burden was lifted and we arose from our knees satisfied that whatever the need of the hour had been, God, through the Holy Spirit, had met that need. After the morning message all of us left the church feeling satisfied that somehow the Holy Spirit had wrought a work that day.

One day after Reverend Walker returned, I related to him the experience of that Sunday morning. A strange look came over his face. He asked the date this incident had occurred. Then he asked the exact time. He then stated that at the very time the church at Lake Worth was groaning and praying in the Spirit, he was desperately ill on board ship in some of the most treacherous waters between those islands. While the church prayed, God touched his body. In that same hour a breeze came up, and the ship, which had been adrift because of the lack of breeze, began to move; and he soon reached his destination. Thus, again, the value of praying in the Spirit is emphasized, not only to the church but to the individual as well.

INSTRUCTION

A word must be said about the value of the Holy Ghost as a teacher. "But the Comforter, which is the Holy Ghost, whom the Father will send in my name, he shall teach you all things" (John 14:26). The Holy Scriptures are Holy Ghost inspired: "holy men of God spake as they were moved by the Holy Ghost" (2 Peter 1:21), and "All scripture is given by inspiration of God" (2 Timothy 3:16).

To understand the Scriptures one must have the Spirit as his teacher and interpreter: "which things also we speak, not in the words which man's wisdom teacheth, but which the Holy Ghost teacheth. . . . But the natural man receiveth not the things of the Spirit of God: for they are foolishness unto him: neither can he know them, because they are spiritually discerned" (1 Corinthians 2:13, 14).

The preachers in the Early Church relied on the Spirit to teach them what to say. When the high priest and rulers perceived that Peter and John were "unlearned and ignorant" men, they "marvelled" at the way they spoke (Acts 4:13). It is recorded of Stephen's preaching: "they were not able to resist the wisdom and the spirit by which he spake" (Acts 6:10).

Why were they thus able to impart such profound truths with such unusual ability? It should be pointed out that not all learned students of the Bible have been believers of its pages; on the other hand, some very unlearned people have had strong faith in God's Word. What often evades critical scholars may come very easily to the humble and ordinary person.[37] René Pache points out that human teachers may change their doctrine and theories, but those who allow themselves to be taught by the Spirit draw directly upon the source of un-

---

[37] Bernard Ramm, *The Witness of the Spirit* (Grand Rapids: Wm. B. Eerdmans Publishing Co., 1960), p. 95.

changing truth: "Having inspired the Scriptures He enables us to understand them."[38]

COURAGE

Pentecostal preachers have proclaimed this experience of the Holy Ghost and tongues speaking despite ridicule, opposition, and charges of heresy. They have done so because they were taught by the Spirit the reality and scriptural basis for such an experience. They have refused to be moved from their position or to change their theology. Unpopular though it may have been, they have consistently preached this Bible truth until it has been accepted and experienced by men and women, not only in Pentecostal churches but in the established historic churches as well.

Even though Pentecostals have relied heavily upon the inspiration and teaching of the Holy Spirit, this is not to say they have neglected education. One of the places where this last-day outpouring of the Holy Ghost fell was in a Bible school in Topeka, Kansas. The Church of God recognized the need of training its workers, and on January 1, 1918, it opened its first school, now named Lee College, "for the training of young men and young women for efficient service on the field."[39] The Bible was to be its principal textbook.[40] The Pentecostal Holiness denomination established Emmanuel College which opened January 1, 1919. The Assemblies of God opened its first educational institution in 1922. Other Pentecostal denominations have established schools and colleges for the training of workers and ministers.

From the beginning of these schools the Pentecostal churches have expanded and improved both choice and quality of

---

[38] René Pache, *The Person and Work of the Holy Spirit* (Chicago: Moody Press, 1954), p. 152. Used by permission, Moody Press, Moody Bible Institute of Chicago 60610.

[39] *Minutes of the Thirteenth General Assembly of the Church of God* (Cleveland, Tenn.: Church of God Publishing House, 1917), p. 300.

[40] *Ibid.*

courses offered, so that now schools and colleges operated by Pentecostals are accredited by regional and national accrediting associations. They are determined to have excellence of scholarship along with excellence of salvation. They are equally determined that academic pursuits shall not usurp spiritual attainment. In all Church of God colleges classes open with prayer. Many times the Spirit descends and revival results. This is as it should be, that in "all things he might have the preeminence."[41]

These educational efforts are vital to the evangelization of the world. Paul advises the ministry to study in order to have God's approval: ". . . correctly analyzing and accurately dividing—rightly handling and skillfully teaching—the Word of Truth."[42] Knowledge, saturated with the Holy Ghost, is mighty in assaulting the strongholds of Satan and presenting the liberating truths of God to a world who needs Christ.

Before concluding this study, three additional benefits of tongues speaking need to be presented: edification of the church, convincing of the unbeliever, and involvement for service.

EDIFICATION OF THE CHURCH

Through believers' speaking in tongues, the church is edified: "I would that ye all spake with tongues, but rather that ye prophesied: for greater is he that prophesieth than he that speaketh with tongues, except he interpret, that the church may receive edifying" (1 Corinthians 14:5). Paul is simply saying that the church can be edified by speaking in tongues provided an interpretation is given. Again Paul says, "Wherefore let him that speaketh in an unknown tongue pray that he may interpret" (1 Corinthians 14:13). "If any man speak in an unknown tongue . . . let one interpret" (1 Corinthians 14:27). I have been in services where someone spoke in the

---

41 Colossians 1:18.
42 2 Timothy 2:15, *Amplified New Testament.*

unknown tongue, an interpretation was given, and all the saints were blessed. When the interpretation is given, not only is the one who speaks in other tongues edified, but they who hear the interpretation also rejoice and are edified in that which God has spoken to the church.

The oldest annual camp meeting in the Church of God is the Florida State Camp Meeting at Wimauma. Attendance runs into thousands; on the weekends between five and six thousand are present for the services. On many occasions when people are loudly praising God, an individual will be moved upon by the Holy Ghost to speak a message in tongues. When the person begins to speak, all other voices are stilled as the message is given and interpreted. At the conclusion of the message the congregation, as one voice, gives praise to God.

At the 1964 General Assembly of the Church of God, the meetings were conducted in the Dallas Memorial Auditorium, Dallas, Texas. The auditorium is so large that it is necessary to use an amplifying system for all to hear. In one service the Holy Ghost moved upon a person in the balcony to speak a message in tongues. The audience was stilled and every syllable spoken was clearly heard in all parts of the auditorium. In another part of the auditorium someone else interpreted the message. Being supernaturally moved upon by the Holy Ghost, both the messenger and the interpreter were clearly heard by the congregation without the benefit of the public address system, and the vast audience was edified.

During a camp meeting in Georgia one particular service in the evening is especially remembered. The saints were rejoicing, some praising God, some dancing in the Spirit, some speaking in tongues. Instead of the evangelist preaching that night, God sent a special wave of power. Many spoke in unison in other tongues. People were convicted and began coming to the altar for prayer. Personal workers laid their hands on the seekers, and that night over fifty were filled with the Holy Ghost and spoke in tongues as the Spirit gave utterance.

Speaking with tongues is also a means of rest and refreshing to the church. "Whom shall he teach knowledge? and whom shall he make to understand doctrine? them that are weaned from the milk, and drawn from the breasts. For precept must be upon precept, precept upon precept; line upon line, line upon line; here a little, and there a little: for with stammering lips and another tongue will he speak to this people. To whom he said, This is the rest wherewith ye may cause the weary to rest; and this is the refreshing" (Isaiah 28:9-12). Thus we find years later, it is said that the churches were edified—established, improved, refreshed—and were walking in the fear of the Lord and in the comfort of the Holy Ghost (Acts 9:31). In the midst of all this they were enjoying growth and expansion for the glory of Almighty God.

CONVINCING OF THE UNBELIEVER

Speaking in other tongues is to convince and convict the unbeliever: "Wherefore tongues are for a sign, not to them that believe, but to them that believe not" (1 Corinthians 14:22).

God quite often uses speaking in tongues to convict the unbeliever of his ungodliness and to convince him that he should seek forgiveness. Testimony after testimony could be given of instances where the Holy Ghost spoke through an individual a message in tongues which was understood by people who were of a different nationality and language. There is available today evidence of persons' speaking miraculously in tongues of almost every language, and of the hearers' being convinced of their needs and seeking God. To attempt in this study to catalogue all of the evidence would be impossible, but I think it would be well to cite a few instances.

John Sherrill tells of Jacob Rabinowitz, a Jewish rabbi who

attended a Pentecostal service in Pasadena, Texas, and went forward for prayer. An Irishman, praying for Him, spoke in tongues. The language in which he spoke was Hebrew. Upon learning that the Irishman did not understand a word of Hebrew, nor could he speak that language, the rabbi was converted to Pentecost.[43]

Stanley Frodsham relates an incident of a man who spoke in tongues in the Russian language. Several Russians were present. The Spirit fell on them as well as on others. He also tells of three different Jews who were converted because of someone's speaking in tongues in the Hebrew language.[44]

He also records Mrs. Lillian Thistlewaite's story: "On one occasion, during the sermon there was a message in tongues. At the close of the meeting a man arose and said, 'I am healed of my infidelity; I have heard in my own tongue a Psalm I learned at my mother's knee.' "[45]

Frodsham related another experience of Mrs. Yerger of California: "In a campaign in Phoenix, Arizona . . . a Swedish woman . . . gave a message in tongues . . . [an Apache] Indian girl came to the front and in awe-stricken tones said: 'this woman speaks my language. She says Jesus is coming soon. Indian girl better get ready.' She did" and assisted her two sisters to find the Lord also.[46]

Vessie D. Hargrave, a missionary for many years, and who presently is serving as General Director of Foreign Missions and as a member of the Executive Council of the Church of God, recently related to me three incidents that he personally had witnessed. At a camp meeting in Weatherford, Texas, a young girl received the Baptism of the Holy Ghost, walked down the aisles, and went outside (where he was standing).

[43] John L. Sherrill, *They Speak With Other Tongues* (New York: McGraw-Hill Book Co., 1964), pp. 99, 100.

[44] Stanley Frodsham, *With Signs Following* (Springfield, Mo.: Gospel Publishing House, 1946), p. 20.

[45] *Ibid.*, p. 22.

[46] *Ibid.*, p. 244.

She was speaking in tongues. Brother Hargrave had lived many years in Mexico and understood Spanish well. He said that although she did not know Spanish, she spoke it perfectly. Some Mexican laborers who were standing about the tabernacle moved in closer when they heard this girl. She was praising the Lord in Spanish with such expressions as, "It is so wonderful. This life is so wonderful. You, too, can enjoy this experience with God." While she continued to praise the Lord in tongues and invite others to accept the experience of the Holy Ghost, several people fell trembling to their knees, weeping, praying, and seeking God. This was a most glorious example of the Holy Ghost's speaking in a language unknown to the speaker, but known to the hearer.

In November, 1964, Dr. Bob O'Bannon, missionary superintendent of the Middle East, and Vessie D. Hargrave were in Assiout, Egypt. An illiterate Egyptian camel driver came to the altar to seek God. He received his Baptism in the Holy Ghost, and this old man, who did not know a word of the English language, spoke in the English language while under the influence of the Spirit.

The Reverend Hargrave also relates that in 1942 while he was in Texas, a Nazarene preacher was seated beside him on the platform. The Spirit of the Lord fell on a girl who turned to this Nazarene minister and spoke in the Yiddish language. This minister, who was Jewish, understood what was said. He was convinced of the reality of this Holy Ghost baptism, fell on his knees, became converted to Pentecost, and became a minister in the Church of God.

In 1953, while attending a convention in Santo Domingo, Dominican Republic, along with some other American ministers, the writer witnessed an outpouring of God's Spirit. Many were baptized with the Holy Ghost. Among those receiving the baptism was a national who in the Spirit spoke the English language which she had never learned.

The Reverend E. J. Boehmer, for many years General Sec-
retary-Treasurer of the Church of God, related his experience
of receiving the Baptism of the Holy Ghost. He was in Los
Angeles attending the old Azusa Street Mission. One of the
worshipers there spoke in other tongues as the Spirit gave utterance. She spoke in the German language and he understood her
perfectly. Later he went to her wanting to know what part
of Germany she was from. She said she was not from Germany,
nor did she speak the German language. The second time he
went back to the service the same thing occurred. Convinced
that it was of the Lord, Boehmer sought the experience and
was baptized with the Holy Ghost.

One could go on and on relating such experiences, but these
will suffice for this study. Such experiences serve as signs to
convince unbelievers that tongues speaking is of God—miraculous.

INVOLVEMENT FOR SERVICE

Pentecostals have been characterized as a people who win
people. It is said that their success is due to three principal
factors: they have active participation in all of the worship;
they aim at the heart rather than the head, and they do not
quench the Spirit with rigid forms. It could also be added that
they have succeeded because of faith in the infallible Word
of God, holiness in daily living, active participation of the
members in soul-winning, and, most of all, because of the
presence and power of the Holy Ghost in their lives. Klaude
Kendrick has said, "The Pentecostals . . . care for their religion—care enough both to give to and live for it. Active
devotion, deep sincerity, and vital enthusiasm have characterized their unusual success."[47]

---

[47] Klaude Kendrick, The Promise Fulfilled (Springfield, Mo.: Gospel Publishing House, 1961), p. 216.

IV. CONCLUSION

The author believes that he has clearly established that speaking in tongues was of great prominence and of great value to the Early Church and that it is of great prominence and of equal value to the church of today. A statement by Frank W. Lemons provides a fitting conclusion: "The Church of Pentecost perseveres to this day and continues to write voluminously of His wondrous acts—not on parchments or in paper books alone, but in visible lives of redeemed men and women. The world is challenged to read and to discover that Christ lives and that His power has not diminished."[48]

---

[48] Frank W. Lemons, *Our Pentecostal Heritage* (Cleveland, Tenn.: Pathway Press, 1963), p. 173.

Glossolalia:
Its Value to the Individual

James L. Slay

James L. Slay is Field Representative of Church of God World Missions. He has served as state overseer, instructor at Lee College, on the Lee College Board of Directors, and on the Editorial and Publications Board. He conducted a one-year preaching mission in the Republic of South Africa, and during his ministry he has traveled in sixty foreign countries. He earned the Bachelor of Science degree, with a major in psychology and a minor in sociology, and the Master of Education degree in educational psychology and counseling, from the University of Chattanooga. He has authored two books, Rescue the Perishing *and* This We Believe, *and has written numerous articles and sermons for religious periodicals.*

James L. Slay

Glossolalia:
Its Value to the Individual

I. A BIBLE DOCTRINE

The smoke of battle that has so long obscured the real issues involved in the glossolalia phenomenon is, at long last,
beginning to fade away, and we are now able to discuss this
Bible doctrine with a modicum of objectivity and rationality.
The opponents of this truth were so radically opposed to the
experience that they could not possibly see it as beneficial to
the individual. As a matter of fact, most theologians ridiculed
the idea of contemporary glossolalia and were very critical of
those who even professed belief in this apostolic enduement.

Those attempting to refute the divine reality of glossolalia
have not been, for the greater part, irenic nor understanding.
Their outbursts against the doctrine have really run the gamut
of criticism. Alexander Mackie says, "We have noticed that
the gift of tongues has always begun with an individual in
whom the presence of some disease can definitely be traced.
. . . there is evidence pointing to the fact that the tongues are
either a fraud or pathological or both."[1] The same writer, to

---

[1] H. J. Stolee, *Speaking in Tongues* (Minneapolis: Augsburg Publishing House,
1963), p. 76, citing Mackie.

escape having to defend the Biblical accounts of glossolalia, states elsewhere that, "The most easy solution of all New Testament problems is, of course, the purely arbitrary but not unpopular one of regarding as textual interpolations such New Testament passages as involve difficulty in exegesis. . . . it is possible to recognize in the account of Pentecost a tradition, modified by an idealizing and myth-making tendency."[2] In other words, if the text is contrary to your belief then count it as an interpolation or myth. This has been the practice of others also.

These quotations above, from a man writing specifically about the gift of tongues, are stated to inform the reader that the concensus of opinion has been that those who professed to speak with tongues, rather than being benefited or blessed thereby, were thought to be, if not totally ignorant, fraudulent or sick, at least theologically and spiritually naive. Because of this, many of the proponents of the doctrine and recipients of the experience took the defensive. In their desire to authenticate speaking in tongues, the Pentecostal believers have spent most of their time proving the doctrine to be scriptural, overlooking the very vital truth that there is really a rationale—a divine reason—for this awe-inspiring and amazing phenomenon. They knew they had a Biblical experience that blessed and inspired; therefore, there was a real desire that others know that what they possessed and believed in was truly Biblical. To them no other proof was needed beyond that of its Biblical authenticity.

Dr. Barnes has aptly written that glossolalia ". . . is an important endowment and is not in its place to be undervalued. It may be of great service in the cause of truth and if properly regulated and not abused, I would rejoice if these extraordinary endowments were conferred on all. I have no envy against any who possess it; no opposition to the endow-

---

[2] Alexander Mackie, The Gift of Tongues (New York: George H. Doran Company, 1921), p. 17.

ment; but I wish that it should not be overvalued."[3] We agree
with this author. There was a reason for glossolalia initially;
there is a need for it now. Great benefits can and will accrue,
if it is scripturally accepted and practiced.

We must not, however, be too quick to find fault with
those who oppose speaking in tongues. Many of those who
have been so harsh in their sermons and writings were perhaps sincere, if not objective. We must remember that we are
herewith dealing with a realm of spirituality that comes not
from intellectual attainment, but is the result of a hunger and
thirst for more of Him and His power. The Pentecostal believer therefore should not be criticized because he has been
enjoying the benefits of a blessing which he may, at times,
not deem it necessary, or even be able, to explain intellectually. As a matter of fact, the doctrine we are now discussing
has to do with the work of the Spirit in helping our infirmities.[4] It is for this reason that we are blessed with this
supernatural enduement. We do not condemn learning, nor
do we condone ignorance; yet, we must ever realize that there
is a spiritual dimension that can be attained only by a simple
childlike faith in Him and in His Word. Paul was right when
he said, ". . . the world by wisdom knew not God."[5] He
was also speaking the truth when he said, "Though I speak
with the tongues of men and of angels, and have not charity,
I am become as sounding brass, or a tinkling cymbal."[6]

The tongues phenomenon should serve as a link or bridge
to bring believers together. If it has been the source of confusion, it has been so because of an unwillingness on the part
of many to believe the unequivocal statement of the Word and
because "we have this treasure in earthen vessels." Schelling,

---

[3] Albert Barnes, *Notes, Explanatory and Practical on the First Epistle of
Paul to the Corinthians* (New York: William Robinson, 1838), p. 280.
[4] Romans 8:26.
[5] 1 Corinthians 1:21.
[6] 1 Corinthians 13:1.

the eminent German theologian, calls the Pentecostal miracle "Babel reversed."[7]

The mass of evidence in the New Testament should surely convince any sincere Christian that this doctrine is Biblical. If it is Biblical, then there must be some reason for it. One of the basic laws of hermeneutics, or the science of Biblical interpretation, is the law of emphasis. If speaking in tongues was not to be an important teaching of the Church, why should the Holy Spirit place so much emphasis on the phenomenon in the book of Acts? Why would Paul devote three chapters of 1 Corinthians to explain the fact and function of an experience that was to cease? There was a need for glossolalia at Pentecost and all during the apostolic period. Dr. Remensnyder says in *The Post Apostolic Age*, "This power He communicated to His disciples whom He sent forth. Without such a signal proof of divine sanction our Lord knew it would be absolutely impossible to get the ears of men in introducing a religion so totally foreign to human ideas."[8] The happening at Pentecost was no *luxus-wunder*—no superfluous and unnecessary miracle. There was a definite need for it then, and that need persists no matter what men may think or feel.

The need for glossolalia today is great, perhaps even greater than ever before. In this scientific age we must have empirical proof. We must experience reality. Bruner says, "Science has been defined as 'a passion for facts.' The early church was born out of a great experience that was based upon facts. The Day of Pentecost and the church that began on that day are actual facts of history."[9] No one who believes the Bible can deny the existence of this phenomenon. There was

---

[7] Philip Schaff, *History of the Christian Church* (Grand Rapids: Wm. B. Eerdmans Publishing Company, 1950), I, pp. 238, 239, citing Schelling from *Einl in d Philos. der Mythologie*, p. 109.

[8] Stolee, *op. cit.*, p. 26, citing Remensnyder.

[9] B. H. Bruner, *Pentecost, a Renewal of Power* (New York: Doubleday, Doran and Company, 1928), p. 14.

a need for it in the days of Peter. Surely there is an even greater need in this day of materialism and rationalism. "Only those elements in the Christian religion which are expressible in and through a genuine human experience are likely to have any great influence upon an age that is in an open revolt against dogma."[10] Carl Rogers says, "Experience is for me the highest authority."[11] These words from an unbeliever aptly express the scientific trend. In glossolalia we have that experience. He who speaks ecstatically knows full well what has happened, and even though he finds it inexplicable, it brings forth joy unspeakable. Too many have been blessed by this phenomenon to permit anyone to say it is not now operational.

With these introductory thoughts in mind, and having briefly stated that there is a reason or rationale for glossolalia, let us now go on to a more specific accounting of the facts which prove this phenomenon to be beneficial to the individual. By the term *individual* it is meant more specifically the one speaking in tongues; however, the hearer, whether believer or unbeliever, can also be benefited by the manifestation.

First of all, this study proposes to show that the individual is made a better witness and soulwinner by this bestowal. Second, it will also be shown that glossolalia is an important aid in worshiping God whether it be in private devotions or in the public service.

II. GLOSSOLALIA AS AN AID TO WITNESSING

ON THE DAY OF PENTECOST

The disciples had been with Jesus as His almost constant companions for nearly three years. They had beheld His marvelous works, heard His wonderful words, and been thrilled

---

[10] *Ibid.,* p. 10.
[11] Carl R. Rogers, *On Becoming a Person* (Boston: Houghton Mifflin Company, 1961), p. 23.

by His presence. Yet, in spite of all this, along with the wonder of His resurrection, they were still in need of something from above. After His resurrection "he appeared unto the eleven as they sat at meat, and upbraided them with their unbelief and hardness of heart, because they believed not them which had seen him after he was risen"[12] Why this upbraiding? Why this unbelief? The disciples were only acting as mere mortals; they had been with Him, but He had not yet come to be in them. That was why He "commanded them that they . . . wait for the promise of the Father, which, saith he, ye have heard of me."[13] The disciples had seen and heard much during their association with our Lord, but this knowledge was not enough to make them able and effective witnesses. Before they could even begin to carry out the Great Commission, they would have to "receive power." The evidence that they had received this power was the glossolalia phenomenon.

The disciples, and the remainder of the 120, obeyed the command of their Lord and tarried. Some had wondered if He would not "restore again the kingdom to Israel"[14] and therefore fulfill their long-lived messianic hopes. They were told, however, that the time for this was not then. Witnessing had to be done. An unbelieving world had to be convinced and reproved "of sin, and of righteousness, and of judgment."[15] This they could not do until the promise had been fulfilled.

After giving these commands to His faithful followers, the Lord was carried up into heaven. Now that their leader and Saviour was gone, there was nothing left for them to do but tarry until the promise be fulfilled. According to Kelsey, "The only stability these men had was to sit still and wait as they had been told, both by Jesus and in a vision; being men who had known suffering and hope, they did just that. They stayed together and prayed, not knowing what might come. It was

---

12 Mark 16:14.
13 Acts 1:4.
14 Acts 1:6.
15 John 16:8.

then that the experience of glossolalia first occurred. This experience was evidence to them that God's Spirit was with them. It helped give them the conviction which sent them courageously into a hostile world."[16]

Let us think for a while on this initial outpouring and how it really benefited the recipient as well as the earnest and sincere onlooker. The 120 did not know what was going to happen. They were not seeking tongues; however, the coming of His Spirit in fullness elicited this marvelous phenomenon. Surely they were amazed; they had reason to be joyfully astonished. Now they were made to realize what Christ meant when He said, "I will not leave you *orphans:* I will come to you."[17] They knew now just what He meant when He said, "when the Comforter is come, whom I will send unto you from the Father, even the Spirit of truth, which proceedeth from the Father, *he shall testify of me.*"[18] How could they doubt the reality of this infilling? They spoke, but it was the Spirit who "gave them utterance."[19] They were all filled with the Holy Ghost; being full of Him there was room for no one else. The 120 furnished the organs of speech, but the thoughts being expressed were His thoughts. He, the Holy Spirit, was literally putting words into their mouths. They were now His witnesses; the tongues phenomenon made them to know this.

Jesus, during the period between His resurrection and ascension, had told His disciples that it was "expedient [or better] for you that I go away: for if I go not away, the Comforter will not come unto you. . . ."[20] A casual reading of this will cause wonder. What could possibly be better than living in the presence of the Only Begotten Son of the Father? The coming of the Spirit at Pentecost erased all doubt as to what He had in mind when this statement was made. The 120, and

---

[16] From *Tongue Speaking* by Morton T. Kelsey. Copyright © 1964 by Morton T. Kelsey. Reprinted by permission of Doubleday & Company, Inc., p. 19.
[17] John 14:18. (Scofield margin.)
[18] John 15:26. Italics ours.
[19] Acts 2:4.
[20] John 16:7.

more especially the eleven, had been living in His presence. "Pentecost transcended this sense of His Presence: it was something corresponding to the difference between 'with-ness' and 'in-ness'."[21] Before Pentecost the Spirit dwelt with them; now He was in them.[22] There were no doubts now; as a matter of fact, His indwelling had expelled them all. Before Pentecost they thought as fleshly or carnal men; now they were Spirit-filled, so filled in fact that they could not speak their words or even think their thoughts. Pentecost without glossolalia would not have really evidenced the complete submission of the individual believer to the Holy Spirit.

"The purpose of 'tongues' is to evince the supernatural presence of God with his people."[23] If the 120 were to form the nucleus of the Early Church; if they were to be worthy and faithful witnesses, then they must not only speak of Him, but let Him speak through them. They must undergo a mental catharsis and become channels of the Spirit. D i o n y s i u s Areopagiticus in A.D. 50 said, "the most godly knowledge of God is that which is known by unknowing."[24] These men and women who first spoke in tongues at Pentecost had known Christ in person, but after the coming of the Holy Spirit they were able to know Him in a new and more amazing dimension. The men who walked with their Lord on the Emmaus Road did not know who He was until "their eyes were opened."[25] Pentecost and the glossolalia brought about a similar and happy awareness. Lancelot Whyte tells us that "it was an essential feature of the mystical tradition that the most important insights are not gained by the deliberate pursuit of knowledge, but by what Keats called the 'negative capability' or ability to

[21] Joe Brice, Pentecost (London: Hodder and Stoughton, 1936), p. 27.
[22] John 14:17.
[23] William G. Moorehead, Outline Studies in Acts, Romans, First and Second Corinthians, Galatians and Ephesians (New York: Fleming H. Revell Company, 1902), p. 143.
[24] Lancelot Law Whyte, The Unconscious Before Freud (New York: Basic Books, Inc., 1960), p. 80, quoting Dionysurs Areopagiticus.
[25] Luke 24:31.

make oneself empty and to receive."[26] The 120 were to be witnesses, and to be proper witnesses they had to experience the phenomenon that occurred at Pentecost.

What were the initial effects of the ecstatic utterances on those present in Jerusalem on the Day of Pentecost? The 120 in the upper room were "all filled with the Holy Ghost, and began to speak with other tongues, as the Spirit gave them utterance."[27] What had happened to this little remnant was soon "noised abroad." "All heard the disciples speaking in their own (the multitudes') tongues the mighty works of God. This produced amazement in some and mockery in others who regarded the men as intoxicated (Cf. Eph. 5:18). Thus do men still see the same wonders but their interpretation of them depends on their attitude."[28] Peter's sermon, delivered to those assembled because of the glossolalia phenomenon, led to the conversion of three thousand souls, but there were many more who were not at all moved by the mighty demonstration of the Spirit. According to Alleman, "the utterances of exalted emotions can be understood only by those who share the emotion."[29] The unbeliever can never be effectively touched by the Spirit in conviction unless he wills to do so.

In spite of the fact that not all believed, the results on the Day of Pentecost were most gratifying. Jesus had fulfilled His promise to His faithful followers; the 120 had been so empowered by the Spirit that they became His witnesses and spoke of the wonderful works of God in such a manner that men of fifteen or more nationalities heard them praising God "in our tongues."[30] Those who spoke in tongues could have recounted the events of Christ's life in the normal fashion, but it would not have made the impact needed at that time.

---

[26] Whyte, *op. cit.*, p. 80.

[27] Acts 2:4.

[28] Herbert C. Alleman, *New Testament Commentary* (Philadelphia: The Board of Publication of the United Lutheran Church in America, 1936), p. 403.

[29] *Ibid.*

[30] Acts 2:11.

Why did the infilling of the Spirit elicit glossolalia in this public and spectacular manner? The answer is seen in the miracle's lasting effect on all who were filled and those who were willing to believe. Barton says:

> The ecstasy and "speaking with tongues" was to them ocular evidence that the days of Samuel, Elijah, and Elisha had returned. Joel's prophecy was now in process of fulfillment. Here was ocular and audible evidence that Jesus was the Messiah and that the Messianic Age had actually begun. Whereas they had formerly felt like the Russian peasants in the days of the empire who used to say, "God is in heaven and the emperor far away," now they knew that God was near to empower, to protect, to guide, to lead to triumph.[31]

God knew what was needed by both recipient and onlooker. Glossolalia met this dual need.

AFTER PENTECOST

The Apostolic Church. After the Day of Pentecost, the tongues phenomenon continued to aid the apostolic church in the matter of witnessing, in the same, if not so spectacular fashion. Glossolalia was still the sign or evidence that the Spirit had come in His fullness. Grosheide, agreeing with this said, "Glossolalia is a sign of the presence of the Holy Spirit."[32] When He comes in His fullness He gives vocal evidence. The human or natural man will surrender all before giving up the power of self-expression. When this happens, it is evident that His Presence prevails and predominates. More will be said about this self-abnegation later on.

There are in Acts five definite records of individuals and groups' being filled with the Holy Ghost. In three of these accounts, there are explicit statements unequivocally stating that glossolalia was a sign or a witness that the Holy Spirit had

---

[31] George A. Barton, *The Apostolic Age and the New Testament* (Philadelphia: University of Pennsylvania Press, 1936), p. 14.

[32] F. W. Grosheide, *Commentary on the First Epistle to the Corinthians. In the New International Commentary on the New Testament.* F. F. Bruce, gen. ed. (Grand Rapids: Wm. B. Eerdmans Publishing Company, 1953), p. 336.

come in His fullness. Luke's account of the infilling at Pentecost says, "they were all filled with the Holy Ghost, and began to speak with other tongues, as the Spirit gave them utterance."[33] In the house of Cornelius, the Gentiles received the same experience that the 120 received on the Day of Pentecost. Naturally, the Jews were astonished by this wonderful outpouring, but they could not in any way doubt its reality and divine origin "for they heard them speak with tongues, and magnify God."[34] Here glossolalia was the sign or witness that every man, be he Jew or Gentile, could receive the Holy Spirit as they did on the Day of Pentecost. Luke was also very lucid when he gave to us the account of the outpouring at Ephesus. Here were found certain disciples who knew nothing at all about the Holy Ghost. They were sincere, however, and in search of the truth. They listened to the preaching of Paul and submitted to the ordinance of Christian baptism. After this Paul laid his hands upon them, and "the Holy Ghost came on them; and they spake with tongues, and prophesied."[35] Here again we find clear evidence that the coming of the Spirit upon the believer was accompanied by speaking with tongues.

No one can deny the clarity of these accounts. Here is proof beyond a doubt that glossolalia was the initial evidence that the believer had been spiritually indwelt; but what will be said about the other two events? Some who fail to believe in glossolalia as the initial evidence of the Spirit's indwelling will hasten to say that there is no mention of tongues in the account of the Spirit's reception by the Samaritans. This may be true, but such is surely implied. Let us read carefully what the Scripture has to say:

> Now when the apostles which were at Jerusalem heard that Samaria had received the word of God, they sent unto them Peter and John: Who, when they were come down, prayed for them that they might receive the Holy Ghost:

---

[33] Acts 2:4.
[34] Acts 10:46.
[35] Acts 19:6.

(For as yet he was fallen upon none of them: only they were baptized in the name of the Lord Jesus.) Then laid they their hands on them and they received the Holy Ghost. And when Simon saw that through laying on of the apostles' hands the Holy Ghost was given, he offered them money, Saying, Give me also this power, that on whomsoever I lay hands, he may receive the Holy Ghost.[36]

Simon had witnessed an empirical or sensual experience that gave immediate and valid evidence that the Holy Ghost had come in His fullness. There was no great time lapse here for close or long observation of a change. What happened was immediate. Surely, in keeping with the remainder of the Lucan record, glossolalia is here most assuredly implied.

Although there is no mention of Paul's having spoken in tongues during the visit of Ananias in Damascus, he without a doubt did speak in tongues. This may seem to be a rather bold and unwarranted assumption, but in the light of Paul's own words, it is not. The apostle, writing to the Corinthian church, said, "I thank my God, I speak with tongues more than ye all."[37] This would surely lead us to believe that his experience with the glossolalia phenomenon was equal to that of any other Christian of his day. How could he have spoken in tongues more than they all, if others had experienced glossolalia on being filled and he had not? Paul's assertion astonished a great and noble Greek scholar.[38] The record remains the same, however, and can surely serve to guide us today.

From the history of Acts we can readily see that glossolalia served as a sign or witness that the Spirit had come in His fullness. Having obtained this witness, the recipient received power to tell forth the message of salvation. Added to this fact is also the effect the phenomenon had on the observer. Glossolalia certainly had a part to play in the winning of the three thousand on the Day of Pentecost. It was also enough to

---

[36] Acts 8:14-19.

[37] 1 Corinthians 14:18.

[38] A. T. Robertson, *Word Pictures in the New Testament* (Nashville: Broadman Press, 1931), IV, p. 183.

attest to Peter and his friends that the Gentiles were to be numbered among the redeemed. They needed evidence in apostolic times, and the Holy Spirit gave them just that. Without this, the struggling little band, who were strangers to all, could never have been able to start His Church on its glorious march.

The Church Today. The question will now arise concerning glossolalia for today. All that has been thus stated could well have been true for another day, but many will say that such an experience is not for us now; it is not even needed. One minister who seems to have changed his views concerning the significance of the Pentecostal experience writes about Pentecost and uses the name in his title, yet says that there will never be another Pentecost and it is wrong to pray for the Pentecostal experience.[39] Thank God that not all agree with him. Permit us to quote another who writes on Pentecost; "Pentecost is the answer. Pentecost is the Something Better. Pentecost is the need of the church today. 'Ours is a Christianity without force, passion, or effort,' cried a modern prophet, 'a suburban piety, domestic and kindly, but unfit to cope with the actual moral case of the world. We cannot deal to any purpose with the deep damnation of the race. Our word is but a lovely song; the people hear, but do not fear; they are enchanted but unchanged.' "[40] Many years ago William Burns, the Scottish firebrand, said, "the work of God would flourish by us if it flourished more richly in us."

The Church has never been so in need of all His power. Surely our God, who is Love, would never withhold from us that which has never been needed as now. Many speak of a changeless Christ in a changing world. With this we heartily agree: He has not changed; and, because of this, cannot we have the same blessing that was needed and enjoyed by those in other days?

[39] Ockenga, Harold J., *Power Through Pentecost* (Grand Rapids: Wm. B. Eerdmans Publishing Company, 1959), p. 26.
[40] Brice, *op. cit.*, p. 22.

III. GLOSSOLALIA AS AN AID IN WORSHIPING

Not only does speaking in tongues convince the believer, and others as well, that the Holy Ghost has come in His fullness to witness; the phenomenon also benefits the individual greatly in the matter and manner of worship. Those who were filled with the Holy Ghost on the Day of Pentecost "knew that God was near to protect, to guide, to lead to triumph."[41] He who had come upon them and so possessed them had come according to promise and prophecy.[42] The blessing was not for them alone, but for all whom the Lord should call in the ages to come.[43] The fact that they spoke in tongues left no room for doubt. The worship of one so near and real was not to be a task, nor was it to be a ritual. They would be happy in rendering praise and prayer to One who had been willing to dwell in them. How happy should we be to realize that glossolalia "was of importance not only for them, but for the church at large in all future times. . . ."[44]

We live today in an age of stopwatches and split seconds. This is a time characterized by cacophony and chaos. Doubts and fears assail and we need not only a "reason of the hope"[45] that is within us, but also some inward feeling that He is there. Writing on 1 Corinthians 14 in 1838, Albert Barnes said, "nothing is of more importance in the church than the doctrine respecting the influences and endowments of the Holy Spirit."[46] This great scholar felt a need for glossolalia in his quiet and orderly days. Perhaps this will explain the fact that there is an even greater need for the endowment in this troubled time. Kelsey, a contemporary writer says, "Another significant aspect of glossolalia is its emotional value to the speaker; the fact that it is accompanied in nearly all cases by

---

[41] Barton, op. cit., p. 14.
[42] Joel 2:28; John 14:16-18.
[43] Acts 2:38, 39.
[44] Barnes, op. cit., p. 242.
[45] 1 Peter 3:15.
[46] Barnes, op. cit., p. 243.

a sense of joy and a deep religious emotion."[47] The carnal man does not have an innate propensity that makes divine worship a joyous and vibrant experience. This comes only to those who have experienced Him in His fullness. It is a part of the redemptive plan to give to His own the Paraclete. He comes to go along with us and in us. The witness of His presence can only bring joy, a joy not dependent on outward circumstances, but on an inward condition.

Paul most certainly recognized the value of tongues in the private and public worship of the believing individual. That is why he wrote so explicitly in 1 Corinthians 12, 13, and 14. At times we want to praise the Lord. This desire can come in public worship or private devotions. At other times we want to pray during moments of trial and uncertainty; we really do not know what to do nor how to pray. In each of these situations, the Spirit's presence can help us.

PRAISE IN WORSHIP

On the Day of Pentecost there was "succession of ecstatic ejaculations from souls overflowing with praise and adoration to God for all His wonderful works and especial personal blessings."[48] The glossolalia mentioned in Acts 2:4 has been compared to the "merry, unmeaning shouts of boyhood, getting rid of exuberant life, uttering in sounds of joy for which manhood has no words."[49] They were expressing an inward emotion without intellectualizing. The person praising God in other tongues is literally at a loss for words to express his feelings and happily finds the Holy Ghost making up for this deficiency. Many have been heard to say that they could not find words to express themselves. They knew they felt or saw something marvelous, but lacked the ability or words for adequate expression. If this be true in explaining natural phe-

---

[47] Kelsey, *op. cit.,* p. 2.
[48] Hayes, *op. cit.,* p. 35.
[49] Marcus Dods, *The First Epistle to the Corinthians* (London: Hodder and Stoughton, 1900), p. 316.

nomena, then it should be even more so in the realm of the Spirit. As mere mortals we are of the flesh, and most of the time live in a natural realm. We know the things of man because we are motivated by sensate desires. The only way to know the things of God is by the Spirit of God. When we become so overwhelmed by a sense of praise to Him that words fail us and the Spirit speaks ecstatically through us, then we have reached a new and fuller dimension of praise.

Some may feel that they do not need this help in praising the Lord and may have harsh and bitter things to say about those who believe in and enjoy His help in utterances of praise. By doing this they not only fail to recognize a scriptural truth, but also tend to regard the fleshly man as being fully capable of giving to Him the highest or ultimate praise. The ministry of the Holy Ghost is primarily that of making known and glorifying the Father through the Son. This work is done by the Holy Ghost through and with us. We cannot render perfect or unadulterated praise without His help. The Holy Spirit literally clothes Himself with us and in so doing uses us as an instrument fully tuned for perfect praise.

> There are three passages in the Old Testament—Judges 6:34, 1 Chronicles 12:18, and 2 Chronicles 24:20—which on a surface reading would seem to indicate that the dedicated men mentioned, Gideon, Amasai and Zechariah, were, as illustrated by the familiar story of Elijah casting his mantle upon Elisha, clothed or mantled by the Holy Spirit, but the R.V. and others make it clear that the converse idea is more correct, namely that the Holy Spirit clothed Himself with Gideon, Amasai and Zechariah. Because some garments are so closely identified with the wearers, following the shapes and contours of the bodies, these are called "habits." These three men became not only temples of the Spirit wherein His sacred presence dwelt, but habits of the Spirit who inhabited them, "habitations of God through the Spirit" (Ephesians 2:22). Their life became the life of the Spirit; the Spirit thought through their minds, felt through their hearts, looked through their eyes, spoke through their lips, and wrought through their hands. It is the Holy Spirit's prerogative to glorify Christ,

and this He does when He clothes Himself with our humanity and honors Christ in every circumstance of life.[50]

The Holy Spirit used in Old Testament times certain rare individuals to show in miniature what He would do on a grand and universal sense in the future. When Luke wrote his Gospel, he spoke "of all that Jesus began both to do and teach."[51] In Acts he tells us that the work of our Lord is to be carried on to a glorious finish by His Church which should be composed of Spirit-filled believers. Jesus said that the Holy Ghost, once He had come, would glorify the Son.[52] How can we better render praise to His honor and glory than by utterly giving ourselves to the Spirit in ecstatic praise. How feeble do we feel when we use our poor thoughts and inadequate words. Yet, how wondrous it is when He takes over and with our breath and our lips articulates with such force and fervor that we, even though suppliant vessels, can enjoy and appreciate the rapture of it all. The person speaking in tongues the praises of God does not have to know exactly what he is saying. He is saying what should be said, but doing so by the inspiration of the Spirit. Glossolalia, according to Hayes, "is an energizing by the Spirit and is independent of the intellect of man."[53] We are to praise Him at all times and not always wait for the whelming of the Spirit. The Spirit takes over when our words seem inadequate. Paul had this in mind when he wrote to the Corinthians, "I will pray with the Spirit, and I will pray with the understanding also."[54]

The human mind, especially if it is critically and rationally oriented, cannot seem to fully grasp nor comprehend the greatness and goodness of God. We cannot, without faith, know the real meaning and impact of divine love and redemption. The

---

[50] J. A. Wright, "The Holy Spirit's Work in the Believer," *The Elim Evangel,* XLVI, No. 34 (August 21, 1965), pp. 531, 532.
[51] Acts 1:1.
[52] John 16:13, 14.
[53] D. A. Hayes, *The Gift of Tongues* (Cincinnati: Jennings and Graham, 1913), p. 14.
[54] 1 Corinthians 14:15.

human limitations of man act to moor him to his mundane and sensate environment. That is why he needs help from on high if he is to worship "in Spirit and in truth" (John 4:23). The apostles knew more about our Lord than any who have lived before or since, but they could not adequately worship Him until the Holy Ghost came in His fullness on the Day of Pentecost. They had seen Him turn water into wine and bring forth from death His friend Lazarus; they had listened to Him as He delivered His Sermon on the Mount; yet, they were told to tarry for the enduement of power. They had knowledge, but it was knowledge that could be better transmitted and accepted if done so under the aegis of the Spirit. One writer in explaining the event at Pentecost said that once the Holy Ghost had descended upon the apostles, He would "become their inner master, instructing them from within."[55] From this we may learn that the quickening of the Spirit transcends the human intelligence and permits worship and praise that is not adulterated by human limitations.

What the apostles saw and heard about Jesus mystified them. What we ordinarily see, hear, and read concerning Him may be a mystery also since much of it is beyond the realm of the commonplace and human experience. The gift of tongues, however,

> is the sign that all which hath hitherto come to pass, the entire mystery of the Incarnation and Atonement, is now no more understood "in the letter" but "in the Spirit." . . . His ascension into heaven is His "withdrawal" from the circumference of things, from the external world, to the centre—to be the inmost reality of all.[56]

What was once a mystery and beyond the realm of human understanding now is made clear by the indwelt Spirit. The coming of the Holy Ghost has endowed us with a new *elan vital* that enables us to praise and worship as we should.

---

[55] Dom Emmanuel Flicoteaux, *The Splendor of Pentecost*, trans. Mary L. Helmir (Baltimore: Helican Press, 1961), p. 11.

[56] Alan W. Watts, *Myth and Ritual in Christianity* (New York: The Vanguard Press, 1953), p. 189.

PRAYER IN WORSHIP

Another aspect of worship is prayer. By the concept of prayer, we do not mean the mere recitation of phrases, often composed by others. Prayer, to really become operational and experiential and beneficial, is nothing more or less than spiritual communion with God. Prayer brings us into a personal and vital relationship to God. Daily we are related to Him in the natural realm, but too seldom do we have this spiritual confrontation. The same limitations that hinder us from perfect praise also keep us from effective and inspirational prayer. The disciples did not know how to pray. That is why they asked Jesus to teach them to pray.[57] Paul, in his letter to the Romans, said, "for we know not what we should pray for as we ought."[58] In this statement the apostle not only reaffirms our lack of ability in knowing how to pray, but also tells us that we also know not for which things we should pray. This would be a very distressing plight were it not for the fact that the apostle hastens to let all men know that the Spirit will aid us in meeting this deficiency. We may not know what we need, nor even realize that there is a need, but "he that searcheth the hearts knoweth what is the mind of the Spirit, because he maketh intercession for the saints according to the will of God."[59]

We believe that Paul wrote under divine inspiration; we also believe that his words are for us. So all should rejoice in the fact that our lack of ability is more than compensated for by the inward and knowledgeable ministry of the Spirit. The sounds made by the burdened soul may not make sense to the hearer, and often are not heard by anyone save our heavenly Father, but they do attest to the fact of His presence and give comfort to us then and in days to come.

The person who prays ecstatically during his private de-

[57] Luke 11:1.
[58] Romans 8:26.
[59] Romans 8:27.

votional life finds much comfort and consolation and finds little or no criticism for his out-of-the-ordinary manifestations. He who prays in this manner in a public worship service, however, should not only use wisdom but should also realize that he can and will be misunderstood by some who will not want to believe. The glossolalia at Pentecost was to some the babblings of drunken people. To others it was the witness of His indwelling. The same condition prevailed during the apostolic period and exists even until this moment. It was for this reason that Paul wrote to the Corinthian church and to us as well. Pentecost had created a new religious experience and "a new language of its own, one of more immediate speech with God in ecstatic prayer (1 Corinthians 12:2, 14)."[60] This new experience was of a spectacular nature. God would have it be so; however, it was given to man to help him and to glorify God. We need to realize that the Holy Ghost is ever present to help us pray even now.

IV. AID TO REGULATION AND ORDER IN WORSHIP

Not only does the charismatic element enter into the areas of praise and prayer in worship, it is also seen as a governmental or regulatory enduement for Christian worshipers. In 1 Corinthians 12, Paul carefully outlines the ministry of the Spirit as to diversity, distribution, and value. Two of the nine gifts have to do with glossolalia: "divers kinds of tongues" and "the interpretation of tongues."[61] It was through the distribution and activation of these gifts that the Holy Spirit empowered the church. Without these supernatural endowments, the apostolic group would have found it virtually impossible to spread the gospel and to worship Him "in Spirit and in truth." The gifts of the Spirit were placed in individuals in the church

[60] James Vernon Bartlet, Ten Epochs of Church History: The Apostolic Age, Its Life, Doctrine, Worship and Polity (New York: Charles Scribner's Sons, 1899), p. 12, in footnote.
[61] 1 Corinthians 12:10.

for the profit of all. All men did not have the same gift or ministry; there was, however, a blessing to be shared in the operation of the gifts. It was with this thought in mind that Paul wrote concerning the gifts. He did not write to condemn; he wrote to offer instruction and to present a note of warning.

Glossolalia was an aid to government in apostolic times. Luke in giving to us the account of the happenings at Antioch, prior to Paul's being set forth, recognizes the authority of the indwelling and ever-present Holy Ghost. He plainly tells us that ". . . the Holy Ghost said, Separate me Barnabas and Saul for the work whereunto I have called them."[62] Here again we must believe the record. The Holy Ghost said what He had to say through the lips of some individual who was in touch with God and able to convey to the Antioch Christians the divine command. There is reason to believe that glossolalia was the method used by the Spirit in making known His will to those present. The name of the person or persons giving the message is not important. What is vital is the fact that "the Holy Ghost said." He is recognized as a Person present and concerned.

The Holy Ghost is presently willing and able to work in the church today. Just as we are unable to reach the ultimate in prayer and praise without His help, so it is that we cannot always know His mind for the church without His intervention. By this we do not mean that there should be some manifestation of the glossolalia phenomenon before any judgments are made. This is a very extreme and unscriptural view. There are times, and they occur rather often, when the Holy Spirit wants to speak not only to the individual but to the church as well. This He can and will do if He is Lord of the occasion. The Scriptures tell us that where "the Spirit is Lord there is liberty."[63]

The fourteenth chapter of 1 Corinthians was written to

---

[62] Acts 13:2.
[63] 2 Corinthians 3:17. (Trans. from original Greek.)

thoroughly explain the operation and regulation of glossolalia in the church. Since it does not come within the purview of this study to make a thorough exegetical study of this portion, we will only state those scriptures which relate to tongues as being beneficial. As a matter of fact, the purpose of this study is to show that glossolalia is beneficial to the individual—both believers and non-believers.

There seems to have been quite a bit of confusion as to who is to derive benefit from tongues. Some say it is a sign to the believer and not to the unbeliever. Others say emphatically that it is a sign to the unbeliever and not to the believer. There is some scriptural warrant for both assertions. The difficulty arises in the matter of interpretation and exegesis. Paul in 1 Corinthians 14:4 clearly states, "He that speaketh in an unknown tongue edifieth himself." This is clear evidence that tongues are beneficial and testify of His indwelling to the individual, if not to anyone else. Here Paul is referring to the edification of the Christian. In verse 22 of the same chapter, the apostle says, ". . . tongues are for a sign, not to them that believe, but to them that believe not." This verse deals with glossolalia as an outward sign that affects the hearer. In both scriptures, tongues are the subject; however, in the first instance Paul speaks of the personal edification of the one speaking ecstatically, while in the second place he deals with glossolalia as a sign to the unbeliever who hears but fails to understand. The only way to fully resolve the matter is to accept the evident truth that tongues can benefit both the speaker and the hearer if the phenomenon is properly and scripturally practiced. It was for this purpose that Paul so painstakingly wrote in full detail the will of God concerning glossolalia in public worship.

Hayes, who wrote rather objectively concerning glossolalia, shares with us the idea that there are spiritual benefits derived therefrom. In defining the tongues phenomenon he says:

It was an individual experience and a method of personal worship and adoration. It was a spiritual rhapsody of vocal expression in terms unintelligible to both speaker and hearer, and in it the mind of the subject was inactive and the conscience of the spectator and audience was unmoved. An unbeliever might be struck with the strangeness of the phenomenon, and he might conceive it to be an evidence of a divine possession; and in that sense it might be a sign to him and lead him to conversion.[64]

This writer feels that glossolalia, even if it be an uninterpreted outburst of ecstatic praise, would not only edify the speaker but might possibly convict the earnest spectator. This has been known to have happened on numerous occasions. There are times when the ecstatic utterance has meaning for all and accomplishes its purpose only if it be interpreted. It is for this reason that the Holy Ghost has endowed some with the gift of interpretation. It is also why Paul said, "let one interpret." An interpretation is not always a translation or a rendering from one language to another in equivalent words or grammatical terms. An interpretation is a declaration of the meaning and may be very differently stated from the precise form of the original. The Greek word for interpret does not mean to translate, but "to explain thoroughly."

A careful study of 1 Corinthians 14 will shed much light on glossolalia. Paul, in writing this chapter, wanted it to be understood that he was not against glossolalia *per se.* Had he shared the opinion of many he would not have gone so far as to say, "I thank my God, I speak with tongues more than ye all."[65] Nor would he have closed this vital section with the admonition to "forbid not to speak with tongues."[66] We must not forget, however, that he was very careful and deliberate in letting it be known that the gift of tongues can be of limited value to the assembled group unless there be an interpreter. That explains his words in verse 19 and the value he rightly placed on prophesying. Prophesying is really equal to tongues

---

[64] Hayes, *op. cit.,* p. 15.
[65] 1 Corinthians 14:18.
[66] 1 Corinthians 14:39.

and interpretation, although it might not appear to be as miraculous. In tongues and interpretation there are two miraculous acts; in prophesying there is only one.

The benefits derived from glossolalia and the use of the gift in the church are set forth in the fourteenth chapter of First Corinthians. This chapter attests to the truth that the glossolalia phenomenon can and does benefit the individual. Tongues and the interpretation of tongues are gifts placed in the church by the will of God and through the Spirit. This enduement is a vital part of the charismata, and as it blesses the individual, quite naturally it will have a salutary effect upon the church since the church is composed of individuals. As healthy cells make healthy body tissue and produce robust bodies, so do edified and spiritual members make a strong church that can accomplish the work for which it was purchased and commissioned.

Before concluding this study concerning the operation of glossolalia phenomenon in the church, it might be well for us to appraise the condition of His church today. Many books have been written concerning the ministry of the Spirit and Pentecost. Nearly all are in accord in asserting that we need apostolic and Pentecostal power. At the same time, however, very few seem to realize that Pentecostal and apostolic power calls for dedication and consecration and that it may produce manifestations that would prove distasteful to many. More than thirty-five years ago E. Stanley Jones, said, "Had the Christian church followed out the intimations and implications of what took place at Pentecost, we would have been saved from the narrow contentious centuries and from the graveclothes that still bind religion today."[67] The church cannot move forward, in a spiritual sense, without the driving force that came upon the 120 at Pentecost. How true is the statement, made by Jones at the end of his book concerning the

---

[67] E. Stanley Jones, *The Christ of Every Road* (New York: The Abingdon Press, 1930), p. 97.

church and Pentecost: "We cannot go further until we go deeper."[68]

"Spiritual gifts, being essential, are perpetual."[69] They were essential to the life and progress of the primitive church; likewise, they are vital to us today. Not only is the Holy Spirit for us; we are for the Holy Spirit. All that He ever had is ours; all that we have is His. There is a constant need today for reiterating the exhortation of Paul to the Corinthians: "forasmuch as ye are zealous of spiritual gifts, seek that ye may excel to the edifying of the church."[70] We can, even in this twentieth century, have the apostolic blessing if we follow the apostolic pattern. Ockenga, nearly twenty-nine years ago, said:

> The goal of any congregation ought to be approximation to the apostolic church. We should try to repeat the form and content of the apostolic church. The argument of expediency has not only developed unscriptural forms of the church, but it has also explained away the Spirit's gift to the church, so that the church in this day is greatly impoverished by the lack of the ministry of the Holy Ghost.[71]

The individual and the church will find it rather difficult and many times impossible to really enjoy the full blessings of Calvary without recognizing the fact that He told those who had been to Calvary to tarry until Pentecost. At Calvary they were changed; at Pentecost they were energized. We must never forget that Calvary was the mountain peak of His redemptive plan. We must also remember that to glorify and exalt Christ there is a great need for His presence and fullness.

Speaking of what happened at Pentecost, Flicoteaux said:

> The Holy Ghost is as Dom Vonier calls Him the "glorifier of Christ." The glory of Our Lord here below, therefore, is much more than a memory preserved by believers of all that He is and of all that He has done; His glory is a

---

[68] *Ibid.,* p. 271.
[69] James M. Campbell, *After Pentecost What?* (New York: Fleming H. Revell Company, 1897), pp. 141, 142.
[70] 1 Corinthians 14:12.
[71] Harold J. Ockenga, *The Spirit of the Living God* (New York: Fleming H. Revell, 1947), p. 173.

Divine Person. Thus there is no ground to fear that the glory of the Saviour may ever suffer the slightest diminution in this world.[72]

V. CONCLUSION

The glossolalia phenomenon has been much maligned and often misunderstood. This is quite natural inasmuch as God's ways are higher than our ways; what may appear foolish and weak to man is in reality the wisdom of God. Paul, in writing to the worldly-wise Corinthians said, ". . . God hath chosen the foolish things of the world to confound the wise: and God hath chosen the weak things of the world to confound the things which are mighty: and base things of the world, and things which are despised, hath God chosen, yea, and things which are not, to bring to nought things that are: that no flesh should glory in his presence."[73]

Man, fallen man, is a very proud and self-centered individual. He glories in his ability to express his desires and impress upon others his independence and his self-achieved accomplishments. All of this disappears when one is utterly and completely dominated by the Holy Ghost. Speaking in tongues may seem foolish to many, but it is strong and valid evidence of complete self-abnegation. That is why the doctrine is given such a prominent place in the New Testament. God must be glorified and the church edified. This has happened and will happen in spite of unbelief on the part of many. The Holy Ghost will continue to speak through us as we yield ourselves to Him day by day.

He is ever present and willing to aid us in witness and worship. When we are able to believe His promise and yield all to Him, He will come to dwell within us as He did those in former times. Everyone should be very grateful for this latter rain. If the "former rain" was vital in founding the Early

---

[72] Flicoteaux, op. cit., p. 47.
[73] 1 Corinthians 1:27-29.

Church, then a continuous outpouring is also needed to perpetuate the work so marvelously begun. The same life-giving breath that animated us as infants still remains with us; it has not diminished at all. The life of the Christian is one of victory, for himself and others, only if he is possessed by the Spirit. We know we are possessed by the Holy Ghost when He speaks through our prayers and praises to our heavenly Father. In this way, too, He reveals to a wasted world that He lives in us.

Glossolalia in Perspective

Lewis J. Willis

Lewis J. Willis is Editor in Chief of Church of God Publications and Editor of the Evangel, *the world's oldest Pentecostal weekly. Because of his excellent work as editor, the* Evangel *earned the 1964 "Denominational Periodical of the Year" award which is given each year by the Evangelical Press Association. For ten years he was Director of Sunday School Literature and Editor of the* Lighted Pathway. *Prior to his entrance into the editorial field he was State Youth Director of Florida, and later, National Youth Director, and a member of the National Sunday School and Youth Board. His ministry has taken him into forty countries. An alumnus of Lee College, he has served on the General Education Board and as Chairman of the Lee College Board of Directors.*

Lewis J. Willis

Glossolalia in Perspective

I. THE PHENOMENON OCCURS

In an upper room in Jerusalem one hundred twenty persons prayed fervently and expectantly.[1] These souls were assembled in response to the precise command of Christ who had said, "behold, I send the promise of my Father upon you: but tarry ye in the city of Jerusalem, until ye be endued with power from on high" (Luke 24:49). For some ten days they "were continually in the temple, praising and blessing God" (Luke 24:53). Through this communion they had achieved a unity of spirit and purpose which always characterizes true believers.[2] Suddenly, mysteriously, and very majestically the mighty effusion of the Holy Ghost engulfed them.

In assessing the drama of the moment in his book *Our Pentecostal Heritage*, Frank W. Lemons observed:

It was an event of history with a lofty, far-reaching purpose. That purpose was the execution of the Great Commission. It was forever to be the norm of the Christian faith. In spite of the fact of the finished work of redemption, the cross, the

[1] Acts 1:14, 15.
[2] Acts 2:1.

247

resurrection, the forty days the resurrected Lord was with His followers, and the grand ascension witnessed by them, Jesus commanded them to suspend all operations—even to postpone their world missions enterprise—until that day, long planned and set aside in the inter-theistic councils of the triune God for the descent of the Holy Ghost. The day, of course, was the Day of Pentecost.[3]

Thus, the dynamic history of Christendom converged upon this group of humble folk. In that blessed moment the prophecies and expectations of many hundreds of years burst forth to momentous fulfillment. The words of Scripture are more profoundly descriptive than any others to be fashioned:

And when the day of Pentecost was fully come, they were all with one accord in one place. And suddenly there came a sound from heaven as of a rushing mighty wind, and it filled all the house where they were sitting. And there appeared unto them cloven tongues like as of fire, and it sat upon each of them. And they were *all filled* with the Holy Ghost, *and began to speak with other tongues,* as the Spirit gave them utterance (Acts 2:1-4).[4]

G. Campbell Morgan described the scene as follows: "Jerusalem saw and heard a company of about one hundred and twenty men and women all 'speaking'—probably all singing, or chanting—'the mighty works of God.' . . . In many tongues and dialects, with perfect distinctness, this chanting, this ecstatic utterance of the newly baptized company of disciples, broke upon the astonished and listening ear of that assembled multitude."[5]

Present in Jerusalem on that memorable day were Jews, "*devout* men, out of every nation under heaven" (Acts 2:5; italics ours). When this unusual worship, with its strange litany was "noised abroad," these men crowded about the worshipers to witness the phenomenon. What they beheld

---

[3] Frank W. Lemons, *Our Pentecostal Heritage* (Cleveland, Tenn.: Pathway Press, 1963), p. 17.

[4] Italics ours.

[5] G. Campbell Morgan, *The Acts of the Apostles* (Westwood, N.J.: Fleming H. Revell Co., 1926), p. 37.

astounded them, for in relation to their own religious experience it was sufficiently different to be arresting, and bewildering, or even provoking.

Their reactions traversed a wide gamut of emotions. Some were "confounded."[6] Others were "amazed,"[7] while yet others "marvelled."[8] Even as those "devout men"[9] sought to accommodate this uncommon religious exercise, they began to be "in doubt, saying one to another, What meaneth this?" (Acts 2:12). Others, with even less spiritual perception, "mocking said, These men are full of new wine" (Acts 2:13).

Thus, from the first moments of the Pentecostal effusion, the marvelous exercise of the Holy Ghost with the concomitant phenomenon of speaking in tongues has stimulated wonder, bewilderment, and criticism. Subsequently, at every point in history when glossolalia has been manifested within the Church, there has arisen simultaneously a tempest of debate usually culminating in cautious interest, careful censure, or caustic derogation. It is not astounding, therefore, that considerable concern about or sharp exception to the current Pentecostal revival is presently taking place.

There are many good and noble persons who honestly inquire concerning the glossolalia phenomenon. Too often, however, the critics of glossolalia evidence a distressing lack of understanding concerning the basic exegesis of the mainline Pentecostals. Splendidly trained and highly respected persons ofttimes speculate and hypothesize to a weird and fantastic proportion. Frequently the speculations range from matters of part truth to proliferations which are ridiculous and perhaps insulting. It is regrettable that those who are so militant in protecting the Christian faith against Pentecostals do not spend sufficient time discovering precisely what the traditional Pentecostals believe and teach.

---

6 Acts 2:6.
7 Acts 2:7.
8 *Ibid.*
9 Acts 2:5.

II. THE PERSPECTIVE ENUNCIATED

The purpose of this discussion is to draw into proper focus those objections usually made against speaking in tongues. It is believed that as these protestations are measured against the traditional Pentecostal concepts, which in turn are applied to the scriptural accounts of glossolalia, a much improved understanding will be achieved. Inasmuch as tongues speaking is only one, although a distinctive, tenet of the Pentecostals' view of the doctrine of the Holy Spirit, a brief statement of dogma should properly be made so that the inquiry might assume a correct perspective.

Pentecostals subscribe to the traditional doctrine of the Trinity which affirms that three Persons exist in one Godhead and that they are coequal in substance, power, and eternity. It is held that all three agree and are totally involved in the eternal salvation of man. God the Father so loved the world that He gave His only Son for man's redemption. God the Son willingly and freely offered Himself for man's redemption. God the Holy Spirit exerts the redemptive process to the souls of believers. All are intent upon the deliverance of sinners.

In their notable work *Introduction to Christian Theology*, Drs. H. Orton Wiley and Paul T. Culbertson give an encompassing statement relative to the posture and work of the Holy Spirit which parallels the Pentecostal position splendidly. They observe:

> While the full dispensation of the Holy Spirit does not begin until Pentecost, the Spirit himself as the third Person of the Trinity was from the beginning operative in both creation and providence. It was the Spirit who brooded over the waters and brought order and beauty out of chaos (Gen. 1:2); and it was the Spirit who breathed into the face of man and made him a living soul (Gen. 2:7; Job 33:4). He has been the Agent in the production of all life, and is therefore, by prophetic anticipation, the Lord and Giver of life.
>
> .　　.　　.　　.　　.　　.　　.　　.　　.　　.
>
> Pentecost marks a new dispensation of grace—that of the

Holy Spirit. This new economy is not to be understood as superseding the work of Christ but as ministering to, and completing it. Jesus indicated that *all things that the Father hath are mine: therefore said I, that he shall take of mine and shall shew it unto you* (John 16:15). As the Son revealed the Father, so the Spirit reveals the Son and glorifies Him.

.   .   .   .

Pentecost was the inauguration day of the Holy Spirit, and the pentecostal Gift was the gift of a Person—the Paraclete or Comforter. This Gift Jesus promised to His disciples as the Agent through whom He would continue His office and work in a new and effective manner.[10]

From eternity,[11] therefore, the Holy Trinity has purposed, planned, and provided for the salvation of man. God the Father freely gave His only Son.[12] God the Son freely gave Himself as the one perfect sacrifice for sin.[13] God the Holy Spirit faithfully applies the atoning work of Christ to believing souls.[14] Thus, Pentecostals believe that the work of the Holy Trinity and that of the Church of the Living God is specifically to rescue lost souls through the agency of the Holy Ghost.

The Holy Spirit is essential in the whole process by which man is brought to Christ, established in the Christian faith, and prepared as a faithful witness of the Christ whom he has made Lord of his life. First, the Holy Ghost convicts and convinces man of his sin.[15] Second, the Holy Ghost is the agent in the regeneration of the soul unto a restored position with Christ.[16] Third, concomitant with regeneration is the baptism into the body of Christ by the Holy Spirit.[17] Fourth, attending the baptism into the body of Christ is the

---

[10] H. Orton Wiley and Paul T. Culbertson, *Introduction to Christian Theology* (Kansas City: Beacon Hill Press, 1964), pp. 246, 249, 250.
[11] 1 Peter 1:20; Revelation 13:8.
[12] John 3:16; Romans 8:32.
[13] Hebrews 9:14; 1 Peter 1:19.
[14] Romans 5:5; 1 Corinthians 12:3; Galatians 4:6.
[15] John 16:8-11.
[16] Ephesians 2:1; Titus 3:5.
[17] 1 Corinthians 12:13; Galatians 3:27.

fruit of the Spirit.[18] Fifth, in addition to His work in regeneration, the Holy Spirit is also involved in the process of the sanctification of the believer unto complete dedication.[19]

At this point the believer has been convicted of sin, brought to repentance and confession, regenerated and restored, cleansed and fully dedicated. He is abiding in Christ and is faithfully bearing the fruit of the Spirit. Now, the believer should expect to receive the gift of the Holy Ghost[20] even as Christ explained, "ye know him; for he *dwelleth with you,* and shall *be in you"* (John 14:17; italics ours).

The urgent need for believers to receive the Holy Ghost is specifically stated by Christ and is utterly believed by Pentecostals. The Lord said, "But ye shall receive power, after that the Holy Ghost is come upon you: and ye shall be witnesses unto me both in Jerusalem, and in all Judaea, and in Samaria, and unto the uttermost part of the earth" (Acts 1:8). The Baptism with the Holy Ghost does not make one more holy, but it does bring the believer to a place of spiritual readiness and power so that he is an effective witness to the saving graces of the Lord Jesus Christ.

In accordance with the Scriptures, Pentecostals believe that those who are baptized in the Holy Spirit speak with other tongues.[21] Again, in keeping with the scriptural record, Pentecostals believe that the speaking with tongues is the initial, empirical evidence of the Baptism in the Holy Ghost. They do not believe that speaking in tongues is the only evidence, nor do they hold that in and of itself speaking in tongues constitutes the "fulness of the Spirit." They simply believe that glossolalia is the first overt and audible evidence that one has been baptized in the Holy Spirit. Those who are really baptized of the Spirit will soon be engaged in the collaborating evidence—that of witnessing for Christ.[22]

[18] John 15:5; Romans 5:5; Galatians 5:22-24.
[19] 2 Thessalonians 2:13; 1 Peter 1:2.
[20] Acts 2:38; 10:45.
[21] Acts 2:4; 10:46; 19:6.
[22] Acts 1:8; 8:4.

III. THE PROTESTS EVALUATED

Over against this brief statement of the traditional Pentecostal position, let us apply those objections which are most often offered to glossolalia. There are many such complaints, and we will consider each of them carefully, though of necessity briefly, in relation to the Scriptures, history, and human experience. For purposes of facility and clarity these protests are divided under the following categories: (1) The Phenomenon Is Based Upon an Improper Exegesis. (2) The Phenomenon Was Strongly Criticized by Paul. (3) The Phenomenon Is a Fallacy of the Emotions and Divisive in Nature.

CATEGORY I: THE PHENOMENON IS BASED UPON
AN IMPROPER EXEGESIS

This assertion, of course, is completely arbitrary and probably indicates some prejudice on the part of the protester. There are many areas of dispute within Christian dogma, but a spirit of cordial investigation should pervade the theological community. Let us expect, therefore, that a charitable attitude will prevail as we examine the following dissents.

Glossolalia as Witnessed Today Is Mistakenly Equated With the Tongues at Pentecost

Those who make this assertion imply that they doubt the authenticity of twentieth-century glossolalia. Either these persons feel that a valid experience of tongues speaking has not continued since Pentecost or else they assume that the phenomenon as experienced among contemporary Pentecostals is not genuine. Kelsey, an Episcopal clergyman, succinctly appraised the dilemma with the observation that "there are two basically different points of view about the dangers inherent in the direct experience of God and speaking in tongues. On one side is the view of Aristotle, Aquinas, and most of Western Christianity to the present, which theoretically denies its reality and value. On the other side is the attitude of Plato, the New Testament, the fathers, and Eastern Orthodoxy, and in our time of the Pentecostals, that such experience is extremely important if man is to know God."[23] Let us examine the issues.

There Has Not Been a Valid Continuation of Glossolalia Since Pentecost

This allegation is in sharp contradiction with the established records. There is rather conclusive scriptural proof that the Pentecostal effusion reached throughout the apostolic church and that "speaking in tongues" accompanied the Baptism of the Holy Spirit. Dr. Ira Jay Martin III, whose views are not always compatible with the traditional Pentecostal position, nevertheless, has given us an insight that is pertinent at this point. He wrote:

> Our attention is now drawn to the place and significance of tongue-speaking in the Apostolic Church. It goes practically without saying that glossolalia did appear in the early Christian fellowship. The scriptural records point out quite clearly the gradual spread of the phenomenon throughout the Empire. Appearing for the first time in Christian circles in Jerusalem at the time of Pentecost (Acts 2:1-42), it manifested itself in Caesarea (10:44-48, 11:15-17), Ephesus (Acts 19:1-7, Cf. Ephesians 5:18-20), Corinth (1 Cor. 12-14), and possibly Rome (Cf. Mark 16:17) or wherever the Longer Ending of Mark's Gospel was written. Other scriptural references give intimations of its presence in Samaria (Acts 8:14-17), Thessalonica (Cf. 1 Thess. 5:19, 20) and Colossae (Cf. Col. 3:16). To plot these particular cities and towns on a map of the first century world is to realize how widespread glossolalia was in the Apostolic Church.[24]

Thus, we see that the glossolalia phenomenon seemed to have reached the full scope of the Early Church and to

---

[23] From *Tongue Speaking*, by Morton T. Kelsey. Copyright © 1964 by Morton T. Kelsey. Reprinted by permission, pp. 228, 229.

[24] Ira Jay Martin III, *Glossolalia in the Apostolic Church* (Berea, Ky.: Berea College, 1960), p. 63.

have encompassed many if not most believers. Contrary to the view of some who maintain that only the apostles and a few other select believers received the Holy Ghost baptism, there is ample scriptural evidence that speaking in tongues was exceedingly widespread and seemed to be the vogue among early believers.

Morton T. Kelsey, among the contemporary writers, has contributed measurably to the dialogue between the tradition church and mainline Pentecostals. Let us look to his writing as he traces the pattern of glossolalia from apostolic days until the present.

> If the practice had been confined to Biblical times and had not occurred again, it would be far easier to dismiss the matter there. If, however, glossolalia continued among those who established the foundations of the church, amid the most adverse circumstances, it deserves our careful attention. . . . Many of the writings of those who sought to explain Christianity to a hostile world have come down to us. These authors, the church fathers as they are called, are little known to readers today, even the highly educated reader of today, but many of these men were just as perceptive and able as the most capable pagan writers of the first centuries of our era. It is significant that among these intellectually sophisticated writers glossolalia was known and accepted as one of the special gifts which are given to Christians.[25]

Kelsey continues by evaluating those conditions and developments within world history which greatly affected the *status quo* of glossolalia.

> With the fall of the Western part of the Roman Empire in the fifth century the stream of Christian thought and life divided and separated. Two very different traditions of Christianity developed. The Greek or Orthodox tradition in the East and the Latin or Roman tradition in the West developed different attitudes toward the gifts of the Spirit in general and speaking in tongues in particular . . .
> In the West the government disintegrated under the barbarian invasions. The church remained as virtually the

[25] Kelsey, *op. cit.*, p. 32.

only organization of civilized life and was forced to take
upon it many of the functions of secular authority. Thus,
of sheer necessity, it became intensely practical and this-
worldly . . . In such a tradition individual experience of
the gifts of the Spirit was soft-pedaled. Authority rather
than individual religious expression was stressed. There was
little place for tongues which had already caused Paul and
the church fathers some real difficulty.
In the Eastern Roman Empire the church grew up under
contrasting conditions. . . . The Greek church remained
far more otherworldly mystical. It continued the Greek bent
of introspection, and individuality. . . . The East developed
a mystical, individualistic, otherworldly, introverted Christianity. In this tradition the individual gifts of the Spirit
flourished. The door was never closed to experiences like
tongues.[26]

According to Kelsey, in a recent visit to the United States
the Patriarch of Constantinople discussed the matter of glossolalia with at least one church leader. "When asked if speaking in tongues was known among his people, the Patriarch replied that it has been a continuing experience among them
through all the ages, although confined chiefly to the mon-
asteries, and that there are provisions in their church to
govern it."[27]

Collaborating evidence may be obtained from many
sources including the *Encyclopaedia Britannica* which reports: "During later church history, Glossolalia occurred
among the mendicant friars of the 13th century, the little
prophets of Cevennes, the Camisards, the Jansenites and the
Irvingites. Tradition has it that the gift of tongues was found
also among early Quakers and Shakers, as well as the converts of John Wesley and George Whitefield; and St. Francis
Xavier and St. Vincent Ferrer are said to have possessed
it."[28]

About the turn of the century a universal stirring of the
Holy Spirit began which encompassed many lands and many

[26] *Ibid.*, pp. 41, 42.
[27] *Ibid.*, p. 7.
[28] "Tongues, Gift of," *Encyclopaedia Britannica* (1965 ed.), XXII, 289.

persons. Numerous writers have described this latter-day effusion but none more clearly than Dr. Charles W. Conn, church historian, who said, "In seasons of fervent prayer, one or two of the members were so enraptured with the One to whom they prayed that they were curiously exercised by the Holy Spirit . . . in ecstasy they spoke in languages unknown to those who heard the utterances. . . . Soon others began to have similiar ecstatic experiences, and, regardless of the place, time, or circumstances contingent to the experience, one manifestation was uniform in all: they spoke in tongues, or languages, unknown to those who listened in wonder and hope."[29]

Today, some seventy years later, it is conservatively estimated that there are at least ten million persons around the world who have received the Holy Ghost baptism with the accompanying evidence of glossolalia. Of those, therefore, who question whether there has been a valid continuation of speaking in tongues we would ask that they ponder prayerfully the vibrant testimony of Scripture, history, and human experience which unanimously echoes the words of the Apostle Peter who attributed to the Holy Ghost that "which ye now see and hear" (Acts 2:33).

That Phenomenon Witnessed Today Among Pentecostals Is Not Genuine Glossolalia

The accusation here, of course, is that Pentecostals are hypocrites and their tongues speaking is mere gibberish. This is a most serious indictment and places awesome responsibilities upon the complainant. One wonders at the audacity of such a charge in the light of the sanctity of the blessed experience and in the face of millions who affirm even to death that they are recipients of the Blessed Comforter of whom Christ said, "I will send unto you from the Fa-

---

[29] Charles W. Conn, *Like a Mighty Army* (Cleveland, Tenn.: Church of God Publishing House, 1955), p. 24.

ther, even the Spirit of truth, which proceedeth from the Father, *he shall testify of me.*"[30]

Naturally, such a charge is offensive to Pentecostals. It is not surprising, however, that exception to glossolalia continues to pervade even a substantial part of the Christian community. Such was the situation at Pentecost. Even though those present were aware that a most marvelous phenomenon was occurring when they witnessed the speaking with tongues at that initial effusion, because it was uncommon and inexplicable they suspected it. Their emotions were characterized from being "amazed,"[31] to being "in doubt."[32] Their comments ranged from "What meaneth this?"[33] to "These men are full of new wine."[34]

Pentecostals are aware that because the general context of glossolalia is rather mystical that it poses unusual difficulties for many. Paul in his regulatory discourse with the Corinthians observed that the uninitiated observer would not be able to fully appreciate the exercise of the Holy Spirit.[35] Aside from eliminating the excesses and abuses which plagued the Corinthian church, however, Paul made it very clear that glossolalia should continue.[36] The lack of understanding or appreciation on the part of critics must not deter the true believer from speaking with other tongues as the Spirit gives the utterance,[37] for the blessing is promised "unto you, and to your children, and to all that are afar off, even as many as the Lord our God shall call" (Acts 2:39).

Perhaps there are those who profane glossolalia with jabber-babble or twattle-twaddle. This prostitution, how

---

[30] John 15:26. Italics ours.
[31] Acts 2:12.
[32] Ibid.
[33] Ibid.
[34] Acts 2:13.
[35] 1 Corinthians 14:9-11.
[36] 1 Corinthians 14:39.
[37] Acts 2:4.

ever, certainly does not apply to the mainline Pentecostals. The languages at Pentecost were clear, distinct, and precise. The ecstatic speech of those who are exercised of the Holy Ghost today remains uncluttered and heavenly. "God has not yet stooped to repetitious and meaningless banality. Gibberish is not the language of the Spirit! As on the Day of Pentecost, God today speaks with the tongues of those endued with the Holy Spirit. The unknown tongue is not the stammering of excited vocal organs, but rather the clear utterances of spiritual ecstasy. When the Spirit speaks . . . it will be exalted praise or convicting exhortation; it will not be in dead, pompous, monotonous, or pointless verbiage. When the Holy Ghost wills to speak through lips of flesh, it will be in phrases as exalted and errorless as the language of the Bible, for He is the Author of it, too."[38]

Glossolalia Is Considered Unscripturally to Be a Necessary Evidence of the Holy Spirit Baptism

The point at issue here is not whether the Holy Spirit baptism may be received by believers today. Again, the problem is not primarily whether glossolalia may accompany the Baptism of the Holy Ghost. The question rests with the belief by traditional Pentecostals that speaking with other tongues is the initial evidence of the Holy Spirit baptism and that *all* who receive the Holy Ghost speak with tongues.

Before this proposition is examined, it should be observed that Pentecostals believe that in addition to glossolalia there are other important evidences of the Baptism of the Holy Ghost. The Holy Spirit is to be a Paraclete or Comforter.[39] He is to be a Teacher.[40] He reveals the Son.[41] He is to provide power for witnessing.[42] These benefits as well as "the fruits

---

[38] Charles W. Conn, *Pillars of Pentecost* (Cleveland, Tenn.: Pathway Press, 1956), p. 57.
[39] John 14:16.
[40] John 14:26.
[41] John 15:26.
[42] Acts 1:8.

of the Spirit"[43] will also characterize the life of the baptized believer. Unless these additional evidences are concomitant with glossolalia, the tongues speaking becomes "as sounding brass, or a tinkling cymbal" (1 Corinthians 13:1).

The basis for the Pentecostals' belief that glossolalia is the initial, overt, physical evidence of the Holy Spirit baptism is the accumulated scriptural evidence provided by Luke in the Acts of the Apostles. In each instance where the account is reported in detail, speaking in tongues either is specifically mentioned or is strongly implied as concomitant with the experience of Holy Ghost baptism. Dr. Ira Jay Martin III observed, "The manifestation of glossolalia was immediately accepted as unquestionable evidence of spirit-possession, yea of the very Holy Spirit, itself (Acts 2:33, 38)"[44]

Even those who are extremely reserved in respect to glossolalia agree that the phenomenon of glossolalia accompanied the initial outpouring of the Holy Spirit.[45] Let us note that the scriptural description is, ". . . they were *all* filled with the Holy Ghost, and *began to speak with other tongues* as the Spirit gave the utterance" (Acts 2:4; italics ours). Clearly on this occasion all who received the Holy Ghost spoke with tongues and the speaking in tongues was the first physical evidence that the Holy Spirit had possessed them. "This was the first perceptible expression *from within* the disciples that they had been filled with the Spirit. . . . Consummately, the manifestation of glossolalia was the attestation that the Holy Spirit was dominant *within* them, having perfect control of the tongue which no man can tame (James 3:8)."[46]

This account is certainly the most distinct and precise description revealed in Scripture of the pattern involved

---

[43] Galatians 5:22, 23.
[44] Martin, *op. cit.*, p. 63.
[45] Acts 2:1-12.
[46] William G. MacDonald, *Glossolalia in the New Testament* (Springfield, Mo.: Gospel Publishing House, [n.d.]), pp. 4, 5.

when persons received the Holy Ghost. This is, of course, as it should be since this was the introduction of the gift of the Holy Ghost which Peter declared "ye now see and hear" (Acts 2:33), and of whom he promised "is unto you, and to your children, and to all that are afar off, even as many as the Lord our God shall call" (Acts 2:39).

Dr. Chester K. Lehman feels that "according to Peter the manifestation of the supernatural was to give adequate outward attestation to the internal experience of being baptized with the Holy Spirit. God provided physical phenomena as outward evidence for believing in the internal spiritual experience which lay beyond sense perception."[47]

In the Samarian revival, when Peter and John came to pray for those who had not received the Holy Ghost, the Scripture records, "Then laid they their hands on them, and they received the Holy Ghost" (Acts 8:17). While no mention is made of glossolalia, many scholars believe that they did indeed speak with tongues. Simon certainly saw some graphic evidence which impelled him to offer money for the knowledge to impart the phenomenon he beheld.[48] E. H. Plumptre says, "The words imply that the result was something visible and conspicuous. A change was wrought; and men spoke with tongues and prophesied."[49]

Again in the account of the Baptism with the Holy Ghost as experienced by Paul in Damascus no mention is made specifically of glossolalia (Acts 9:17, 18). Plumptre, however, strongly supports the Pentecostal view that Paul did speak with tongues. He said:

> The narrative clearly implies that here, as in chapter viii. 17, the being "filled with Holy Ghost" was connected with the laying on of hands as a condition, and it is so far a proof

[47] Chester K. Lehman, *The Holy Spirit and the Holy Life* (Scottdale, Penn.: Herald Press, 1959), p. 69.
[48] Acts 8:18, 19.
[49] E. H. Plumptre, *The Acts of the Apostles,* Vol. VII of *Ellicott's Commentary on the Whole Bible,* Charles John Ellicott, ed. (Grand Rapids: Zondervan Publishing House, 1954), 50. Used by permission.

> that that gift was not one which attached exclusively to the
> Apostles. It was, we may well believe, manifested in this
> instance as in others, by the ecstatic utterance of "the
> tongues" . . . and by the gift of prophetic insight.[50]

There is absolutely no question but that Paul did speak with
tongues as he himself emphatically stated.[51]

In the marvelous effusion at the house of Cornelius the
scriptural record is beautifully clear. "While Peter yet spake
these words, the Holy Ghost fell on all them which heard
the word. And they of the circumcision which believed were
astonished . . . because that on the Gentiles also was poured
out the gift of the Holy Ghost. For they heard them speak
with tongues, and magnify God" (Acts 10:44-46). The two
very significant aspects of this occurrence to our discussion
is that "all" received the Holy Ghost, and the Jews were sure
of it because "they heard them speak with tongues."

An observance by MacDonald is apt at this point. He said,
"Though the fiery tongues and the heavenly hurricane-like
wind were missing, the net result was, as Peter said, 'the same
gift.' This throws the weight of evidence, in Peter's analysis,
upon glossolalia and magnifying God (10:46) as the index of
normal Pentecostal experience (2:4-11)."[52]

One of the most emphatic proofs of glossolalia as the initial and identifying evidence of the Holy Ghost baptism is
revealed in Peter's defense before the council in Jerusalem.[53]
It was necessary for the apostle to convince the brethren at
Jerusalem that Cornelius and the other Gentiles in his house
had received the Holy Ghost even as the Jews had at Pentecost. "The crucial factor in this episode was the glossolalia
which made Peter and his six colleagues know with certainty
that the Gentiles had received identically the same experience
that he and the others had at the Pentecost Feast. Peter calls
it the 'same gift' (11:17) and states *four* times (10:47;

---

[50] *Ibid.*, p. 60.
[51] 1 Corinthians 14:18.
[52] MacDonald, *op. cit.*, p. 9.
[53] Acts 11:1-18.

11:15, 17; 15:8) that these men have received the Holy Spirit just as he and his companions had."[54]

More than twenty years after Pentecost Paul, making a missionary journey, came to Ephesus and found brethren who did not even know "whether there be any Holy Ghost" (Acts 19:2). "On hearing Paul's explanation of the meaning of John's baptism, 'they were baptized in the name of the Lord Jesus. And when Paul had laid his hand upon them, the Holy Spirit came on them; and they spoke with tongues and prophesied' (Acts 19:5, 6). The speaking with tongues and prophesying served to confirm to these disciples that their experience of being baptized with the Holy Spirit was identical with that of the other believers at Pentecost."[55]

In assessing the evidence let us contemplate the thoughts of René Pache. He said, "Lastly, the disciples at Ephesus spoke with tongues after receiving the Spirit (Acts 19:6). They were in the same situation in which we find ourselves today, coming after Pentecost and Cornelius. Their example goes to show quite simply that God in His sovereignty can grant the gift of tongues to whomsoever He desires."[56] Pentecostals concur and also believe that these scriptural accounts should clearly establish the fact that all those who receive the blessed Holy Spirit baptism do speak with tongues and that glossolalia is the first physical sign which signifies that the Comforter has come.

Glossolalia Is Unfortunately Confused With the Gift of Tongues

The point of objection here is based on the belief of some that the glossolalia of Pentecost and the subsequent instances in Acts were demonstrations of the gift of tongues and not

---

[54] MacDonald, *op. cit.*, p. 8.
[55] Lehman, *op. cit.*, p. 74.
[56] René Pache, *The Person and Work of the Holy Spirit* (Chicago: Moody Press, 1954), p. 87. Used by permission, Moody Press, Moody Bible Institute of Chicago 60610.

an initiatory or evidential glossolalia as the Pentecostals teach. The problem, therefore, is to determine the distinctions between "evidential" or "devotional" tongues and "ecclesiastical" or the "gift" of tongues. We may then apply these characteristics against the tongues phenomenon of the Acts to determine if indeed it were the gift of tongues.

It is clear that Paul is speaking of two distinct manifestations of glossolalia in his letter to the Corinthians.[57] The crux of his regulatory discourse to this church was to place in proper perspective the functions of glossolalia in respect to personal edification and ecclesiastical edification with the guiding motivation always being (agape) love.

At this point no attempt will be made to render an evaluation of the Corinthian problem. Let us simply inventory the basic benefits as well as the regulations governing devotional tongues as set forth by Paul in the discussion. We will then apply the same procedure to the gift of tongues.

We should first observe that devotional tongues function as a means of communion or perhaps intercommunion with God. "For he that speaketh in an unknown tongue speaketh not unto men, but unto God" (1 Corinthians 14:2). This medium of worship may be exercised also by praying in tongues[58] and by singing in tongues.[59] Since this is a personal, private communion, the person speaking in a devotional tongue primarily edifies himself[60] whether it be in private devotion or in congregational worship. The exercise of devotional tongues, however, is not to be undisciplined and without order.[61] All spiritual manifestation should be directed toward the common good.[62]

The gift of tongues is for congregational edification. If there is to be an exercise of glossolalia issuing through the

57 1 Corinthians 12-14.
58 1 Corinthians 14:15; Romans 8:26, 27.
59 1 Corinthians 14:15; Ephesians 5:19; Colossians 3:16.
60 1 Corinthians 14:4.
61 1 Corinthians 14:23.
62 1 Corinthians 12:7.

gift of tongues,[63] concordant with it should be the exercise of the gift of interpretation by which an understanding and concomitant edification would come to the congregation. Should there not be an interpreter present, then the glosso-lalist should not assume the posture of a public messenger but "speak to himself and to God" (1 Corinthians 14:28).

We deduce, therefore, that devotional tongues are employed principally for praise and adoration during personal communion with God. The gift of tongues is in operation generally during congregational worship, always in conjunction with the gift of interpretation, and definitely regulated in operation.[64] Properly exercised, these two gifts equate the gift of prophecy. Within the propriety of this function, glossolalia becomes a sign to the unbeliever.[65]

In respect to the objection posed at the beginning of our discussion, it would appear that perhaps it is the critics of Pentecostals rather than the Pentecostals who are confused concerning the respective operations of devotional tongues and the gift of tongues. It would seem apparent that according to the identifying functions as specifically stated by Paul, the exercise of glossolalia in the Acts could not have been a manifestation of the gift of tongues. First, the exercise was clearly one of personal praise and adoration to God.[66] Second, the gift of interpretation does not seem to have been employed. Third, all those exercised of the Holy Ghost spoke in tongues simultaneously[67] which would have violated perhaps the most stringent rule stated by Paul regarding the regulation of the gift of tongues.[68] We may conclude, therefore, that the glossolalia of Acts was not only initiatory and evidential but also devotional and distinctly different in function from the gift of tongues.

---

[63] 1 Corinthians 12:10.
[64] 1 Corinthians 14:27.
[65] 1 Corinthians 14:22.
[66] Acts 2:11; 10:46.
[67] Acts 2:4; 10:44-46; 19:6, 7.
[68] 1 Corinthians 14:23, 27, 28.

Glossolalia Is Substituted for Foreign Languages Given Only to Evangelize Mission Fields

Although some very beloved scholars have felt evangelization of persons foreign in language to that spoken by the preacher to be the function of glossolalia, it is difficult to comprehend how an objective study of the Scripture could possibly reveal such a view. The Baptism with the Holy Ghost was to supply power for witnessing[69]—witnessing in one's own language. In no place does Scripture indicate one was to be enabled to witness in a language foreign to his own. The act of speaking in tongues was to be a sign to the unbeliever[70] and edification to the believer.[71]

From the specific description in Acts 2:11 and the parallel structuring in the subsequent occurrences of tongues speaking in the Acts, glossolalia seemed to be intelligible language. A study of the one instance[72] where the reporting is specific, however, definitely shows that preaching the gospel was not the primary purpose of the phenomena of tongues. Actually the 120 persons who spoke with tongues on this occasion were engaged in the exercise of glossolalia when the crowd gathered and were able to *overhear* words of praise pertaining to the "wonderful works of God"[73] It is a scene of personal devotion, not a preaching effort.

Although hearing languages spoken by persons who had never learned them was amazing and dramatically arresting, this was not the method God employed in bringing His message to the people. Even while the 120 continued in their private ecstasy,[74] the Apostle Peter, in his native tongue, preached a mighty sermon saying, "Repent, and be baptized every one of you in the name of Jesus Christ for the re-

---

[69] Acts 1:8.
[70] 1 Corinthians 14:22.
[71] 1 Corinthians 14:4.
[72] Acts 2:1-41.
[73] Acts 2:11.
[74] Acts 2:33.

mission of sins, and ye shall receive the gift of the Holy Ghost" (Acts 2:38). About three thousand responded to the gospel message.

There is no doubt but that the Holy Ghost could and has enabled some to communicate to others in languages they had never learned. Such persons as Saint Dominick and others[75] have been reported to have been able, without the aid of an interpreter, to engage in a ministry of preaching and instruction in a foreign language they had never learned. In such a case we have a situation of intercommunication. Not only did Dominick speak in the language of the people, but he also understood what he spoke as well as that which was spoken to him. Evidently in such instances the Holy Ghost exercised upon these persons the gift of miracles,[76] thus enabling them to reason and communicate in a language they had never learned. That phenomenon is quite apart from devotional glossolalia.

CATEGORY II: THE PHENOMENON WAS STRONGLY CRITICIZED BY PAUL

This assertion is undoubtedly made because of Paul's corrective directives included in his regulatory letter to the Corinthians. Very likely precise attention is directed to his rather detailed discourse on the charismatic gifts.[77] Before examining these particular matters, however, let us give attention to the general conditions prevailing at Corinth which gave rise to the perversion of glossolalia as well as to many other corruptions.

Corinth by its strategic location on the isthmus between the Adriatic and Aegean Seas became the amalgamator of Western and Oriental culture and trade. The result was a people possessed of excessive independence, imagined intel-

---

[75] George Barton Cutten, *Speaking With Tongues* (New Haven: Yale University Press, 1927), pp. 38, 39.
[76] 1 Corinthians 12:28.
[77] 1 Corinthians 12-14.

lectual superiority, and horrid immorality.[78] One writer gave this description of the populace in Corinth when he wrote of

> this mongrel and heterogeneous population of Greek adventurers and Roman bourgeois, with a tainting infusion of Phoenicians; this mass of Jews, ex-soldiers, philosophers, merchants, sailors freedmen, slaves, trades-people, hucksters and agents of every form of vice.[79]

Kling gave added insight to the miscellany of the people with his words, "The city was then in the height of its prosperity, puffed up with the pride of wealth and the vanity of carnal science, and captivated by a fondness for sophistical dialectics and pompous rhetoric . . ."[80]

From this Epicurean atmosphere emerged the church at Corinth. Unfortunately, the church did not escape some perverting influences in its conflicts with the prevailing culture. Niebuhr discussing this conflict said:

> It appears in the early struggles of the church with the empire, with the religions and philosophies of the Mediterranean world, in its rejections and acceptances of prevailing mores, moral principles, metaphysical ideas, and forms of social organization.[81]

At the time Paul wrote to the Corinthians, therefore, there were a great many problems seriously plaguing the church. In addition to the profanation which had arisen concerning glossolalia, a few of Paul's other complaints against the church are reflected in his

> condemnation of the Corinthians' attitude towards the monstrous case of incest (5:1-13) and the solemn warning against thinking lightly of sins of the flesh (6:12-20), but

---

[78] Bobby E. Lyons, "Charismatic Gifts: An Exegesis of 1 Corinthians 12:1-11" (unpublished Master's thesis, Columbia Theological Seminary, Decatur, Ga., 1965), p. 13.

[79] From *The Letters to the Corinthians*, tr. William Barclay. Published 1957, The Westminster Press. Used by permission, p. 4, quoting Farrar.

[80] Frederick Christian Kling, *The Epistles of Paul the Apostle to the Corinthians*, Vol. XX in *Lange's Commentary on the Holy Scriptures*, John Peter Lange, ed. (Grand Rapids: Zondervan Publishing House, [n.d.], p. 7. Used by permission.

[81] H. Richard Niebuhr, *Christ and Culture* (New York: Harper & Brothers, 1951), p. 10.

also the nature of the reply to the Corinthians' letter (7:1-11:1). The whole treatment of this marriage problem and of the right behavior with regard to idol-meats is influenced by the thought of the manifold and ceaseless temptations to impurity with which the new converts to Christianity were surrounded . . .[82]

Let us understand then: "Taken as it stands, 1 Corinthians is the most intensely practical of all St. Paul's letters. It was written to meet immediate needs of his converts . . ."[83] Among the several needs represented in this church was that of a better understanding of the functions of the charismatic gifts and particularly glossolalia. It is perfectly clear, however, that Paul's approach was to regulate the gift and certainly not to prohibit it.

Glossolalia Was Seen by Paul as a Heresy

One of the most conspicuous facts demonstrated in Paul's regulatory discourse with the Corinthian brethren was that even though glossolalia had fallen into some irregularities, nevertheless it was a usual exercise of worship among the apostolic churches. While much is made of the strong discipline which the apostle exerted in respect to the abuses associated with speaking in tongues at Corinth, this stringent, corrective procedure was required only because these persons were guilty of profaning an evidence of the Baptism of the Holy Ghost, and not because it was prohibitive to speak with tongues.[84] These persons had fallen into irreverence and excess toward this religious function even as they had in regard to the proper respect for their minister[85] and the correct attitude toward the Lord's Supper.[86]

---

82 Archibald Robertson and Alfred Plummer, *A Critical and Exegetical Commentary on the First Epistle of St. Paul to the Corinthians (The International Critical Commentary,* Edinburgh: T. and T. Clark, 1961), p. xvi.
83 Alan H. McNeile, *An Introduction to the Study of the New Testament,* Second edition (Oxford: At the Clarendon Press, 1953), p. 136.
84 1 Corinthians 14:5, 39.
85 1 Corinthians 3:3-7.
86 1 Corinthians 10:15-22.

There is absolutely no statement nor any implication in Paul's entire treatment of the charismata that suggested that glossolalia was unorthodox. "Note particularly that he never questions the genuineness of their gifts. There is not one single line in which he suggests (as so many hastily do today) that they had 'counterfeit' gifts inspired by deceiving spirits. All through these three chapters he proceeds on the assumption that *they had right gifts, but used them wrongly.*"[87]

The fact that Paul employed three chapters[88] of his letter to the Corinthians to reconcile the functions of the gifts of the Spirit is a significant indication of the value he placed on the operation of these gifts within the church. In chapter 12 he eloquently projected the thesis that while there are many diversities, divisions, and distributions of the gifts,[89] they all operate within the context of unity[90] so that the manifestation of the Spirit is for the common good.[91] Chapter 13 is a cogent, sublime treatise on the one proper and acceptable motivation for the exercise of the gifts: love. Predicated upon these bases, in chapter 14 the apostle seeks to regulate the exercise of the gifts, with particular attention given to glossolalia. "The temporary disorders in connection with spiritual gifts at Corinth did not arise out of anything in the nature of the gifts themselves, but only out of certain weaknesses in the believers who were exercising them."[92] The problem, therefore, was not a matter of orthodoxy but of orderly operation.[93]

Glossolalia Is Not to Be Exercised by All

The impetus for this assertion is found in Paul's didactic question, "Do all speak with tongues?" (1 Corinthians 12:30).

---

[87] Donald Gee, *Concerning Spiritual Gifts* (Springfield, Mo.: Gospel Publishing House, [n.d.]), p. 82.
[88] 1 Corinthians 12-14.
[89] 1 Corinthians 12:4-6.
[90] 1 Corinthians 12:11-14.
[91] 1 Corinthians 12:7.
[92] Gee, *op. cit.*, pp. 6, 7.
[93] 1 Corinthians 14:40.

A careful reading of this chapter should convince any objective reader that Paul is here referring to spiritual gifts and not to devotional tongues as differentiated in chapter 14. This particular verse correlates perfectly with verses 10 and 11. Here the apostle clearly states that by the Holy Spirit God has placed in the Church the gift of tongues, even as He has the other gifts, but that the Spirit operates these gifts through those persons whom He chooses. "The Holy Spirit is a person and is the center of spiritual unity in the church, being as He is the one who distributes all the different gifts, and works out, in and through the individual members, the wonderful works of the Christ of God."[94]

Not everyone exercises the gift of tongues, just as not everyone has the gift of prophecy or works miracles or has the word of wisdom. The gifts of the Spirit all reside within the Church and are exercised by the Holy Ghost only as He wills.[95] "It can be said that while there is variety of gifts, they are all unified by their common source, the Holy Spirit, and by their common motivation, love."[96]

Paul's statement, "I would that ye all spake with tongues" (1 Corinthians 14:5), is a straightforward, declarative statement. Even when he gave the firm regulations about the exercise of the gifts of tongues and interpretation, he seemed to be careful to make provision for those who would yield to devotional tongues by saying "let him speak to himself, and to God" (1 Corinthians 14:28). Luke leaves no question in his report about those who received the Holy Ghost. He said, "They were *all* filled with the Holy Ghost, and began to speak with other tongues" (Acts 2:4; italics ours.). Again he reports, "the Holy Ghost fell on *all* them which heard the word . . . For they heard *them speak with tongues*" (Acts 10:44, 46; italics ours). Not all persons are exercised by

---

[94] John W. Shepard, *The Life and Letters of St. Paul* (Grand Rapids: Wm. B. Eerdmans Publishing Co., 1956), p. 248.
[95] 1 Corinthians 12:11.
[96] Lyons, *op. cit.*, p. 33.

the gift of tongues, but all persons who receive the Holy Spirit speak with evidential and devotional tongues.

Glossolalia Is the Least of All the Gifts

This objection has often been made to the phenomenon of glossolalia. It would seem that the objector is saying, "Speaking in tongues is a gift from God but it is not so great a gift as some others of God's gifts; therefore, it is not a profitable gift and should be rejected." This is obviously a weak, if not an absurd, argument. Who can rightly say which of God's gifts are small or great? ". . . all the gifts alike are from God. They are the gifts of His grace. His is the Spirit who inspires them in all their varieties."[97]

Paul's purpose in 1 Corinthians 12-14 was to correct a situation where a group of persons sought to dominate the public worship with an uncontrolled display of tongues speaking. Such practices, at the best, could only serve to satisfy some personal aggrandizement. "The apostle, therefore, when he heard that this gift was coveted for the mere purpose of ostentatious display, took occasion to reprove the Corinthians for that perversion."[98]

In order to impress upon the Corinthians that for the understanding and consequential edification of the whole church it was far better for the worship service to be intelligible to the congregation, Paul said, "in the church I had rather speak five words with my understanding, that by my voice I might teach others also, than ten thousand words in an unknown tongue" (1 Corinthians 14:19). With consummate logic the apostle establishes the regulation that in the ministering of the Word the gift of prophecy or the gifts of tongues and interpretation would best be exercised rather than devotional glossolalia.

---

[97] *The Interpreter's Bible* (Nashville: Abington-Cokesbury Press, 1953), X, 150.
[98] George Smeaton, *The Doctrine of the Holy Spirit* (London: The Banner of Truth Trust, 1958), p. 52.

We should understand clearly, however, that "the Apostle does not either forbid glossolaly or suffer prophecy to run riot uncontrolled. Both were gifts of the Spirit, and each had its place in the manifestations of spiritual life . . ."[99] Of himself Paul said, "I thank my God, I speak with tongues more than ye all" (1 Corinthians 14:18). To speculate, therefore, on the smallest or greatest of the spiritual gifts is both presumptuous and fatuous since the Scripture does not classify their importance. God would have all the gifts, by the Holy Spirit, exercised in His Church "decently and in order" to the edification of believers.

Glossolalia Has Ceased

This contention arises from Paul's statement in 1 Corinthians 13:8 when he said, ". . . whether there be tongues, they shall cease." Any serious student of the Word realizes, of course, that the apostle is speaking of the conditions which will exist in the "perfect age."[100] The theme of the chapter is "Charity Never Faileth." Over against the endurance of tongues is placed the stamina of charity, and charity prevails. The same equation is applied to prophecies and to knowledge, and the result is the same.[101] Because love is the essence of God[102] it will serve as the only sufficient motivation for the gifts of the Spirit during this dispensation, and when all things are complete and finished, it will serve as the sustaining atmosphere of the eternal heaven.

When Paul wrote, "But covet earnestly the best gifts: and yet shew I unto you a more excellent way" (1 Corinthians 12:31), he did not mean that he would introduce something to replace the spiritual gifts. The "more excellent way" had to do with the underlying and undergirding impetus and

---

[99] Henry Barclay Swete, *The Holy Spirit in the New Testament* (London: Macmillan and Company, Ltd., 1919), p. 188. Used by permission.
[100] 1 Corinthians 13:10.
[101] 1 Corinthians 13:8.
[102] 1 John 4:8.

power which would condition the exercising of the gifts. Issuing from the very nature of God was (*agape*) love that "never faileth."[103]

In contemplating the vital relationship of love to the gifts of the Spirit, Frank Boyd observed:

> Without this love, the whole complement of spiritual "gifts" are nothing (zero), as far as accomplishing God's purpose in their use. Just as our speech should be "always with grace, seasoned with salt," so even tongues given impulse by the Spirit of God, should flow through a channel richly sweetened by the love of God.[104]

Henry Halley adds his thoughts: "The Gift of Speaking like an Angel, of Prophesying, of having All Knowledge, of Faith that Moves Mountains, of Charity to the last dollar, even Martyrdom, all [are] of no use unless we have the Spirit of Christian LOVE."[105]

The thrust of 1 Corinthians 13:8, therefore, is that prophecies, knowledge, and tongues, motivated and sustained by godly love, will continue to function to the glory of Christ and to the extension of the kingdom of God until the end of the age. Then, when "that which is perfect is come,"[106] prophecies, knowledge, and tongues, as we know them now, will not be needed nor be functional.

CATEGORY III: THE PHENOMENON IS A FALLACY OF THE EMOTIONS AND DIVISIVE IN NATURE

This is, of course, a most serious allegation. Should these charges be true, then Pentecostals would at the best be a group of religious neurotics or a conglomeraton of

---

103 1 Corinthians 13:8.
104 Frank M. Boyd, *The Holy Spirit* (Springfield, Mo.: Gospel Publishing House, [n.d.]), p. 86.
105 Henry H. Halley, *Bible Handbook*, Copyright 1962, Halley's Bible Handbook, Inc. 23rd edition, p. 549. Used by permission of Zondervan Publishing House.
106 1 Corinthians 13:10.

sanctimonious hypocrites! Neither is true. While Pentecostals are no less exposed to the problems and pressures which exact a quotient of emotional illnesses than their neighbors, they also are as well adjusted in their domestic, social, and religious functions. To criticize the fervor with which Pentecostals worship or to look askance upon their break with traditional liturgy is to suspect the verity and orthodoxy of the apostolic church, for those early believers were hardly traditional in their worship.[107]

Glossolalia Indicates an Abnormal Intrapsychic Function, Perhaps Schizophrenia or Even Demon Possession

It is rather amazing to contemplate the tenacity of man as he seeks to match his intellectual capabilities against the miracles of God and evolve a plausible, humanistic explanation. An explanation is impossible, however, "Because the foolishness of God is wiser than men; and the weakness of God is stronger than men" (1 Corinthians 1:25). Again, it is impossible for "the natural man receiveth not the things of the Spirit of God: for they are foolishness unto him: neither can he know them, because they are spiritually discerned" (1 Corinthians 2:14). Perhaps this gives insight into the reason that many persons, not being able to accept glossolalia intellectually, relegate it to a sphere of emotional or mental illness.

While he does not fully share the Pentecostals' view on glossolalia, Dr. John F. Walvoord has made some observations helpful to our discussion. He said, "By its nature, a spiritual gift had reality, and being supernatural, needs no naturalistic explanation. The phenomenon of speaking in tongues was accepted by believers as a work of the Holy Spirit. All attempts to relate speaking in tongues with the ravings of heathen mystics and soothsayers, as some do, must

---

[107]Acts 2-9.

be rejected as in effect an attack on the accuracy of the scriptural revelation."[108] Collaborating this view are the thoughts of Dr. Ira Jay Martin III, "It is worthy of note that Apostolic glossolalia was never attributed to the spirit of any of the non-Judeo-Christian gods or goddesses. It appears to have been thought of as the special gift of Yahweh's Spirit . . . There appeared to have been some generally accepted standards for judging individuals seized by evil spirits. Yet glossolalia was not one of those criteria."[109]

The effort, therefore, to relate Pentecostal glossolalia with evil spirits or false religions will not withstand objective scrutiny. Nor is there any validating study establishing tongues speaking as a schizophrenic tendency. To the contrary, Kelsey reports, "Although I have found no study comparing the forms of irrational speech in schizophrenia with Christian glossolalia, one psychologist who is familiar with both has pointed out to me that there is little outward similarity between them. And he went on to say that it is surprising how seldom one meets up with schizophrenic individuals who have experienced religious tongues."[110]

Let us conclude then that there is no factual reason to classify the Christian glossolalist as being emotionally unstable or as demon possessed. We do believe that communion with God brings all responses of man into correlation and purpose. We believe the work of salvation encompasses the whole man. It would seem that the collected psyche as well as the collected organism of man should receive spiritual nurture. It should not seem strange, therefore, for the psyche and/or the emotions of man to be stimulated, released, or to be involved in some aspect of spiritual catharsis in true worship. The Apostle Paul seemed to have no hesitation in affirming that

---

108 John F. Walvoord, The Holy Spirit. Copyrighted and published by Dunham Publishing Company. P. 182. Used by permission of the publishers.
109 Martin, op. cit., pp. 29, 31.
110 Kelsey, op. cit., p. 203.

one of the basic functions of glossolalia was to edify the individual.[111]

Glossolalia Is Associated With Persons Who Are Immature and Unable to Function Well With Others

Pentecostals are normal ordinary persons who are neither immortal nor infallible. Having evolved from the cold stilted atmosphere of mere religiosity, they received the Holy Ghost with exuberance and enthusiasm. It is not unexpected that they are sometimes exercised by an overflowing of the Holy Spirit. These persons, however, live stable, productive lives in the community and are generally considered good solid citizens. They can hardly be classified less mature than some of their neighbors who engage in a cheering frenzy at a ball game on Friday night, indulge in excessive cocktails on Saturday night, and seek to begin their search for equilibrium by Sunday night!

While Lapsley and Simpson are willing to characterize Pentecostals as "problem oriented people who consume much time and energy in attempting to cope with life,"[112] they are forced to concede that Pentecostals "are persons who have enough credulity to be able to reduce all their problems to the one global problem of the battle between good and evil, and to view its solution uniformly in terms of supernatural intervention."[113] One would debate strongly the assertion that Pentecostals are any more "problem oriented" than their neighbors, for all are subjected to the pressures of a world made cruel by sin. On the other hand, it would appear that perhaps Pentecostals are more mature than most if they are able to bring their problems into focus—and especially in relation to the "sufficient grace"[114] of God.

---

[111] 1 Corinthians 14:4.
[112] James N. Lapsley and John H. Simpson "Speaking in Tongues: Infantile Bobble or Song of the Self?" *Pastoral Psychology*, XV, No. 146 (September, 1964), 16, 17.
[113] *Ibid.*
[114] 2 Corinthians 12:9.

To say that glossolalists are not able to function well with others is to vary from the facts. In many cities Pentecostals serve with great honor and high respect in civic, social, and religious activities. It is certainly not uncommon for a Pentecostal to be an officer in the ministerial association or to serve as a chaplain in the local hospital. Pentecostals are to be found among most of the professions and are highly respected by their colleagues. Recently a Pentecostal served as president of a national organization of evangelicals,[115] and presently another Pentecostal is serving as president of an affiliate[116] of the same organization. There are presently thirty-five Pentecostal chaplains serving the spiritual needs of our military throughout the world. Who will dare say Pentecostals will not work with others? Could it be that there are some who refuse to work with Pentecostals?

Glossolalia Stimulates a Religious Pride and Causes Schisms Among the Brethren

On occasion one does hear an observation to the effect that glossolalia is divisive and tends to generate a noxious pride. Now, two assertions are projected here. Let us consider each of them in order. The first allegation is that glossolalia is divisive. To a degree this probably is true. It has been observed that at Pentecost "very evidently there was a sharp division of the people, as well as of opinions concerning the spiritual manifestation."[117] This division of opinion continued throughout the apostolic age and during the subsequent centuries since. Today the Pentecostals are as certain about their experience of the Baptism with the Holy Ghost with the evidence of glossolalia as were those 120 at

---

115 Thomas F. Zimmerman, General Superintendent of the Assemblies of God, served as President of the National Association of Evangelicals (1960 and 1961).

116 E. C. Thomas, Publisher, Church of God Publishing House, served as President of the National Sunday School Association (1965-66).

117 *The Wesleyan Bible Commentary* (Grand Rapids: Wm. B. Eerdmans Publishing Company, 1964), IV, 506.

Pentecost. Apparently there are those yet today who are as hostile to glossolalia as then. To this degree, therefore, I suppose glossolalia is divisive.

Kelsey, however, has made some observations which seem to be pertinent to our discussion at this point. He wrote:

> Tongues undoubtedly causes conflict, but is conflict necessarily evil from a Christian point of view? Can there be any growth and development without conflict? I am not sure that Christianity is always meant to bring peace and harmony as a soothing salve, however much the ministers of the church (myself included) would like it to be so. How often we overlook the arrogance and enmity generated by the early Christians as they attempted to bring Jewish brethren and pagan friends to the light! They stirred up so much conflict that they were stoned and fed to wild beasts. Paul's life could scarcely be termed free of conflict. And I am reminded of the little quoted statement of Jesus from the Gospel of Luke: "I have come to set fire to the earth, and how I wish it were already kindled! I have a baptism to undergo, and how hampered I am until the ordeal is over! Do you suppose I came to establish peace on the earth? No indeed, I have come to bring division" (Luke 12:49).[118]

While there is a large measure of disagreement among theologians in respect to glossolalia, is it not true that extreme variances of opinion exist concerning other aspects of church dogma? Who can estimate the wide gulf separating those who embrace the concepts of predestinarianism and those who hold to the tenets of free will? Will Calvin and Arminius ever embrace? What of the wide distances separating a unity of thought between the premillennialists and the postmillennialists? Does one really suppose that a single mode of water baptism will ever be acceptable to those who would sprinkle, or dip, or immerse? All these facets of doctrine are divisive in the same manner as glossolalia.

Now, let us consider the matter of glossolalia stimulating a religious pride. To be sure, Pentecostals are as capable of falling into error as any devout believers. Should any person

---

[118] Kelsey, op. cit., p. 230.

become obsessed with a spirit of religious superiority because he speaks with tongues, he would be guilty of some of the same faults of the Corinthians and deserving of the same reproof. But our Episcopalian writer observes: "Pentecostals are often more self-critical than most people realize. They are well aware of the difficulties inherent in their religious way, and those in the major Pentecostal bodies are trying to correct the abuses of other days."[119]

It must be observed that if the criticisms that glossolalia is divisive and promotes a religious pride are based upon the Pentecostals' enthusiasm to apprise others of the marvelous benefits of the Holy Ghost baptism, then the matter assumes a different posture. Pentecostals feel impelled to witness of their blessing. Twentieth-century Pentecostals should respond as did those first-century Pentecostals. "When the deluge of spiritual power came down upon this infant church, the record says, 'they were all filled with the Holy Ghost, and began to speak . . .' (Acts 2:4). This was the secret of their success. They were filled brimful of the Holy Ghost. All difficulty, timidity, fear, and impotence were gone. They were now qualified and authorized to witness. They began to speak not only in tongues, but in witnessing boldly to the saving grace of Jesus Christ."[120] Hence, if this evangelistic fervor to witness is misinterpreted to be divisive or evidence of a religious pride, we refute it by observing, "We cannot but speak the things which we have seen and heard" (Acts 4:20).

Glossolalia Is Magnified Out of Proportion by Pentecostals

Over the years considerable attention has been focused upon glossolalia more often than not by those who were either curious or perhaps hostile. "The sincere Pentecostal has

---

119 Ibid., p. 83.
120 Wade H. Horton, Pentecost Yesterday and Today (Cleveland, Tenn.: Pathway Press, 1964), p. 67.

never been preoccupied with this gift alone, for he sees it as only one of many gifts given for the 'wholeness' of the Church; therefore, he does not worship or meet just to speak in 'tongues' for speaking in 'tongues' sake (such motive would be vain and idolatrous), but rather he meets to worship God and be furnished for every good work."[121]

It would appear from criticisms spoken and printed by important religious voices that Pentecostals consider glossolalia to be the end result of the indwelling Spirit. This is a gross and tragic mistake. Dr. Ray H. Hughes has a statement here. He observes:

> Speaking with tongues is the initial witness or evidence that the Spirit has come to accompany the individual in fulfilling his task of world evangelization. Speaking in tongues is not the height of the Holy Ghost experience, but it is merely the starting point. It is the beginning not the graduation. The experience of the Baptism is not an end in itself but only a means to an end—pointing men to Christ.[122]

Dr. Hughes continues, "Now for the true purpose of Penecost. When the Spirit came, the disciples went. They went everywhere and preached Christ. The secret of their success was that 'the Spirit gave them utterance.' This accounts for the contents of their message. When the Spirit came, He focused attention on Christ."[123]

Giving emphasis to this affirmation is a statment from James L. Slay, respected author and preacher. Writing in *This We Believe* he said:

> This glorious promise of the Father was not merely the presence of someone to render aid in time of need. The ministry of the Holy Ghost in the life of the believer has other than ameliorative purposes. There is a reason behind

---

121 Paul L. Walker, "Charismatic Development in the Contemporary Church" (Atlanta: Hemphill Church of God, 1964), p. 19. (Mimeographed.)
122 Ray H. Hughes, *What Is Pentecost* (Cleveland, Tenn.: Pathway Press, 1963), p. 19.
123 *Ibid.*, p. 20.

this help from the Spirit other than our own welfare and spiritual betterment. This fact is notably expressed in the content of John, chapter 15. The disciples, and such are we, were to be bearers of fruit. God wants us to be "good for something." Jesus wanted the Twelve to bear fruit. He wants us to bear fruit. This cannot be done unless we remain in Him and He remains in us. The Christ life in us is the life of the Spirit. We cannot have the mind of Christ unless we submit our wills to Him. As Christ dominated the life of His disciples, so must the Holy Ghost dominate our lives. We who were servants of sin are now to be filled with the Spirit and to become servants of God (Romans 6:17; Ephesians 5:18).[124]

We see, therefore, that primarily Pentecostals do not magnify glossolalia but rather the encompassing benefits of the Baptism with the Holy Ghost. "Accompanying the Baptism of the Holy Ghost are power for witnessing, strength to be a better Christian, guidance in everyday affairs of life, and a constant companionship and comfort in accord with the Biblical promise."[125] These are the benefits which Pentecostals would proclaim to the world!

IV. THE PATTERN ESTABLISHED

Thus, we have examined glossolalia as an integral aspect of the Pentecostal effusion which engulfed the apostolic church and has continued since. We have established that "speaking in tongues has been a practice of some of the church through Christian history."[126] We conclude with Dr. Jonathan Goforth that, "This Divine empowering is for us as for them. We, too, may do the works which our Lord did, yea, and the greater works. The Scriptures convey no other meaning to me than that the Lord Jesus planned that the Holy

---

124 James L. Slay, *This We Believe* (Cleveland, Tenn.: Pathway Press, 1963), p. 85.
125 Thomas F. Zimmerman, "The Pentecostal Position," *Church of God Evangel*, LIV (March 2, 1964), p. 4.
126 Ralph E. Knudson, *Theology in the New Testament* (Valley Forge: The Judson Press © 1964), p. 179. Used by permission.

Spirit should continue among us in as mighty manifestation as at Pentecost."[127]

We have shown that glossolalia is concomitant with the Baptism of the Holy Ghost as an evidential and devotional manifestation. It is our belief that the Baptism with the Holy Spirit with the speaking in tongues applies its benefits to the total experience of man. We agree, "It is a verifiable phenomenon of Christian experience that an individual man, laid hold upon by the Spirit of God, can have his whole life lifted to a level of spiritual force and efficiency which previously would have seemed quite impossible."[128]

According to the Scriptures, we believe that all who receive the Baptism of the Holy Ghost do speak with tongues. We do not believe, however, that glossolalia is an end within itself. We fully agree with that princely preacher Bishop Webb who said, "The Holy Spirit not only dwells in the church as his habitation, but also uses her as the living organism whereby he moves and walks forth in the world, and speaks to the world and acts upon the world. He is the soul of the church which is Christ's body."[129]

Let us conclude then that the Scriptures set forth the formula "that in the mouth of two or three witnesses every word may be established" (Matthew 18:16). Accordingly, with the specific presentation of "speaking with tongues" from several instances in the Word, with impressive collaborating evidence from church history, and with the testimony of myriads who experienced glossolalia, it would seem that the matter would be clear to the honest inquirer.

Therefore, let every inquiring heart sincerely examine the body of facts on which this doctrine is based. The Bible sets

---

[127] Taken from "*By My Spirit*," by Jonathan Goforth, published by Zondervan Publishing House, used by permission, p. 11.

[128] James S. Stewart, *Thine Is the Kingdom* (Edinburg: The St. Andrews Press, 1956), p. 72.

[129] A. J. Gordon, *The Ministry of the Spirit* (Minneapolis, Minn.: Bethany Fellowship, Inc., 1964), p. 60, quoting Bishop Webb, *The Presence and Office of the Spirit*, p. 47.

forth the plan, pattern, and purpose of Pentecost. History reveals the penetration, progress, and persistence of the Holy Spirit baptism. More than ten million persons presently portray to the world the power and permanence of glossolalia. The promise announced by the Apostle Peter continues to ring true, "For the promise is unto you, and to your children, and to all that are afar off, even as many as the Lord our God shall call" (Acts 2:39).

Bibliography

1. GLOSSOLALIA AND THE SCRIPTURES

Barnes, Albert. *Notes on the New Testament.* 11 vols. Grand Rapids: Baker Book House, 1949.

Bruce, F. F. *The Acts of the Apostles: Commentary on the Greek Text.* Grand Rapids: Wm. B. Eerdmans Publishing Company, 1951.

Bruce, F. F. *Commentary on the Book of the Acts. In the New International Commentary on the New Testament.* Grand Rapids: Wm. B. Eerdmans Publishing Company, 1954.

Brumback, Carl. *"What Meaneth This?"* Springfield, Mo.: The Gospel Publishing House, 1947.

Carter, Charles W. and Earle Ralph. *The Acts of the Apostles.* Vol. II of *The Evangelical Commentary,* ed. George Allen Turner. Grand Rapids: Zondervan Publishing House, 1959.

Conn, Charles W. *Acts of the Apostles.* Cleveland, Tenn.: Pathway Press, 1965.

Conn, Charles W. *Pillars of Pentecost.* Cleveland, Tenn.: Pathway Press, 1956.

Conybeare, W. J. and J. S. Howson. *The Life and Epistles of St. Paul.* Grand Rapids: Wm. B. Eerdmans Publishing Company, 1957.

Courtney, Howard P. *The Vocal Gifts of the Spirit.* Los Angeles: B. N. Robertson Company, 1956.

Fausset, A. R. *Bible Encyclopaedia and Dictionary.* Grand Rapids: Zondervan Publishing House, n.d.

Godet, F. L. *Commentary on the Epistle of St. Paul to the Corinthians.* 2 vols. (1886). Reprinted in the *Classic Commentary Library.* 24 vols. Grand Rapids: Zondervan Publishing House, 1957.

Gordon, A. J. *The Ministry of the Spirit.* Philadelphia: The Judson Press, 1894. Reprinted by Bethany Fellowship, Inc., Minneapolis, Minn., 1964.

Gould, E. P. *A Commentary on the Epistles to the Corinthians.* Vol. V of *An American Commentary on the New Testament,* ed. Alvah Hovey. 7 vols. Philadelphia: The American Baptist Publication Society, 1882.

Hackett, Horatio B. *A Commentary on the Acts of the Apostles.* Vol. IV of *An American Commentary on the New Testament,* ed. Alvah Hovey. 7 vols. Philadelphia: The American Baptist Publication Society, 1882.

Hastings, James (ed.). *A Dictionary of the Apostolic Church.* 2 vols. New York: Charles Scribner's Sons, 1922.

The International Standard Bible Encyclopedia. Edited by James Orr. 5 vols. Grand Rapids: Wm. B. Eerdmans Publishing Company, 1939.

285

Kling, Christian Friedrich. *Corinthians*. Vol. XX of *Lange's Commentary on the Holy Scriptures* (1866). 24 vols. Grand Rapids: Reprinted by Zondervan Publishing House, n.d.

Knudsen, Ralph E. *Theology in the New Testament*. Valley Forge: The Judson Press, 1964.

Lechler, G. V. *The Acts of the Apostles*. Vol. XVIII of *Lange's Commentary on the Holy Scriptures* (1886). 24 vols. Grand Rapids: Reprinted by Zondervan Publishing House, n.d.

Meyer, F. B. *Back to Bethel*. Chicago: Moody Press. n.d.

Pearlman, Myer. *Knowing the Doctrines of the Bible*. Springfield, Mo.: The Gospel Publishing House, 1937.

Phillips, J. B. *The Young Church in Action*. New York: The Macmillan Company, 1955.

Riggs, Ralph M. *The Spirit Himself*. Springfield, Mo.: The Gospel Publishing House, 1949.

Robertson, A. T. *The Acts of the Apostles*, Vol. III of *Word Pictures in the New Testament. The Epistles of Paul*. Vol. IV of *Word Pictures in the New Testament*. 6 vols. New York: Harper & Brothers, 1930.

Schaff, Philip. *Apostolic Christianity*. Vol. I of *History of the Christian Church*. 8 vols. Grand Rapids: Wm. B. Eerdmans Publishing Company, 1950.

Smith, David. *The Life and Letters of St. Paul*. New York: Harper & Row, Publishers, n.d.

Smith, Frank W. "What Value Tongues?" *Message . . . of the Open Bible*, XLV (June, 1963), 4, 5.

Torrey, R. A. *What The Bible Teaches*. New York: Fleming H. Revell Company, 1933.

Trapp, John. *Commentary on the New Testament* (1865). Grand Rapids: Reprinted by Zondervan Publishing House, n.d.

Wierville, Victor Paul. *Receive the Holy Spirit Today*. Van Wert, Ohio: The Way, 1957.

Williams, Ernest S. *Systematic Theology*. 3 vols. Springfield, Mo.: The Gospel Publishing House, 1953.

2. Glossolalia: Apostles to the Reformation

The Ante-Nicene Fathers. American Edition. 14 vols. New York: Charles Scribner's Sons, 1907.

The Ante-Nicene Fathers. American Series. 14 vols. Grand Rapids: Wm. B. Eerdmans Publishing Company, 1956.

Brumback, Carl. *"What Meaneth This?"* Springfield, Mo.: The Gospel Publishing House, 1947.

Butler, Alban. *The Lives of the Fathers, Martyrs and Other Principal*

Saints. 4 vols. Baltimore: John Murphy & Company, 1889.

Cutten, G. B. *Speaking With Tongues.* New Haven: Yale University Press, 1927.

Cross, F. L. "Glossolalia," *The Oxford Dictionary of the Christian Church.* New York: University Press, 1958.

Encyclopaedia Britannica. 24 vols. (14th ed.) XXII, 283.

Ferm, Vergilius (ed.). *An Encyclopedia of Religion.* New York: The Philosophical Library, 1945.

The International Standard Bible Encyclopaedia. Edited by James Orr. 5 vols. Grand Rapids: Wm. B. Eerdmans Publishing Company, 1943.

The Interpreter's Dictionary of the Bible. 4 vols. New York: Abingdon Press, 1962.

Kelsey, Morton T. *Tongue Speaking.* New York: Doubleday & Company, Inc. 1964.

Knox, Ronald A. *Enthusiasm: A Chapter in the History of Religion.* New York: Oxford University Press, 1950.

Loetscher, Lefferts, A. (ed.). *Twentieth Century Encyclopaedia of Religious Knowledge.* 2 vols. Grand Rapids: Baker Book House, 1955.

Miller, Elmer. *Pentecost Examined.* Springfield, Mo.: The Gospel Publishing House, 1936.

Miller, Madeleine S. and J. Lane Miller. *Harper's Bible Dictionary.* New York: Harper & Brothers, 1952.

The Nicene and Post-Nicene Fathers. First Series. 14 vols. Grand Rapids: Wm. B. Eerdmans Publishing Company, 1956.

The Nicene and Post-Nicene Fathers. Second Series. 14 vols. Grand Rapids: Wm. B. Eerdmans Publishing Company, 1952.

Phillips, McCandlish. "*And There Appeared to Them Tongues of Fire,*" The Saturday Evening Post, 237th year (May 16, 1964), 30-40.

Qualben, Lars P. *A History of the Christian Church.* New York: Thomas Nelson & Sons, 1942.

Schaff, Philip. *History of the Christian Church.* 8 vols. Grand Rapids: Wm. B. Eerdmans Publishing Company, 1952.

Steinmueller, John E. and Katheryn Sullivan. *Catholic Biblical Encyclopedia.* New York: Joseph F. Wagner. 1956.

Walker, Williston. *A History of the Christian Church.* New York: Charles Scribner's Sons, 1959.

3. GLOSSOLALIA: REFORMATION TO THE 20TH CENTURY

Alexander, Joseph Addison. *Commentary on the Acts of the Apostles.* Grand Rapids: Zondervan Publishing House, 1956.

Barnes, Charles Randall. *The People's Bible Encyclopedia.* Chicago:

The People's Publication Society, 1921.

Bruce, F. F. *The Acts of the Apostles*. Grand Rapids: Wm. B. Eerdmans Publishing Company, 1960.

Brumback, Carl. *"What Meaneth This?"* Springfield, Mo.: The Gospel Publishing House, 1947.

Cadbury, Henry T. *The Book of Acts in History*. New York: Harper & Brothers, 1955.

Calvin, John. *Calvin's Commentaries*. 45 vols. Grand Rapids: Wm. B. Eerdmans Publishing Company, 1949.

Carter, Howard. *Questions and Answers on Spiritual Gifts*. London: Assemblies of God Publishing House, 1955.

Carver, William Owen. *The Acts of the Apostles*. Nashville: Broadman Press, 1901.

Chafer, Lewis Sperry. *Systematic Theology*. 8 vols. Dallas: Dallas Seminary Press, 1948.

Clarke, Adam. *Commentary on the Holy Bible*. 6 vols. Nashville: Abingdon-Cokesbury Press, n.d.

Clarke, W. K. Lowther. *Concise Bible Commentary*. New York: The Macmillan Company, 1953.

Conybeare, W. J. and J. S. Howson. *The Life and Epistles of St. Paul*. Hartford: The S. S. Scranton Company, 1920.

Cutten, George Barton. *Speaking With Tongues*. New Haven: Yale University Press, 1927.

Davidson, F., A. M. Stibbs, and E. J. Kevan (eds.). *The New Bible Commentary*. Grand Rapids: Wm. B. Eerdmans Publishing Company, 1953.

Drummond, A. L. *Edward Irving and His Circle*. London: James Clarke & Company, Ltd. 1934.

Dummelow, John R. (ed.). *A Commentary on the Holy Bible*. New York: The Macmillan Company, 1941.

Ellicott, John Charles (ed.). *Ellicott's Commentary on the Whole Bible*. 8 vols. Grand Rapids: Zondervan Publishing House, reprint classic, n.d.

Erdman, Charles. *The First Epistle of Paul to the Corinthians*. Philadelphia: The Westminster Press, 1928.

Espasa, Calpe. *Encyclopedia Universal Illustrada*. Madrid, Spain: Espasa-Calpe, 1925.

Ferm, Vergilius (ed.). *An Encyclopedia of Religion*. New York: The Philosophical Library, 1945.

Godet, Frederick. *Commentary on St. Paul's First Epistle to the Corinthians* (1898). Reprinted in the *Classic Commentary Library*. 24 vols. Grand Rapids: Zondervan Publishing House, 1957.

Gray, James Comper, and George M. Adams. *Gray and Adam's Bible Commentary*. 5 vols. Grand Rapids: Zondervan Publishing House, n.d.

Hastings, James. *The Great Texts of the Bible.* 20 vols. New York: Fleming H. Revell Company, 1935.

Hendry, G. S. *The Holy Spirit in Christian Theology.* Second edition. Philadelphia: The Westminster Press, 1964.

Henry, Matthew. *Commentary on the Whole Bible.* 6 vols. New York: Fleming H. Revell Company, 1935.

Hilgenfield, A. *Die Glossalalie in der Alten Kirche* (Glossolaly in the Primitive Church). Lupsic, 1850.

Hobbs, Herschel H. *The Epistles to the Corinthians, A Study Manual.* Grand Rapids: Baker Book House, n.d.

Horton, Harold. *The Gifts of the Spirit.* London: Assemblies of God Publishing House, 1954.

Hughes, Ray H. *Religion on Fire.* Cleveland, Tenn.: Pathway Press, 1956.

The Interpreter's Bible. 12 vols. Nashville: Abingdon-Cokesbury Press, 1953.

Jamieson, Robert, A. R. Fausset and David Brown. *A Commentary Critical, Experimental and Practical on the Old and New Testaments.* 6 vols. Grand Rapids: Wm. B. Eerdmans Publishing Company, n.d.

Jamieson, Robert, A. R. Fausset and David Brown. *Commentary on the Whole Bible.* 2 vols. in one. Grand Rapids: Zondervan Publishing House, n.d.

Kelsey, Morton T. *Tongue Speaking.* New York: Doubleday & Company, Inc., 1964.

Kling, Christian Friedrich. *Corinthians.* Vol. XX of *Lange's Commentary on the Holy Scriptures* (1866). 24 vols. Grand Rapids: Reprinted by Zondervan Publishing House, n.d.

Kuyper, Abraham. *The Work of the Holy Spirit.* Tr. by Henry De Vries. Grand Rapids: Wm. B. Eerdmans Publishing Company, 1941.

Lange, John Peter (ed.). *Commentary on the Holy Scriptures* (1886). 24 vols. Grand Rapids: Reprinted by Zondervan Publishing House, n.d.

Lechler, G. V. *The Acts of the Apostles.* Vol. XVIII of *Lange's Commentary on the Holy Scriptures* (1886). 24 vols. Grand Rapids: Reprinted by Zondervan Publishing House, n.d.

Latourette, Kenneth Scott. *A History of Christianity.* New York: Harper & Brothers, 1953.

Lenski, R. C. H. *Interpretation of the Acts of the Apostles.* Columbus, Ohio: The Wartburg Press, 1944.

Lombard, C. *De la Glossalalie Chez les Premiers Chretiens* (Glossolalia Among the Early Christians). Lausanne, 1910.

Luccock, Halford E. *The Acts of the Apostles.* New York: Harper & Brothers, 1942.

Macaulay, J. C. *A Devotional Commentary on the Acts of the Apostles.*

Grand Rapids: Wm. B. Eerdmans Publishing Company, 1946.

Maclaren, Alexander. *Expositions of the Holy Scripture.* 17 vols. Grand Rapids: Wm. B. Eerdmans Publishing Company, 1944.

Morgan, G. Campbell. *The Acts of the Apostles.* New York: Fleming H. Revell Company, 1924.

Morgan, G. Campbell. *The Corinthian Letters of Paul, an Exposition of I and II Corinthians.* New York: Fleming H. Revell Company, 1946.

Neander, Johann August Wilhelm. *History of the Planting and Training of the Christian Church.* Edinburgh, 1842.

Nicoll, W. Robertson, *et al.* (eds.). *The Expositor's Dictionary of Texts.* 2 vols. New York: George H. Doran Company, 1910.

Nicoll, W. Robertson (ed.). *The Expositor's Bible.* 6 vols. Grand Rapids: Wm. B. Eerdmans Publishing Company, 1940.

Olson, Arnold Theodore. *This We Believe.* Minneapolis: Free Church Publications, 1961.

Pearlman, Meyer. *Knowing the Doctrines of the Bible.* Springfield, Mo.: The Gospel Publishing House, 1937.

Peloubet, F. N. *Peloubet's Bible Dictionary.* Philadelphia: Universal Book and Bible House, 1947.

The People's Bible Encyclopedia. Chicago: The People's Publication Society, 1921.

The Preacher's Complete Homiletic Commentary. 32 vols. New York: Funk & Wagnalls Company, Inc., n.d.

Purves, George T. *Christianity in the Apostolic Age.* Grand Rapids: Baker Book House, 1955.

Rackham, Richard Belward. *The Acts of the Apostles.* In *Westminster Commentaries Series,* ed. Walter Lock. Fourteenth edition. London: Methuen & Company, Ltd., 1951.

Richardson, Alan. *A Theological Workbook of the Bible.* New York: The Macmillan Company, 1953.

Richardson, Cyril C. *The Doctrine of the Trinity.* Nashville: Abingdon Press, 1958.

Ripley, Henry J. *The Acts of the Apostles; with Notes.* Boston: Gould, Kendall, and Lincoln, 1844.

Robertson, Archibald Thomas. *Word Pictures in the New Testament.* 6 vols. Nashville: Broadman Press, 1931.

Robinson, H. W. *The Christian Experience of the Holy Spirit.* New York: Harper & Brothers, 1928.

Rolston, Holmes. *Consider Paul.* Richmond: John Knox Press, 1951.

Schaff-Herzog Encyclopedia: The New Schaff-Herzog Encyclopedia of Religious Knowledge. 13 vols. Grand Rapids: Baker Book House, 1953.

Sherrill, John L. *They Speak With Other Tongues.* New York: McGraw-Hill Inc., 1964.

Smith, David. *The Life and Letters of St. Paul*. New York: Harper & Brothers, n.d.

Smith, William. *Smith's Bible Dictionary*. Chicago: The John C. Winston Company, 1884.

Spence, H. D. M. and Joseph S. Exell (eds.). *The Pulpit Commentary*. 23 vols. Grand Rapids: Wm. B. Eerdmans Publishing Company, 1950.

Stagg, Frank. *The Book of Acts*. Nashville: Broadman Press, 1955.

Thomas, David. *Acts of the Apostles, A Homiletic Commentary*. Grand Rapids: Baker Book House, 1955.

Torrey, R. A. *The Holy Spirit*. Westwood, N. J.: Fleming H. Revell Company, n.d.

Torrey, R. A. *What the Bible Teaches*. Westwood, N. J.: Fleming H. Revell Company, 1933.

Van Dusen, H. P. *Spirit, Son and Father*. New York: Charles Scribner's Sons, 1958.

Walker, D. *The Gift of Tongues and Other Essays*. London: n. n., 1906.

Weisberger, Bernard A. *They Gathered at the River*. Boston: Little, Brown & Company, 1958.

Wesley, John, *et al. One Volume New Testament Commentary*. Grand Rapids: Baker Book House, 1958.

Wesley, John. *The Works of John Wesley* (1872). 14 vols. Grand Rapids: Reprinted by Zondervan Publishing House, n.d.

Wiley, H. Orton and Paul T. Culbertson. *Introduction to Christian Theology*. Kansas City: Beacon Hill Press, 1964.

The Zondervan Pictorial Bible Dictionary. Edited by Merrill C. Tenney. Grand Rapids: Zondervan Publishing House, 1955.

4. Glossolalia in Contemporary Times

The Ante-Nicene Fathers. American Series. 14 vols. Grand Rapids: Wm. B. Eerdmans Publishing Company, 1956.

Atter, Gordon F. *The Third Force*. Peterborough, Ontario: The College Press, 1962.

Bach, Marcus. "Whether There Be Tongues," *Christian Herald*, LXXXVII (May, 1964), 10ff.

"Bishop Jolts Arid Church," *Portland Oregonian*, April 12, 1961.

Blikstad, Vernon M. "Spiritual Renaissance," *Christian Life*, XXVI (May, 1964), 31.

Boyd, Robert. *Lives and Labors of Moody and Sankey*. Toronto: A. H. Harvey, 1876.

Bredesen, Harald. "The Foolish Things," *Trinity*, II (Trinitytide, 1962), 2, 3.

Bredesen, Harald. "Return to the Charismata" (tract). Mount Vernon, New York, n.d.

Catholic Encyclopedia, XIV, 777. New York: Robert Appleton Company, 1912.

"The Challenge of the 'Sects,' " Pentecost, No. 47 (March, 1959), 4.

Conn, Charles W. Like a Mighty Army. Cleveland, Tenn.: Church of God Publishing House, 1955.

David, George T. B. When the Fire Fell. Philadelphia: The Million Testaments Campaigns, 1958.

Dirks, Lee E. "The Pentecostals: Speaking in Other Tongues," National Observer Newsbook: Religion in Action. Silver Spring, Md.: The National Observer, 1965.

Encyclopaedia Britannica (11th ed.), XXVII, 9, 10.

Farrell, Frank. "The Outburst of Tongues: The New Penetration," Christianity Today, VII (September 13, 1963), 3-7.

Frame, Raymond. "Something Unusual," His, XXIV (December, 1963), 18ff.

Frodsham, Stanley Howard. With Signs Following. Springfield, Mo.: The Gospel Publishing House, 1964.

Gee, Donald. All With One Accord. Springfield, Mo.: The Gospel Publishing House, 1961.

Gee, Donald. "Critics and Criticism," Pentecost, No. 35 (March, 1965), 17.

Gee, Donald. "Don't Spill the Wine," Pentecost, No. 61 (September-November, 1962), 17.

The Full Gospel Business Men's Voice, January, 1961.

Greenway, H. W. This Emotionalism. London: Victory Press, 1954.

Harris, Carl. " 'Speaking in Tongues': A Point of Dissention," The Dallas Morning News, June 28, 1964.

Henry, Carl F. "Pentecostal Meeting Makes Holy Land History," Christianity Today, V, No. 17 (May 22, 1961), 25.

Holm, Lewis. "Speaking in Tongues," The Lutheran Standard, II, No. 19 (September 11, 1962), 3ff.

Horton, Harold. The Gifts of the Spirit. London: Assemblies of God Publishing House, 1962.

Kelsey, Morton T. Tongue Speaking. New York: Doubleday & Company, Inc. 1964.

Loetscher, Lefferts, A. (ed.). Twentieth Century Encyclopaedia of Religious Knowledge. 2 vols. Grand Rapids: Baker Book House, 1955.

Luccock, Halford E. The Acts of the Apostles. New York: Harper & Brothers, 1942.

Miller, Madeleine S. and J. Lane Miller. Harper's Bible Dictionary. New York: Harper & Brothers, 1952.

"Millions Read About Revival of Speaking With Tongues," Pentecost,

No. 54 (December, 1960 to February, 1961), 2.

Nichol, John Thomas. "Pentecostalism," Doctoral dissertation, Boston University, Boston, Massachusetts, 1965.

Packard, Vance. The Status Seekers. New York: David McKay Company, 1959.

Phillips, J. B. The Young Church in Action. New York: The Macmillan Company, 1955.

Phillips, McCandlish. " 'And There Appeared To Them Tongues of Fire,' " Saturday Evening Post, 237th Year (May 16, 1964), 30-40.

"Rector and a Rumpus," Newsweek, LXI (July 4, 1960), 77.

Sherrill, John L. They Speak With Other Tongues. New York: McGraw-Hill Inc., 1964.

"Speaking in Tongues," Time, LXXVI (August 15, 1960), 53, 55.

Stone, Jean. "What Is Happening Today in the Episcopal Church?" Christian Life, XXIII (November, 1961), 38-41.

Sweet, William Warren. The Story of Religion in America. New York: Harper & Brothers, 1950.

Thoburn, J. M. The Church of Pentecost. New York: Methodist Publishing House, 1899.

Thomas, Robert L. "The Holy Spirit and Tongues," The King's Business, LIV (May, 1963), 9-11.

Thrapp, Dan L. "Churches Look Closely At 'Gift of Tongues,' " Los Angeles Times, March 17, 1963.

Turner, W. H. Pentecost and Tongues. Shanghai: Modern Publishing House, n.d.

Wierville, Victor Paul. Receiving the Holy Spirit Today. New Knoxville: The Way, Inc., 1962.

Wiley, H. Orton. Christian Theology. 3 vols. Kansas City: Beacon Hill Press, 1952.

5. GLOSSOLALIA: ITS VALUE TO THE CHURCH

Amplified New Testament. Grand Rapids: Zondervan Publishing House, 1958.

Atter, Gordon F. The Third Force. Peterborough, Ontario: The College Press, 1962.

Book of Minutes. Cleveland, Tenn.: Church of God Publishing House, 1922.

Brumback, Carl. Suddenly . . . from Heaven. Springfield, Mo.: The Gospel Publishing House, 1961.

Clarke, Adam. Commentary on the Holy Bible. 6 vols. Nashville: Abingdon-Cokesbury, n.d.

294   THE GLOSSOLALIA PHENOMENON

Conn, Charles W. *Like a Mighty Army.* Cleveland, Tenn.: Church of
God Publishing House, 1955.
Farrell, Frank. "Outburst of Tongues: The New Penetration," *Chris-
tianity Today,* VII, Number 24 (September 13, 1963), 3-7.
Church of God Evangel, I (August 15, 1910).
Frodsham, Stanley H. *With Signs Following.* Springfield, Mo.: The
Gospel Publishing House, 1946.
Gee, Donald. "Do 'Tongues' Matter," *Pentecost,* No. 49 (September,
1958), 17.
Gordon, A. J. *The Ministry of the Spirit.* Philadelphia: American Bap-
tist Publication Society, 1895.
Horton, Wade H. *Pentecost, Yesterday and Today.* Cleveland, Tenn.:
Pathway Press, 1964.
The International Standard Bible Encyclopedia. Edited by James Orr.
5 Vols. Grand Rapids: Wm. B. Eerdmans Publishing Company,
1943.
Juillerat, Howard L. *Brief History of the Church of God,* a Preface
to the *Book of Minutes.* Cleveland, Tenn.: Church of God Pub-
lishing House, 1922.
Kendrick, Klaude. *The Promise Fulfilled.* Springfield, Mo.: The Gospel
Publishing House, 1961.
Kelsey, Morton T. *Tongue Speaking.* New York: Doubleday & Company,
Inc., 1964.
Lemons, Frank W. *Our Pentecostal Heritage.* Cleveland, Tenn.: Path-
way Press, 1963.
McLaughlin, G. A. *Commentary on the Acts of the Apostles.* Chicago:
Christian Witness Company, 1915.
Minutes of the Fiftieth General Assembly of the Church of God. Cleve-
land, Tenn.: Church of God Publishing House, 1964.
Pache, René. *The Person and Work of the Holy Spirit.* Chicago: Moody
Press, 1954.
Pierson, Arthur T. *The Acts of the Holy Spirit.* London: Morgan and
Scott, n.d.
Ramm, Bernard. *The Witness of the Spirit.* Grand Rapids: Wm. B.
Eerdmans Publishing Company, 1960.
Sherrill, John L. *They Speak With Other Tongues.* New York: McGraw-
Hill Inc., 1964.
Simpson, A. B. *The Holy Spirit.* Harrisburg, Pa.: Christian Publication,
Inc., n.d.
Spence, H. D. and Joseph S. Exell (eds.). *The Pulpit Commentary.*
23 vols. Grand Rapids: Wm. B. Eerdmans Publishing Company,
1950.
Versteeg, John M. *Perpetuating Pentecost.* Chicago: Willet, Clark, &
Colby, 1930.

6. Glossolalia: Its Value to the Individual

Alleman, Herbert C. *New Testament Commentary*. Philadelphia: The Board of Publication of the United Lutheran Church in America, 1936.

Barnes, Albert. *Notes, Explanatory and Practical on the First Epistle of Paul to the Corinthians*. New York: William Robinson, 1838. Reprinted by Baker Book House, 1950.

Bartlet, James Vernon. *Ten Epochs of Church History: The Apostolic Age, Its Life, Doctrine, Worship and Polity*. New York: Charles Scribner's Sons, 1899.

Barton, George A. *The Apostolic Age and the New Testament*. Philadelphia: University of Pennsylvania Press, 1936.

Brice, Joe. *Pentecost*. London: Hodder & Stoughton, Ltd., 1936.

Bruner, B. H. *Pentecost, A Renewal of Power*. New York: Doubleday, Doran and Company, 1928.

Campbell, James M. *After Pentecost What?* New York: Fleming H. Revell Company, 1897.

Dods, Marcus. *The First Epistle to the Corinthians*. London: Hodder & Stoughton, Ltd., 1900.

Flicoteaux, Dom Emmanuel. *The Splendor of Pentecost*. Baltimore: Helicon Press, 1961.

Grosheide, F. W. *Commentary On The First Epistle To The Corinthians. In The New International Commentary* on the New Testament. F. F. Bruce, gen. ed. Grand Rapids: Wm. B. Eerdmans Publishing Company, 1953.

Hayes, D. A. *The Gift of Tongues*. Cincinnati: Jennings and Graham, 1913.

Jackson, Foakes and Kersopp Lake. *The Beginning of Christianity*. Part I. London: Macmillan and Co., Ltd., 1933.

Jones E. Stanley. *The Christ of Every Road*. New York: The Abingdon Press, 1930.

Kelsey, Morton T. *Tongue Speaking*. Garden City, N. Y.: Doubleday & Company, Inc., 1964.

Lapsley, James N., and John Simpson. "Speaking in Tongues: Infantile Babble or Song of the Self?" Part II, *Pastoral Psychology*, XV (September, 1964), 16-24.

Mackie, Alexander. *The Gift of Tongues*. New York: George H. Doran Company, 1921.

Moorehead, William G. *Outline Studies in Acts, Romans, First and Second Corinthians, Galatians and Ephesians*. New York: Fleming H. Revell Company, 1902.

Mourant, John A. *Readings In The Philosophy of Religion*. New York: Thomas Y. Crowell Company, 1956.

Ockenga, Harold J. *The Spirit of the Living God*. New York: Fleming H. Revell Company, 1947.

Ockenga, Harold J. *Power Through Pentecost*. Grand Rapids: Wm. B. Eerdmans Publishing Company, 1959.

Robertson, A. T. *Word Pictures In The New Testament*. 6 vols. Nashville: Broadman Press, 1931.

Rogers, Carl R. *On Becoming A Person*. Boston: Houghton Mifflin Company, 1961.

Ropes, James Hardy. *The Apostolic Age, In the Light of Modern Criticism*. New York: Charles Scribner's Sons, 1906.

Schaff, Philip. *History of the Christian Church*. 8 vols. Grand Rapids: Wm. B. Eerdmans Publishing Company, 1950.

Stolee, H. J. *Speaking in Tongues*, a reprint of *Pentecostalism*. Minneapolis: Augsburg Publishing House, 1963.

Tillich, Paul. *Systematic Theology*. Chicago: The University of Chicago Press, 1953.

Watts, Alan W. *Myth and Ritual in Christianity*. New York: The Vanguard Press, 1953.

Whyte, Lancelot Law. *The Unconscious Before Freud*. New York: Basic Books, Inc., 1960.

Wright, J. A. "The Holy Spirit's Work In The Believer." *The Elim Evangel*, XLVI, No. 34 (August 21, 1965), 530-532.

7. GLOSSOLALIA IN PERSPECTIVE

Barclay, William. *The Letters to the Corinthians*. Philadelphia: The Westminster Press, 1957.

Boyd, Frank M. *The Holy Spirit*. Springfield, Mo.: The Gospel Publishing House, n.d.

Conn, Charles W. *Like a Mighty Army*. Cleveland, Tenn.: Church of God Publishing House, 1955.

Conn, Charles W. *Pillars of Pentecost*. Cleveland, Tenn.: Pathway Press, 1956.

Cuttin, George Barton. *Speaking With Tongues*. New Haven: Yale University Press, 1927.

Ellicott, Charles John (ed.). *Ellicott's Commentary on the Whole Bible*. 8 vols. Grand Rapids: Zondervan Publishing House, reprint classic, n.d.

Gee, Donald. *Concerning Spiritual Gifts*. Springfield, Mo.: The Gospel Publishing House, n.d.

Goforth, Jonathan. *"By My Spirit."* Grand Rapids: Zondervan Publishing House, 1942.

Gordon, A. J. *The Ministry of the Spirit*. Minneapolis: Bethany Fellowship, Inc., 1964.

Halley, Henry H. *Halley's Bible Handbook.* Grand Rapids: Zondervan Publishing House, 1962.

Horton, Wade H. *Pentecost: Yesterday and Today.* Cleveland, Tenn.: Pathway Press, 1964.

Hughes, Ray H. *What Is Pentecost.* Cleveland, Tenn.: Pathway Press, 1963.

The Interpreter's Bible. 12 vols. Vol. X, 150. Nashville: Abingdon-Cokesbury Press, 1953.

Kelsey, Morton T. *Tongue Speaking.* New York: Doubleday & Company, Inc., 1964.

Kling, Christian Friedrich. *Corinthians,* Vol. XX of *Lange's Commentary on the Holy Scriptures* (1886). 24 vols. Grand Rapids: Reprinted by Zondervan Publishing House, n.d.

Knudson, Ralph E. *Theology in the New Testament.* Valley Forge: The Judson Press, 1964.

Lapsley, James N., and John H. Simpson. "Speaking in Tongues: Infantile Babble or Song of the Self?" *Pastoral Psychology,* XV, No. 146 (September, 1964), 16, 17.

Lehman, Chester K. *The Holy Spirit and the Holy Life.* Scottdale, Pa.: Herald Press, 1959.

Lemons, Frank W. *Our Pentecostal Heritage.* Cleveland, Tenn.: Pathway Press, 1963.

Lyons, Bobby E. "Charismatic Gifts: An Exegesis of 1 Corinthians 12:1-11." Unpublished Master's thesis, Columbia Theological Seminary, Decatur, Georgia, 1965.

Martin, Ira Jay III. *Glossolalia in the Apostolic Church.* Berea, Ky.: Berea College, 1960.

MacDonald, William G. *Glossolalia in the New Testament.* Springfield, Mo.: The Gospel Publishing House, n.d.

McNeile, A. H. *An Introduction to the Study of the New Testament.* Second edition. Oxford: The Clarendon Press, 1953.

Morgan, G. Campbell. *The Acts of the Apostles.* Westwood, N. J.: Fleming H. Revell Company, Inc., 1926.

Niebuhr, Richard H. *Christ and Culture.* New York: Harper & Brothers, 1951.

Pache, René. *The Person and Work of the Holy Spirit.* Chicago: Moody Press, 1954.

Plumptre, E. H. *The Acts of the Apostles,* Vol. VII in *Ellicott's Commentary on the Bible.* John C. Ellicott, ed. Grand Rapids: Zondervan Publishing House, reprint classic, n.d.

Robertson, Archibald, and Alfred Plummer. *A Critical and Exegetical Commentary on the First Epistle of St. Paul to the Corinthians.* In *The International Critical Commentary.* Edinburgh: T. and T. Clark, 1961.

Shepard, J. W. *The Life and Letters of St. Paul.* Grand Rapids: Wm. B. Eerdmans Publishing Company, 1956.

Slay, James L. *This We Believe.* Cleveland, Tenn.: Pathway Press, 1963.

Smeaton, George. *The Doctrine of the Holy Spirit.* London: The Banner of Truth Trust, 1958.

Stewart, James S. *Thine Is the Kingdom.* Edinburg: The St. Andrews Press, 1956.

Swete, Henry Barclay. *The Holy Spirit in the New Testament.* London: Macmillan and Company, Ltd., 1919.

"Tongues, Gift of," *Encyclopaedia Britannica* (1965 ed.), XXII, 289.

Walker, Paul L. "Charismatic Development in the Contemporary Church." Atlanta, Georgia: Hemphill Church of God, n.d. (Mimeographed.)

Walvoord, John F. *The Holy Spirit.* Findlay, Ohio: Dunham Publishing Company, 1958.

The Wesleyan Bible Commentary. 6 vols. Grand Rapids: Wm. B. Eerdmans Publishing Company, 1964.

Wiley, H. Orton, and Paul T. Culbertson. *Introduction to Christian Theology.* Kansas City: Beacon Hill Press, 1964.

Zimmerman, Thomas F. "The Pentecostal Position," *Church of God Evangel,* LIV (March 2, 1964), 4.

Index of Scriptures

299

Index of Names

303